# Brand.new

V&A PUBLICATIONS

# Brar

**nd.new**

First published by V&A Publications,
2000

V&A Publications
160 Brompton Road
London SW3 1HW

Designed by Stephen Coates, August
Jacket designed by Agenda Design
Associates

Specially commissioned photography:
Graham Brandon, V+A Photography
studio and Andrew Cross

ISBN 185177 3231

A catalogue record for this book is
available from the British Library

Printed in Singapore

Every effort has been made to seek
permission to reproduce those images
whose copyright does not reside with
the V&A, and we are grateful to the
individuals who have assisted in this
task. Any omissions are entirely
unintentional, and the details should
be addressed to the publishers

# CONTENTS

# ACKNOWLEDGEMENTS

In the course of the preparation of both this book and the exhibition Brand.New, the curators have received invaluable advice and assistance from many varied quarters. My first thanks must go to my co-curator, Gareth Williams. His contribution to this book extends far beyond the chapter that bears his name. Secondly, the exhibition organiser, Anna Gustavsson, who has worked tirelessly to make the entire project possible, and Mike Malham, who deftly co-ordinated the design work. We have all been ably assisted by Poppy Hollman from the Exhibitions Department and researchers Emmie Kell, Debra Dawson and Catharina Holmberg.

I would like to thank all the contributors, who offered their expertise and scholarship not only to the book but also to the exhibition during the course of its development. Their details are on the following pages. Thanks are also due to the numerous people from companies, press and publicity offices, business archives and photographic agencies, who helped us in the search for images and information, and took the time to talk with us. In particular, I would like to mention: The London Business School; Phil Mooney and his team at the Coca-Cola Archive; Lynn Downey, Levi Strauss & Co Archive; Antonella Viero, Diesel; Siamack Salari, BMP DDB; Masuhiro Yamaguchi and Yasuhiro Masuda, Sanrio GmbH; Angela Gleinicke, Greenpeace; Amanda Sandford, Action on Smoking and Health; Allan MacDonald, The Media Foundation; The John Lewis Partnership Archive; Harrods Archive; Woolworths Archive; The Anti-Counterfeiting Group; Manchester United Football Club; Liz Lowe, Coca-Cola Great Britain; John Sorrell of Interbrand Newell and Sorrell; Caroline Lynch and Gillian McVie, Purple; George Pincus; Shubhankar Ray; Dave Morris; and Tony Hayward.

The team at V&A Publications have been patient and supportive during the preparation of this book, in particular Mary Butler, Head of V&A Publications, Miranda Harrison, Mary Wessel, Helen Armitage and Geoff Barlow. I am grateful to John Styles and Jonathan Woodham for helpful comments on various drafts of the text. I would especially like to thank Stephen Coates and August Media for the design of the book, and Agenda Design for the cover and the Brand.New logo. The photographs specially commissioned for this book are the work of Graham Brandon, V&A Photographic Studio, who has contributed enormously to this project, and also Andrew Cross. Special thanks also must go to the exhibition design team: Thomas Heatherwick, Kieran Gaffney, Tom Chapman Andrews, Richard Greenwood and Stephen Coates, who have given creative form to our ideas.

Many colleagues at the V&A have offered help and advice with Brand.New: particularly Linda Lloyd Jones, Head of the Exhibitions Department, and Paul Greenhalgh, Head of the Research Department, who have guided the project. All members of the project team for Brand.New have contributed enormously, especially Eithne Nightingale, Francis Pugh, Jane Rosier, Emily Owen, Sarah Gray, Brian Griggs, Lucy Morrison and her team in the Development Department, and Michael Cass and staff of V&A Enterprises. Thanks also to members of the Research Department and the Furniture and Woodwork Department, and to the numerous colleagues and friends who sent us photographs and press clippings, told us their 'brand' preferences, and thought of us whilst out shopping: in particular, Tessa Hore, Andrew Bolton, Ghislaine Wood, Susan McCormack and John Strand. My personal thanks also go to the University of Brighton and the British Academy, who have supported my time at the V&A in the form of a six-year research fellowship, and last but especially not least, Tim Burne.

Jane Pavitt

PAOLA ANTONELLI is curator in the Department of Architecture and Design at the Museum of Modern Art, New York. She has curated a number of exhibitions, including *Mutant Materials in Contemporary Design* (1995), *Thresholds: Contemporary Design from the Netherlands* (1996), *Achille Castiglioni: Design!* (1998), and *Projects 66: Campana/Ingo Maurer* (1998–9). She is currently working on a cycle of exhibitions about the MoMA collection from 1960 to today, in collaboration with Kirk Varnedoe and Josh Siegel.

PATRICK BARWISE is Professor of Management and Marketing, Director of the Centre for Marketing and Chairman of the Future Media Research Programme at London Business School. His publications, with various co-authors, include books on *Television and its Audience*, *Accounting for Brands*, *Strategic Decisions*, *Predictions: Media and Advertising in a Recession*, as well as numerous articles. He is currently writing a book with Andrea Dunham on *The Business of Brands*, to be published by Harvard Business School Press. He is Deputy Chairman of the Consumers' Association and Joint Managing Editor of *Business Strategy Review*.

RUSSELL W. BELK is the N. Eldon Tanner Professor of Business Administration and Professor of Marketing in the David Eccles School of Business (University of Utah, USA). He has also had regular, visiting or honorary university appointments in Canada, Romania, Zimbabwe, Hong Kong, Australia and elsewhere in the United States. His areas of expertise are consumer behaviour, qualitative research, and marketing and development. He is past president of the Association for Consumer Research and current president of the Society of Marketing and Development. He is a Fellow in the Association for Consumer Research and the American Psychological Association. He has published more than 250 books, articles and videotapes, including *Collecting in a Consumer Society* (1995).

AARON BETSKY is Curator of Architecture and Design at San Francisco Museum of Modern Art. He has curated a wide range of exhibitions including *Icons: Magnets of Meaning* (1997). He has published, taught and lectured extensively, and is currently an Adjunct Professor at the California College of Arts and Crafts (CCAC) and a Contributing Editor of *Architecture*, *Metropolitan Home*, *Blueprint* and *ID* magazines. He has published eight books on architecture and design, including *Violated Perfection: Architecture and the Fragmentation of the Modern* (1990), *James Gamble Rogers and the Architecture of Pragmatism* (1994), *Building Sex: Men, Women, Architecture and the Construction of Sexuality* and *Queer Space: The Spaces of Same Sex Desire* (1997).

ANDREW BOLTON is the Joint London College of Fashion/Victoria & Albert Museum Contemporary Fashion Research Fellow. Formerly an assistant curator in the Far Eastern Department of the V&A, much of his research centres on East Asian fashion, on which he has published several essays and articles.

RACHEL BOWLBY is Professor of English at the University of York. Her books include *Just Looking* (1985), *Shopping with Freud* (1993) and *Carried Away: The Invention of Modern Shopping* (2000).

ALISON CLARKE lectures at the Royal College of Art, London, and as Visiting Professor at the University of Applied Arts, Vienna, in the field of material culture and design history. She has published numerous articles around the consumption of everyday artefacts, and is the author of *Tupperware: The Promise of Plastic in 1950s America* (1999).

CHARLOTTE COTTON is an assistant curator of photographs at the Victoria & Albert Museum. She is part of the team there responsible for the national collection of the art of photography and the programme of exhibitions and events for the Canon Photography Gallery. She is curator of the V&A exhibition *Imperfect Beauty* (2000) and author of the accompanying book.

ANDREA DUNHAM is President of Unique Value International, Inc., a New York based management consultancy with global clients. She is co-author of *Unique Value: The Secret of All Great Business Strategies* (1993) and *Building a Global Image*, a 1991 report published by the Economist group. She is currently writing a book with Patrick Barwise, *The Business of Brands*, to be published by Harvard Business School Press. She is a Fellow of the Royal Society of Arts.

KENT GRAYSON is on the marketing faculty at London Business School, where he researches deception and trust in marketing and branding. He also studies a type of direct selling called 'network marketing'.

HELEN JONES is a freelance writer, curator, researcher and lecturer. She is a graduate of the Victoria & Albert Museum/Royal College of Art MA in the History of Design, where her specialist subject was petrol-station design. She was co-curator with Deyan Sudjic of *The Architecture of Democracy* (1999) and is currently visiting lecturer in Design Studies at Goldsmiths University.

GUY JULIER is employed in the School of Art, Architecture and Design at Leeds Metropolitan University. His previous books include *New Spanish Design* (1991) and the *Thames & Hudson Dictionary of 20th-century Design and Designers* (1993). The discussion of branded leisure that appears in this publication is developed further in his forthcoming book *The Culture of Design* (2000).

SHARON KINSELLA is a researcher and lecturer in contemporary media, culture and society in Japan at the University of Cambridge, UK.

CELIA LURY is a Reader in Sociology at Goldsmiths College, University of London and has a DPhil in Sociology from Manchester University. She has written widely on consumer culture, the culture industries and visual culture. She is currently researching a book on brands. The pieces in this book are based on research conducted as part of an RSRC-funded project 'Global Culture Industries:

The Biography of Cultural Products' with Deirdre Boden, Scott Lash, Vince Miller, Dan Shapiro and Jeremy Valentine.

STEFANO L. MARZANO is Managing Director of Philips Design. He was born in 1950 in Italy. He holds a doctorate in Architecture from the Milan Polytechnic Institute. During the early part of his career, he worked on a wide range of assignments for several design firms. In 1978 he joined Philips Design in The Netherlands, as Design Leader for Data Systems and Telecommunication products. He returned to Italy in 1982 to direct the Philips-Ire Design Centre (Major Domestic Appliances), becoming Vice President of Corporate Industrial Design for Whirlpool International (a joint venture of Whirlpool and Philips) in 1989. In 1991 he took up his present post in The Netherlands.

JANE PAVITT is University of Brighton/Victoria & Albert Museum Senior Research Fellow in Product Design & Museology, based in the Research Department at the V&A. Formerly a senior lecturer in design history at Camberwell College of Arts (The London Institute), she has written widely on aspects of design and design history. She is co-curator of the major exhibition Brand.New at the V&A in autumn 2000. She has curated several design exhibitions including *Designing in the Digital Age* (1999) and *The Shape of Colour: Red* (1999). She is the author of *Buildings of Europe: Prague* (2000).

MARK RITSON is an Assistant Professor at London Business School and has a PhD in Marketing from Lancaster University. His research focuses on branding, advertising and consumer culture. His most recent article, 'The Social Uses of Advertising', appeared in the December 1999 edition of the *Journal of Consumer Research*.

GARETH WILLIAMS is co-curator of the major V&A exhibition Brand.New in 2000 and an Assistant Curator in the Department of Furniture and Woodwork at the Victoria & Albert Museum, London, where he specialises in twentieth-century and contemporary furniture. For

the academic year 1999-2000 he was the V&A/University of Sussex Exchange fellow. He has written numerous articles about aspects of furniture design and collaborated with the design group Inflate on their book *Swell* in 1998. He has curated several V&A displays including *Green Furniture* (1996), *...not so simple* (1997), *Swell* (1998) and *Ron Arad, before and after now* (2000). He is the author of *Branded? Products and their Personalities* (2000), also published to coincide with Brand.New.

JONATHAN WOODHAM is Professor of the History of Design at the University of Brighton. He is also Director of the University's Design History Research Centre, which seeks to promote the discipline nationally and internationally, and holds a number of important design archives, the most significant of which is that of the Design Council. He has written widely on the history of design, including *Twentieth-century Design* (1997) and serves on the editorial boards of a number of periodicals, including the *Journal of Design History and Design Issues*.

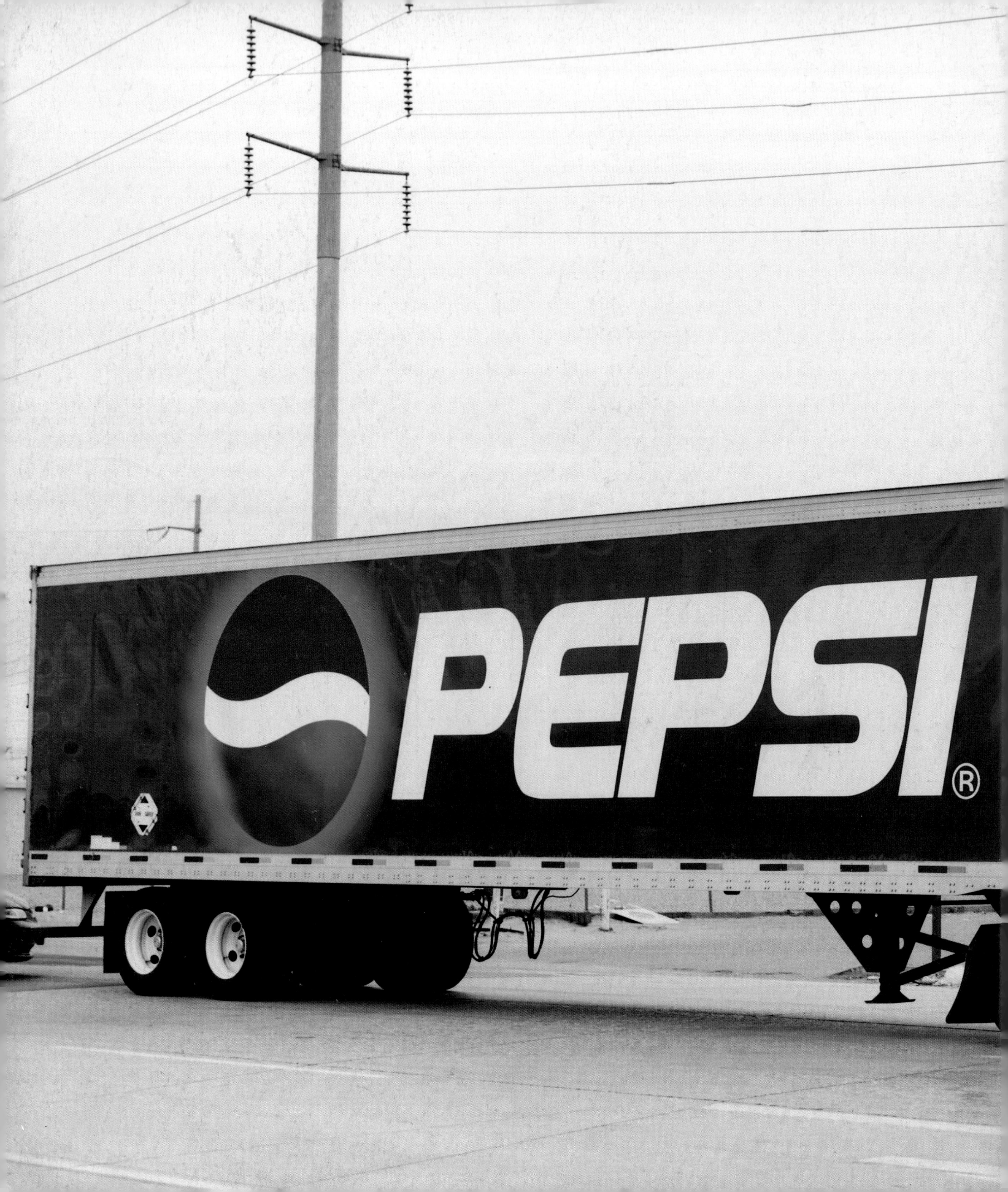
PEPSI®

From cornflakes to cars, our daily lives are increasingly dominated by branded goods and brand names; the brand is the prefix, the qualifier of character. The symbolic associations of the brand name are often used in preference to the pragmatic description of a useful object. We speak of 'the old Hoover', 'my new Audi' or 'my favourite Levi's' – not needing to qualify them with an object description. The brand is at the heart of this process for many of the goods we buy and sell.

The concept of the brand is central to our society. Media interest in the subjects of branding, marketing and corporate concerns has been substantial in recent years, and the fortunes of global corporations such as Microsoft make for regular news features.

The subject of brands is also one that crosses over a diversity of interests. Recent studies in sociology, anthropology, business, marketing and design have chosen to focus on the relationship between brands and consumer behaviour.

In the light of this, we have brought together writers and commentators for whom the brand is the 'point of entry' to their subject approach. As well as the five main chapters that form the body of the book, there is a selection of writings that provide snapshots of brand and consumer behaviour. The contributors range from observers and critics of brand-culture to the 'image-makers' themselves. The subjects cover products, locations and social practices, as they all fall within the matrix of branding.

# CHAPTER ONE

# IN GOODS
# WE TRUST?

JANE PAVITT

> "The logo is the point of entry to the brand."
>
> Milton Glaser, designer, *Graphis*, 1995

The origins of the term 'brand' in its contemporary sense are relatively new. The term derives from the practice of indelibly marking or stamping property, usually with a hot iron. Cattle or sheep would be marked in this way, but it was equally a means of signalling disgrace. Criminals would be 'fixed with a mark of infamy' using a hot iron or tattoo. Branding therefore signalled a loss of esteem that could not be restored and could be publicly recognised. We still talk of people being 'branded a liar'. Branding is principally the process of attaching a name and a reputation to something or someone.

The most recognisable feature of a brand is a name, logo, symbol or trademark that denotes a product's origin. A person, corporation or institution will own the rights to the brand name and employ it as a means of distinguishing their product or service from others. The ways in which this is done is described as branding, the process by which the values of the brand are attached, both physically and by suggestion, to the product. The brand, however, is much more than a

name or trademark. As Patrick Barwise, Andrea Dunham and Mark Ritson propose in their chapter, 'Ties That Bind', the idea of the brand also encompasses the associations that the name has for consumers. The brand image, or brand value, results from the 'dialogue' that takes place between producer or brand owner and the consumer or user. A brand's strength rests upon a close correlation between the image the brand creates through the process of branding, and the reception of that message by the consumer. Any distortions to that message tend to result in a weaker brand – for example, a brand that promotes itself as 'cheap and cheerful' may actually be read as poor quality if the message is mismanaged.

A brand name can be both that of the company or product owner and that of the particular product or product range. A family of branded products, all owned by the same company, may share certain features of their brand image, while still possessing a distinctive character or potential market. Jane Frost, Brand Manager of the BBC, has described this as a kind of 'brand DNA'.[1] Despite their individual character, each brand depends upon the image of the parent-brand. The brand structure of the BBC

(or any broadcast network) is a good example of this. The BBC has a powerful and globally recognised brand image and heritage, associated with quality broadcast, drama and news. It is seen as a reassuring voice heard all over the globe – particularly through the BBC World Service. Its brand values are an asset. Associated with it is a host of family members: Radio 1, 2, 3, 4 and 5live, regional radio stations, two TV channels and so on, not forgetting recent forays into digital broadcasting. Radio 1 and Radio 2 have markedly different brand values (both subject to considerable repositioning in recent years). On each station or channel are a multitude of programmes and personalities, each again with their own brand values. These values and associations are bankable assets, both for the Corporation and individuals associated with it.

So how is brand value established? The invention of a new brand overnight with subsequent rapid marketing is unlikely to be a success. Brands with strong images are the product of a successful nurturing of the relationship between producer and consumer. They also require economic investment, marketing and corporate nurturing. The most recognisable brands tend to maintain their position by establishing loyalty and ubiquity, by becoming the market standard. Early branded products often literally embodied the brand's promise within its name, such as the 'Thorough Washer', an early washing machine, patented in England in 1871. In some cases, the brand name becomes the generic name for that product, such as Hoover, Coke, Walkman or Rollerblade. For certain products, what started out as a brand name has become so generic that it can not be protected by trademark: aspirin, yo-yo, thermos and escalator are all terms that began life as brand names. The familiarity of names such as these demonstrates the rise to prominence of the brand in the last century. Brands are a part of twentieth-century mythology.

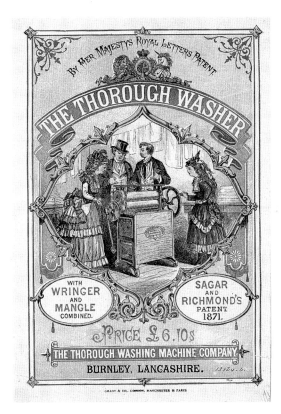

Opposite page: Winston Churchill, BBC broadcast, June 1942 (with current BBC logo below).
Above: Advertisement for the 'Thorough Washer' by the Thorough Washing Machine Co. of Burnley. English, nineteenth century.
Right: Advertising hoarding in Bolton, Lancashire, by Alec Davis. English c. 1898.

# EVERY GARMENT GUARANTEED

**LEVI STRAUSS & CO'S**
**TWO HORSE BRAND**

TRADE MARK

PATENTED    MAY 20 1873

## COPPER RIVETED CLOTHING

BLOUSES, JUMPERS, COATS, VESTS, MENS YOUTHS
AND BOYS OVERALLS, WITH OR WITHOUT BIBS
CARPENTERS APRONS AND SPRING BOTTOM PANTS

ALSO MANUFACTURERS

OF

**SUNSET SHIRTS**

EL REAL
HOSIERY
AND UNDERWEAR FOR
MEN WOMEN CHILDREN
AND DISTRIBUTORS FOR
RUGBY STOCKING
FOR CHILDREN
"THEY WEAR AND WEAR AND WEAR"

"In 19 out of 22 product categories, the company that owned the leading American brand in 1925 still has it today – Nabisco in cookies, Kellogg's in breakfast cereals, Kodak in film, Sherwin Williams in paint, Del Monte in canned fruit, Wrigley's in chewing gum, Singer in sewing machines, Campbell's in soup, Gillette in razors."[2]

The historical development of branding and branded goods is bound up with changes to the production, distribution and retail of goods, and to related demographic and economic shifts. Equally important, however, is the way in which the social history of a brand is often mythologised to become part of that brand's image. The respective histories of Coca-Cola and Levi's parallel neatly the rise of the American mass market, and the biography of each company is an exercise in the making of the American myth. Both products exemplify the ideal of American individualism. Levi's have successfully exploited the image of the American cowboy or rock'n'roll hero in generations of advertising.[3] Coca-Cola's association with the Free West in the post-war period has been, until recently, unshakeable. Images of Coca-Cola drinking American soldiers during the Second World War summed up the idea of America as a land of plentiful consumer products (along with silk stockings and cigarettes). Less tangibly, Coca-Cola may have been a nostalgic reminder of home for homesick GIs, and even of the values for which they might feel themselves to be fighting.[4] This image was successfully re-deployed during the Korean and Vietnam wars, when Coca-Cola kept American troops supplied with the drink, even building extra bottling plants in Vietnam to maintain the 'demand'.[5]

However successful a brand image might be, significant social and even political shifts can result in a loss of popularity. For brands that trade on heritage or national identity, for example, attempts to reposition them can be dangerous. Both Levi's and Coca-Cola, however, have in the past achieved significant 'comebacks' using advertising campaigns that combine the emotional appeal of the product with current concerns. In 1971 Coca-Cola made a successful appeal to a post-Vietnam, post-Woodstock generation of youthful consumers, who could conceivably have been ill disposed to Coke's image of all-American patriotism. The 'Hilltop' advertisement of that year featured a crowd of peace-loving people of all creeds and colours in a natural setting, all enjoying a Coke, and singing a song that was to become famous: 'I'd like to teach the world to sing in perfect harmony … I'd like to buy the world a Coke and keep it company.' The song was subsequently released as a single to huge success, although with its references to Coke

Previous pages: Cover of brochure, 'Evolution of a Pair of Overalls', showing Levi Strauss & Co.'s Two-Horse Brand, c.1907.
Right: Levi Strauss & Co. original jeans label.

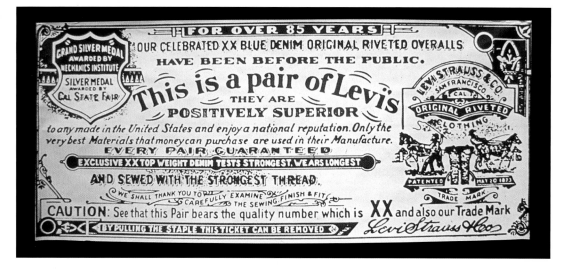

American soldiers serving
overseas were supplied
with Coca-Cola during the
Second World War.
Overleaf: Coca-Cola
reinvented their image
with the memorable 'Hilltop'
TV commercial of 1971.

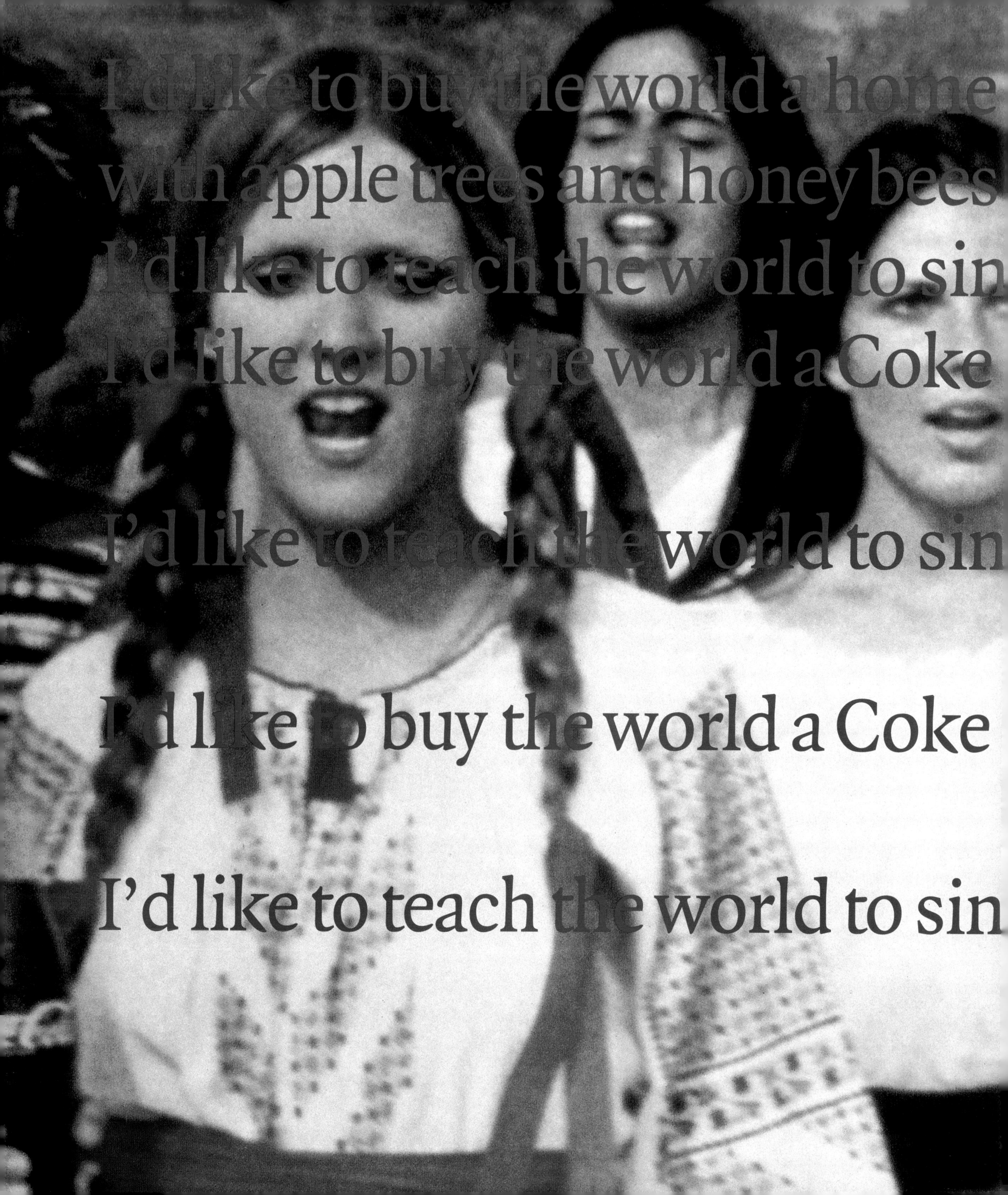

I'd like to buy the world a home
with apple trees and honey bees
I'd like to teach the world to sin
I'd like to buy the world a Coke

I'd like to teach the world to sin

I'd like to buy the world a Coke

I'd like to teach the world to sin

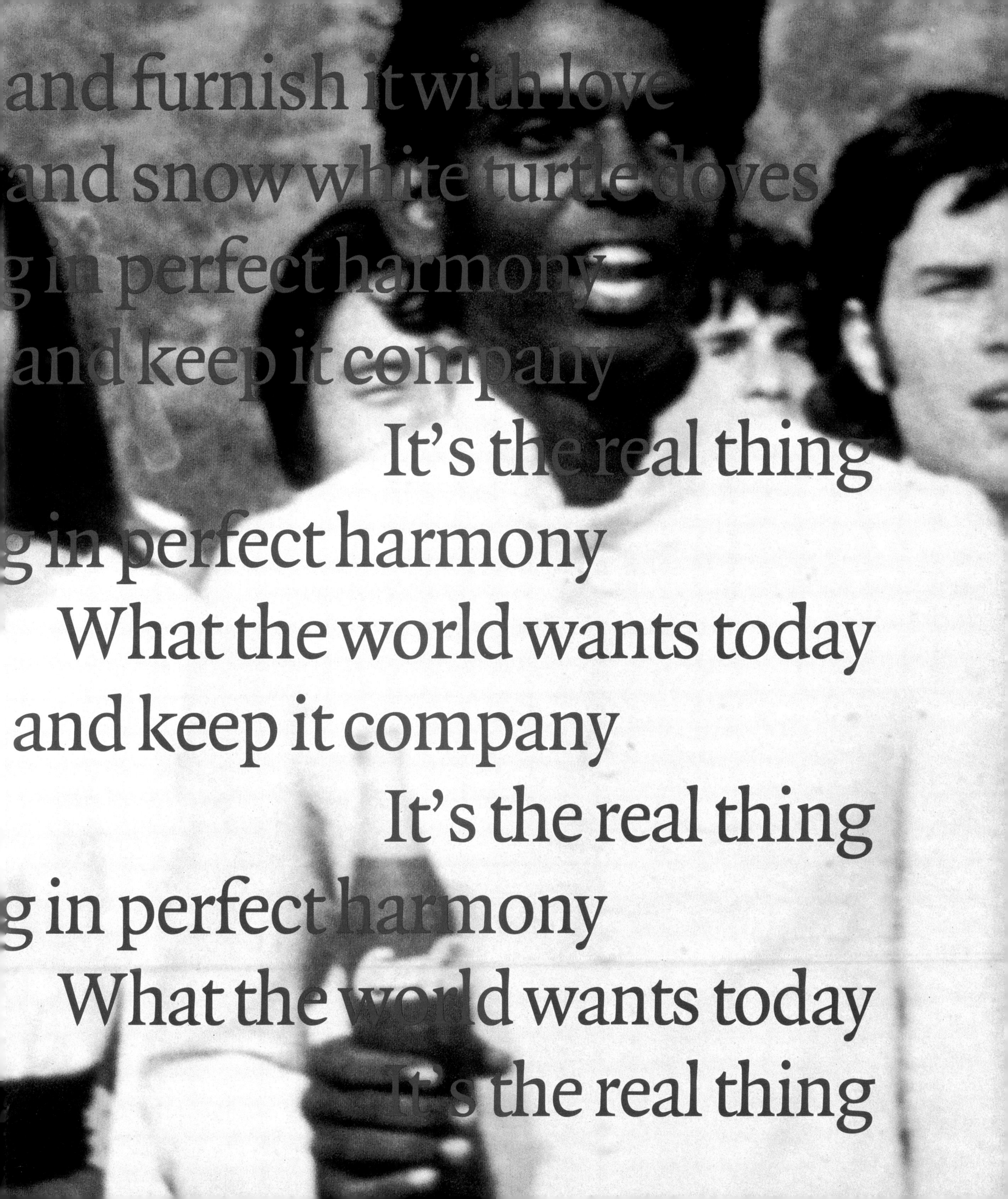

and furnish it with love
and snow white turtle doves
g in perfect harmony
and keep it company
It's the real thing
g in perfect harmony
What the world wants today
and keep it company
It's the real thing
g in perfect harmony
What the world wants today
It's the real thing

Top: Coca-Cola Soda
Fountain, USA, c. 1920.
Above: Coca-Cola bottling,
Junction City, Kansas, USA,
c. 1910.
Right: Cover of Sears,
Roebuck & Co. catalogue,
no. 102, 1896.
Opposite: The Eiffel Tower,
illuminated by Citroën,
Exposition des Arts
Décoratifs, Paris, 1925.

removed.[6] The song and its related imagery became part of Coca-Cola folklore, so much so that the Corporation attempted to revisit the success of the ad in 1989, using the children of the original cast.[7] The success of Levi's television advertising in the 1980s, with their famous 'Laundrette' campaign and others, once more demonstrated how the popular-music charts could be used to reinforce the image of brand. Like most of Levi's advertising, this campaign again utilised the image of a mythologised America.

It is no accident that a number of familiar companies promote themselves as the brands that 'built' America. The growth of national networks of goods circulation and distribution in mid-nineteenth-century America and the increasing regulation of products created a climate where brands could flourish. In a more mobile society, the familiarity of branded goods quickly became an important selling point. Companies rushed to register patents on new products and brand names, as others were quick to move in on the popularity of a new idea. Patent or proprietary medicine was one particularly burgeoning area for brand names. Coca-Cola started life in 1886 (and was patented in 1887) as a medicinal product or 'nerve tonic', sold as a general pick-me-up at a time when a host of similar products were appearing.[8] Available first through cafés or 'soda fountains' and only later as a bottled (and then canned) product, it achieved rapid success by investing in the value and image of its name. In fact, patent-medicine makers were early exploiters of newspaper and billboard advertising and among the first to trade on image above product,[9] by a range of promotional activities and related merchandising. By the late 1890s, Coca-Cola was being claimed in the States as the 'national drink'.[10]

Aside from the growth of advertising, other channels for branded goods were developing, and retail outlets developed into brands in themselves. Large multiple stores, such as Woolworths and J. C. Penney's in America and Thomas Lipton's stores in Britain, began to standardise the quality of service in their outlets. British companies W. H. Smith and John Menzies took control of a network of railway-

station news-stands. Mail Order giants like Montgomery Ward and Sears, Roebuck offered American consumers the opportunity to purchase the same goods regardless of location. All of these companies, founded in the 1870s, 1880s and 1890s, are among the major national (and sometimes international) brand-name retailers today.

Promotion of branded items often focussed on the lifestyle attributes of the product: health, beauty or social status. Goods and their messages contributed to the establishment of popular concepts of self-identity and individualism. In his history of American advertising, Jackson Lears has argued that advertising by the early twentieth century had become 'dominated by the ethos of personal efficiency'.[11] Perfectionism, both physiological and psychological, was inculcated into its messages.[12] Advertising was just one of the mechanisms that helped brands to succeed in establishing the association of physical and social ideas with particular brands. Beauty brands, for example, benefitted from the range of promotional and distribution channels for goods: 'By 1880 a spider's web of establishments – pharmaceutical houses, perfumers, beauty salons, drugstores, wholesale suppliers, the incipient mail order trade, and the

Top: Tradecard of Mowbray
& Son, Tea Dealers & Grocers,
High Street, Newport,
1850-1900.
Above: Tradecard of Hope
Insurance Company, Ludgate
Hill, by John Girton,
1800-1825.

department stores – provided the infrastructure for beauty culture.'[13] Female entrepreneurs such as Helena Rubinstein and Elizabeth Arden established companies that grew into international brands by the mid-twentieth century.

Although we may associate the idea of globalisation in business with the information culture of the late twentieth century, many companies were operating transnationally by the early twentieth century. Coca-Cola resisted international expansion for some time, only agreeing to a European venture in the 1920s,[14] and found different degrees of difficulty in establishing their brand in other countries. Ford began with exporting cars to Britain from America but quickly moved to set up a production plant in Manchester as early as 1911.[15] The prominence of brand names at international expositions in the late nineteenth and early twentieth century contributed to the transnational recognition of some companies. Citroën's 'branding' of the Eiffel Tower at the International Exposition des Arts Décoratifs in Paris in 1925 may well have contributed to the consumer perception of Citroën as not only a manufacturer but also an embodiment of Frenchness.

But at some point in the twentieth century branding became pervasive. The maintenance of brand image and value was the driving force for producers and brand-owners and national – even global – brand names came to dominate local markets. In the post-war West, against the backdrop of the Cold War, to be an active participant in a consumer society became increasingly regarded as a basic human right. The idea of citizenship becomes framed around the idea of consumership and this 'redefinition of rights and obligations articulated itself in the seemingly innocuous language of soft drinks, cars and household appliances'.[16] Critics of this materialist society also tended to see 'Americanisation' as the driving force behind such consumer demands. We may classify this post-war society as the apogee of consumer culture, but the origins of such social and business practices can be traced back much further.

Changes in retail practices and relations in the eighteenth century in Britain heralded the rise of

branded goods. But in Britain, as in other European countries, the full development of branding was inhibited until the later nineteenth century by the absence of legislative protection against piracy for trademarks, packaging and the like. The shift from barter to fixed pricing, the increasing use of advertising and even the embryonic use of the 'brand' as an assurance of quality can be found in late eighteenth-century Europe.[17] Tobacco branding, to give just one example, evolved from the use of trade cards, first used by tobacco merchants in the seventeenth century. In the early nineteenth century, some tobacco importers differentiated their products using different brand names.[18] Trade cards for wholesalers, importers, retailers and service businesses, although not brand names, used descriptive imagery to embody the practices and promises of their trade.

There is certainly evidence for the emergence of retail brands, as opposed to branded products, prior to the mid-nineteenth century. Consumers were more likely to identify goods with the retailer or distributor than with the manufacturer, with the exception of some early manufacturer brands such as Wedgwood. In 1780s' Paris a fashionable and expensive boutique, Le Petit Dunkerque, sold goods at fixed prices and promoted the shop's good name as a kind of brand so that, 'as with today's designer jeans, the label on his goods was more important to his customers than the products themselves'.[19] Wide-scale distribution was well established in Britain by the eighteenth century, as was a consumer taste for novelty and an increasing diversity of product ranges, such as in printed fabrics. The development of new marketing and advertising strategies such as handbills, newspaper advertisements and other promotional activities was underway. However, this is a long way from 'the extensive advertising of branded products characteristic of the end of the nineteenth century, or the concern with the mental processes of the consumer, with empathy and therapy, that has become widespread in advertisements by the mid-twentieth century'.[20] The idea of modern branding had yet to emerge.

As historian and anthropologist James Carrier has

pointed out,[21] until the late 1800s consumers were unlikely to associate goods with the name of the manufacturer, importer or distributor. Goods were more likely to be thought of in terms of the retailer or the place of origin – French lace, Scotch whisky and so on. Retailers had traditionally traded in loose dry, fresh and cured goods, blending, weighing, bottling and wrapping purchases on the premises. Increasingly, manufacturers or importers started to package their own goods, standardising the size of purchases in paper parcels, jars and later tins. This was partly due to the rise of regulation, which fuelled the perception among consumers that packaged and tinned goods were cleaner and protected from impurities. The US Food & Drug Administration, for example, was established in 1906 to regulate corporations selling such goods. Regulation also meant that large and profitable enterprises could flourish, less hampered by rivals with inferior products.

Packaging also allowed manufacturers to standardise pricing, rather than leaving it to the retailer (thus ensuring a regularised percentage of profits, too). As packaging became more distinctive, shoppers learnt to distinguish goods by their brand name and ask for them by brand. According to a survey of Chicago grocers in 1920, more than three-quarters of their customers asked for baked beans by brand name.[22] In a more mobile society, the reliability of finding a familiar brand in stores all over America compensated for the increasing anonymity of shopping. It also meant that retailers began to stock more than one brand of sugar, tea, cereal and so on, so that packaging had to compete on the shelves. Dry goods were more likely to be packaged initially – particularly tea, coffee, spices, sugar and soap. Among the first, and still familiar, brands were Bovril, Cadbury, Rowntree and Oxo.[23] The packaging of butter, ham and other cured foodstuffs started soon after 1900.[24]

As pre-wrapped merchandise eclipsed loose goods, so the role of the retailer changed too. Pre-packaged cigarettes had emerged in Britain in the 1880s with the launch of brands such as Woodbines, and by the 1930s the cigarette dominated the tobacco retail market. The tobacconist, who had once been the purveyor of an assurance of quality to the consumer, now found this role increasingly being played by the brand:[25]

The brand became the new expression of assurance. It laid the foundation for the modern confidence of the purchaser when buying commodities which he could neither try nor test before use. This applies in particular to articles for which a guarantee is given; the branded article means, more or less, a direct relationship between the consumer and the producer.

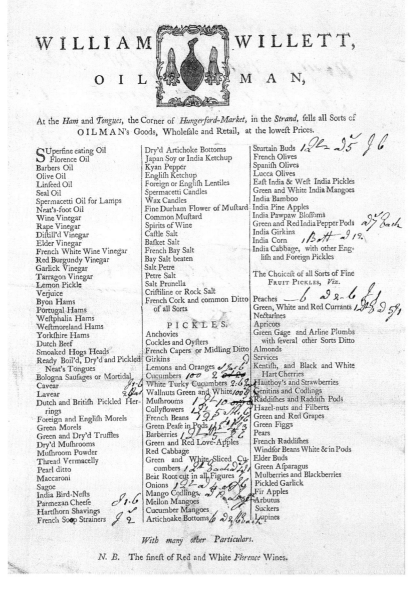

Right: Advertisement for a grocer. William Willett, Oilman's goods, At the Ham and Tongues, the Corner of Hungerford Market, in the Strand, sells all sorts of Oilman's goods, Wholesale and Retail, at the lowest prices: 4 May 1765.

Willings
BESSEMER
gave us
Steel
Give me
OXO
NGTH LIKE THAT
NESTLÉ'S
MILK
RICHEST IN CREAM

Many of the early food and drink brands that still exist today came from strongly paternalistic company structures. Company philosophy was equivalent to brand values, and the advertising slogans tended to reflect this. The names of Kellogg, Cadbury, Rowntree and Mars are associated with the kind of company philosophy that embraced puritan ideals, conservative family values and moderation in all things (except perhaps profit). These, and other early brand owners, based their company behaviour upon issues such as worker welfare and education, health and temperance. Benign organisations, which formed their own worker clubs, schools and social events, tended also to be vociferous opponents of trade unionism and organised worker politics. Ford, Rowntree and Cadbury all invested in education, welfare and housing for employees and their families. Health and goodness, in fact, were frequent early selling points for branded goods, trading on the concerns of shoppers, which were in turn fuelled by an increasingly visible system of regulation. Soft drinks, cigarettes and chocolate often carried the association of being 'good for you'. The Mars Bar slogan 'helps you work, rest and play'

is a variation on a message that had been sold with the product since the 1930s. Forrest Mars Snr, who arrived from the States to set up a confectionery company in England in 1932, marketed his new product to appeal to a depression-hit society that was wary of indulgence. The Mars Bar was therefore promoted as a nutritional product.[26] The consistency of such messages gives these early brands a common identity: they all aimed to inspire trust and loyalty, the first principles of branding.

From the 1930s onwards, almost inevitably beginning in America, as Aaron Betsky points out in 'All the World's a Store', the supermarket became one of the main locations for engagement with the brand. Like its older sibling, the department store, the supermarket created a retail environment where the shopper could look without buying and enter without prejudice. Unlike the department store, the supermarket's image was one of utility, with 'a vaunted lack of display: here it is, nothing fancy, no extras'.[27] Packaged goods could vie with one another on the shelves for the shoppers' attention. The advent of the shopping trolley and self-service meant that the

shopper would select her goods (it almost invariably was 'her') without the direct intervention of the sales assistant. Over-the-counter purchases meant that the 'eye-appeal' of a product or package was less significant. Once in the supermarket, however, the package had to do the work of the shopkeeper and make the sale. Faced with an array of choices, the well-known brand name is a constant upon which the shopper would rely. It is a means of making the choice on behalf of the shopper. Therefore, 'Kellogg's cornflakes' or 'Heinz baked beans' offer reassurance.

The association of the brand name with the product turns the purchase into an engaging experience – packaged with the cornflakes is the promise that this is the authentic product. It carries a feeling of reliability and communicates a sense of care to the family. Advertising, of course, plays on the knowledge that choices made when shopping for the family are bound up with both fear and love.[28]

These are the messages that carry through all the channels for engagement with the brand. Billboards, TV and radio advertising, product placement and

status, desire, fear and need, condensing more complex thoughts into short signals that can be read instantly from a billboard or in moments from a television commercial. It relies upon a vocabulary of emotional triggers that can be commonly understood: art, nature and classical music are reliable indicators of the mood of a certain ad and product. Humour, celebrity endorsement or the use of 'real people' are other well-known narrative strategies. What can not be determined is the range of responses to ads. We may understand the message and the associations, but a level of more personal association is likely finally to determine our response. We may enjoy the ad, admire it, laugh at it, discuss it, but still not buy the product. Consuming the ad may even enable us to have the product experience without needing to consume the product. As Patrick Barwise, Andrea Dunham and Mark Ritson propose in 'Ties That Bind', advertising is a weaker force than we imagine. Particularly with household goods and consumables, the advertisement presumes a prior relationship to the well-known brand and tends to focus on keeping the brand name in consumers' minds.

The package and the ad are not the only outward manifestations of brand value. Brand owners often seek to control the experience of engaging with the brand and encourage us to see purchase as only one aspect of the 'brand experience'. Brand values are also played out in the service offered by companies, and the places in which we encounter brands. Indeed, retail environments are now so completely dominated by the signs of branding that the formal architecture of such spaces disappears, a point expanded upon by Aaron Betsky in 'All the World's a Store'. The creation of brand-specific environments – from NikeTown to Disneyland – is an indication of this. A clearly definable shift in advertising has been the move from a product-centred message (ads that outline the purposive benefits of the product) to an experience-centred message (ads that determine a relationship between the brand and a perceived lifestyle, by association).[31] Guy Julier suggests in his snapshot piece (p. 148) that the emphasis in branding is shifting 'from object to experience', so that our time,

endorsement are all conduits for reinforcing the value of the brand. Advertising is often seen as an alchemic process, taking our emotional weaknesses and fashioning them into demands and desires for goods. The development of the advertising industry and its corollary, marketing, is generally assumed to be based on the dominant American model of the 1950s. In Britain, large American advertising agencies moved in to control a vast proportion of the industry during that decade.[29] As Gareth Williams suggests in chapter five 'The Point of Purchase', totemic publications such as Vance Packard's *The Hidden Persuaders* (1957) confirmed the view that the advertisers and marketers were the key agents of change in the post-war society and the architects of what Tibor Scitovsky called 'the joyless economy'.[30]

Much more recently, studies of advertising have presented it as a polysemous process, where there is a diversity of readings and responses, rather than the manipulator–victim relationship between advertiser–consumer implied by early critics. Advertising makes use of already established codes of

ARMANI

eau pour homme

as well as our goods, is becoming branded.

Brands are 'designed' in a multitude of ways, and this is part of the branding process. Products, whether sportswear or electronic goods, can have the brand values of the company literally 'built-in'. Just as the process of designing is not simply styling but also development and innovation, so branding is not just the addition of a company's logo or corporate colours to a designed product. Some branding is, of course, just that, when unbranded goods are bought and repackaged with the brand name, but this tends to be seen as a relatively unsuccessful example of brand development in the long term. However, when the brand company develops new products, either designed in house or by consultants, the brand image is of significant importance to that development.

Brand image had become so central to the success of a product that it is now as important if not more so than product innovation.[32] In fact, the relationship of product, marketing and branding is so close that it becomes impossible to distinguish the character of an object from that of its branded image – they are one and the same.[33] The design of the product is actually a vehicle for brand value, rather than the other way around. Rather than brands existing to sell more of a product, products are developed as a means of extending and consolidating the brand. A good example of this is the relationship between the couture collections produced by designers for established fashion houses, and the success of house fragrances and cosmetics. The publicity garnered by the seasonal couture collections is crucial for the sales of branded merchandising, which may have little to do with the designer or the fashion house itself: what counts is the name.

This is not to say that companies do not invest in design and product development, as many clearly do. A branded company will tend to develop goods that have a clear relationship to their brand image. Tracking the histories of established industries, one usually finds the reason for a line of development lies in manufacturing knowledge and technical ability. Nokia, the Finnish telecommunications company, has its roots in three nineteenth-century industries:

paper making, rubber and synthetics and the manufacture of cables for telegraph and telephone networks. Outside of Finland, the brand has achieved global recognition only in the last decade, and its origins are largely unknown.

Consumer-goods companies with a strong brand image and awareness often move into areas of product development where the brand values carry across successfully. Richard Branson's empire, Virgin, has tested out the strength of its brand value on everything from clothing to mortgages. When moving into areas of business activity where it has no previous experience, Virgin is relying upon the image of Branson as 'the consumer's friend' who brings personality to faceless industries and business practices. The success of the Virgin brand is firmly tied to the cult of personality. What Branson offers is a specific character of service and a reputation for challenging authoritative brands (for instance, his public battles with British Airways). Virgin makes ironic use of the 'rules' of branding as part of its brand image; when Virgin cola was first launched, the company parodied the myth that the famous 1930s' Coca-Cola bottle was based on the voluptuous curves of Mae West. Virgin produced a similar curved plastic bottle, coloured red, and christened it the 'Pammy', after surgically enhanced *Baywatch* star Pamela Anderson.

Corporations are now more than ever involved in the manipulation and control of image, over and above the production of 'real' things. Sociologist Don Slater has characterised contemporary culture as 'the domination of information, media and signs, the disaggregation of social structure into lifestyles, the general priority of consumption over production in everyday life and the constitution of identities and interests'.[34] This is the idea that we all engage in 'lifestyles' literally fashioned from commodities and forms of entertainment and information gathering, rather than from more traditional providers of identity such as family and work, religious and political belief. As goods take on this greater symbolic function in our lives, so their aesthetic content increases. The roles of the image-makers, including designers, ad agencies and

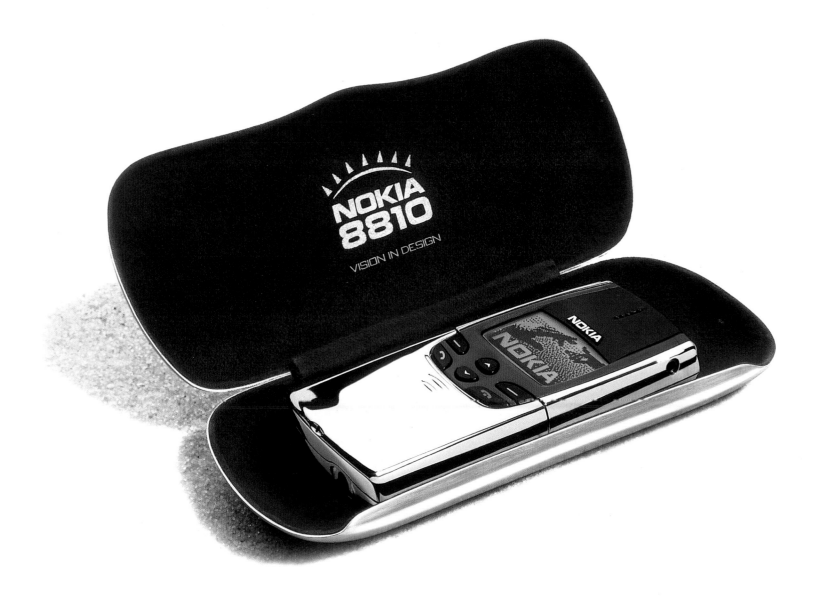

brand managers, take centre stage. Consuming is defined as a more romantic, hedonistic and emotional act. The product is promoted as a 'sign of me' – a signal to others of our status, aspiration or personal values. This is what has been called 'the aestheticisation of everyday life'.[35] Contemporary society is 'saturated' with images and signs, where the aesthetic and symbolic appearance of goods becomes the primary means of everyday experience. The prime role of commodities becomes to express emotional and symbolic value – as signs to be decoded by ourselves and others. Branding is one of the processes by which products become signs. A pair of jeans becomes associated with youthful sex appeal, or a particular bar of chocolate signals the exotic.

Two 1999 ad campaigns present a very literal view of the symbolic properties of objects and their function as indicators of status and fashion. The campaign for the IBM ThinkPad shows the product on a clothes hanger and the Nokia 8810 mobile phone is photographed variously in a perfume bottle, sunglasses case or shown as a powder compact. Both ads employ the qualities of perfume or cosmetics ads – sparse white background, photographed in a way that indicates the casing of the object is somehow 'precious' and stylish. Both campaigns were run in the lifestyle press. Although no person is shown with the products, the implication is that these items are about adornment rather than utility. They are to be worn on the body, like make-up or clothing. A marked tendency in current advertising is to associate a wide diversity of products with the fashion system, so that all goods are seen as 'accessories' to our lifestyle or personality. Signs of sexual or emotional gratification are often used, for example, to advertise everything from ice cream to cat food. Branded products are used to signify our emotional relationships to those around us: friends, families, pets.

We are encouraged by advertisers and the media to see the acquisition of goods as a means to constructing a social persona, and we are all likely to make certain high-risk purchases at certain times as a means of sending signals to others. A sleek and expensive car is a pretty straightforward indication of wealth and career success. In choosing from the bracket of executive cars, however, the signalling becomes more complex. Two cars in the same price range may be associated with very different values, such as successful sex appeal or reliable family values. Volvo is a car that has variable brand associations – a residual image as rather staid, dull and kindly, and a newer brasher one that has been stressed in the ad campaigns for several years. The success of Volvo currently implies that the second brand image is being received and understood, but the residual one is still evident.

Stuart Ewen has called the appropriation of personality by the acquisition of goods 'the assembling of the commodity self'.[36] American artist Barbara Kruger, whose work deals with the relationship between identity and consumerism, expressed this in more ironic terms with her phrase 'I shop therefore I am.' The reading of character through personal goods is the staple practice of a good deal of advertising and also magazine editorial, with features on celebrity shopping habits, favourite car brands, designer labels and even the contents of famous refrigerators. American beer label Schlitz parodied this in its press advert featuring a rummage through celebrity dustbins and the tagline 'You are what you trash.' As Celia Lury has commented: 'Is garbage, the husks of a personal selection of consumer goods, to be understood as a self portrait?'[37]

Although undoubtedly consumption is bound up with a sense of self and group identity, it is not simply enough to think that commodities are a way of telling others about ourselves. Objects do communicate certain accepted social truths, but as the British Conservative Party leader William Hague demonstrated when he wore a baseball cap to the (predominantly Afro-Caribbean) Notting Hill Carnival in London, the signals may be different to those we wish to send out. Hague's appearance at the Carnival was an exercise in the acquisition of what French sociologist Pierre Bourdieu has termed 'cultural capital'. By associating himself with some signs of 'hip' and youthful popular culture, and with an event that is seen, in cultural and racial terms, as highly 'authentic', Hague should have made political capital

out of his actions. Instead, his behaviour was ridiculed in the press, and Hague's projected, personal 'brand' image went somewhat awry.

The use of branded goods to send signals to others is rarely as self-conscious as it might appear. We tend to imbue branded goods with a significance that is out of proportion to their everydayness. Take the sight of President Clinton giving testimony during the 1998 investigation into his relationship with Monica Lewinsky. The President sipped from a can of Diet Coke, an act that was analysed in detail by the world's media almost instantaneously. The President is known for his love of junk food, and the sight of the packaging (rather than a glass) could be taken as a sign of his 'ordinary Joe' Americanness. But Diet Coke rather than ordinary Coke? Some saw this as a sign of emasculation, others as a sign of penitence. In choosing a low-calorie drink, the President perhaps unwittingly presented the world with an image of pleasures denied, a form of calorific sobriety.

The idea that goods act as a kind of language is a precarious one.[38] First of all, the assembling of commodities in one place or on one person is not like constructing a sentence, as there is no apparent grammar. There is rarely a consensus about what is 'in fashion' and 'out of fashion' among more than very selective groupings of people.[39] Branding is an attempt to fix the codes attached to certain goods and to make for a more reliable form of communication. However, once control over the reception of the branded message is lost, the brand itself is weakened. The recent and on-going controversy in Britain over 'grey goods' was more than simply an argument about profit

and loss – it was a battle for control over brand image. Two large supermarket chains, Tesco and Asda, began stocking 'designer brands' at discount prices. The goods on sale were legitimately purchased but from sources other than the brand owners. Genuine label goods, bought at end-of-line ranges, could then be sold at much lower cost than in the 'brand-sanctioned' outlets. However, the availability of discounted brand names on supermarket shelves might be seen to devalue an established luxury brand.

The significance of branded goods to our concept of lifestyle is dependent upon a speedy turnover of product types and brand innovations. Fuelled by flexible systems of goods production and circulation, manufacturing is increasingly responsive to fluctuations of taste and meaning within the market and is, in turn, able to promote fluctuations in order to increase turnover. In the 1950s and 1960s, as Gareth Williams describes in 'The Point of Purchase', critics of industry argued against what they saw as 'planned obsolescence' in consumer goods, against products that were deliberately designed only to last several years. Planned obsolescence is now more applicable to the meaning rather than the functioning of the object. Signs are increasingly unstable and more quickly superseded by new ones than ever before.

The shift from a production- to a consumption-oriented economy is indicative of this. Increasingly, branded companies place the emphasis on service and marketing, rather than on manufacture, which is clear from a look at the 'image industries' involved in the production of highly symbolic goods. In the early years of mass production, producers looked to forge new markets and demands for their products. Production systems were more rigid, and tooling and assembly relatively inflexible. Developing standardised products for mass markets and driving down prices to make goods more attractive were the core aims of most manufacturers. The American mass market was built on this method, as were the beginnings of the Japanese 'economic miracle' after the Second World War. However, Japan was able to develop a more flexible and adaptable system of production, which kept better pace with changes in consumer behaviour and

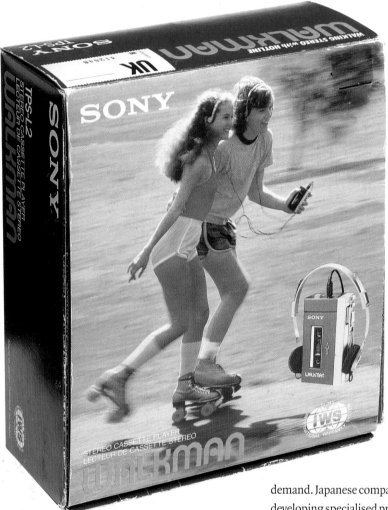

technologies are on hand. Often with a high level of 'crafting' or skill involved in the creation of products, such companies tend to be in the 'luxury goods' bracket. In Italy, the manufacture of home wares, furniture, ceramics, leather goods and other 'lifestyle' products works according to this system.

Alessi is perhaps the best example of a local company with global brand recognition. These Italian industries may be the result of a centuries-old tradition of manufacture in the region, but flexible specialisation does not always refer to the transformation of existing forms of production. The same model can also be applied to two localities for production in California. 'Silicon Valley', so called for its predominance of electronics and information technology industries, and Hollywood, the home of the film and entertainment industry. Both rely upon a network of highly specialised and skilled producers, and a supporting community of creative talents. Both are also outstandingly successful in the art of brand management and image creation.

As markets for new consumer goods became saturated, and demand more sophisticated, specialised and fragmented, so the emphasis on production changed too. Nowadays, manufacturing is characterised by the high level of out-sourcing, where companies no longer own the means of production but sub-contract or buy in from other manufacturers. By maintaining a flexible production or service base, shorter life cycles for goods and constant (but low-cost) product innovation, companies maintain a dynamic image. Often, this innovation will concentrate on marketing, advertising and styling alone. Mass customisation refers to the greater range of product or service variants that companies now offer. When purchasing a car or a mobile phone, for example, the range of 'optional extras' may be such that the customer feels that he or she is creating a unique product from the characteristics on offer. Mass customisation also employs the device of offering 'special' limited editions that are a variation on the basic purchase. The 'theming' of items by fast-food outlets to tie in with a major film release (usually children's cartoons) is a good example of this.

demand. Japanese companies had great success from developing specialised products for niche markets, or generating new market demands, with products such as the Sony Walkman.

In the 1970s, when many large-scale industries foundered due to their cumbersome and inflexible structures, some smaller-scale ones found their ability to adapt made them able to respond to shifts in niche market demand. As economic historians Piore and Sabel have described it 'the spread of flexible specialisation amounts to a revival of craft forms of production.'[40] The practice of flexible specialisation means the production of short-run, specialised goods, often with a high design content. It often develops around an interdependent community network of similar producers, suppliers and creative industries. This in turn supports a community of skilled workers and ensures that the required expertise, materials and

A dominant model of brand behaviour has been termed 'McDonaldisation' after the global fast-food chain. Whilst McDonald's may appear at first as a paradigm of mass production and standardisation – the Henry Ford of Hamburgers – it is an organisation capable of rapid and continuous innovation. On one level, uniforms, recipes, interior architecture and the character of service are similar across the world. The 'Big Mac' has become an economist's unit of value to analyse the difference in the economic status of nations. McDonald's is based on a system of franchising restaurants, where the parent company owns the brand values but not the real estate. McDonald's also create local products for different locations – the infamous 'Maharajah Big Mac' in India or the 'McTeryaki Burger' in Japan. As Russell Belk explains in 'Wolf Brands in Sheep's Clothing'

(pp. 68-9), global brands such as McDonald's nurture their relationship to a particular locality in a number of ways, in order to become 'naturalised'. To quote Edward Rensi, President of McDonald's USA: 'People have a vision of McDonald's being identical in 12,000 restaurants…. We've got products in Texas that we don't have in Boston. There's a lot going on at McDonald's all the time.'[41]

The stereotype of the modern consumer lifestyle is set against a backdrop of global culture. Terms such as 'globalism' and 'globalisation' abound in any discussion of brands and branded consumer goods, and the mythological power of these terms needs addressing. One assumption is that 'über-brands' such as Coca-Cola and McDonald's have achieved such a global penetration of the market that one can almost expect to encounter them on a Himalayan

Opposite: Packaging for Sony Walkman, *c.* 1979.
Right: McDonald's, Shanghai, 1999.

mountain pass or a military base camp in the Antarctic. A second assumption is that globalisation is an entirely new phenomenon, borne out of late twentieth-century cultural and economic shifts, rather than a longer historical process. In fact, it can be argued that the roots of modern globalisation can be found in the early fifteenth century, and that the most dramatic period of global expansion, until now, covered the years 1880–1925.[42] That period, which saw the setting up of the first global competitions such as the Olympics, was also a fertile period for the establishment of today's most familiar brands, including BMW, ICI and HMV.

Despite these precedents, however, it seems we are now more self-conscious about our place in a globalised culture than before. Since Marshall McLuhan's influential concept of the 'global village' first appeared in the 1960s,[43] the idea of an homogenised global culture has been seen as one of the chief characteristics of the late twentieth century. Signs of cultural homogeneity include the rapid advance of new technologies such as the Internet, allowing near instantaneous communication across the globe. The international language of brand names and branded goods, and the presence of Microsoft or McDonald's in towns and cities from Calcutta to Cincinnati, support the view that we are all citizens of a single, Americanised and commodified culture.

Brands are the signifiers of this vision of contemporary culture, with Coca-Cola, McDonald's, Versace, Gucci, Nike and Tommy Hilfiger presented as icons of a homogenised international language of goods. In the global village, shopping, eating and entertainment are products packaged identically in any high street, mall or entertainment park. In the words of one cultural commentator: 'Eclecticism is the degree zero of contemporary general culture: one listens to reggae, watches a western, eats McDonald's food for lunch and local cuisine for dinner, wears Paris perfume in Tokyo and "retro" clothes in Hong Kong.'[44] The brand acts as quality control, reassuring us that a hamburger in Moscow will be the same as in Manchester. Globalisation, it seems, offers the kind of market saturation of which corporations once only dreamed and suggests the domination of market forces over all other cultural practices.

Whereas advertisers present an image of the modern consumer as unfettered global traveller, free to pick and choose from a range of lifestyles, the reality of our everyday lives is very different, and in a series of scenarios we should consider some of the implications of the 'globalised experience'. First of all, the process of globalisation has to be observed through what has been called 'the prism of the local'.[45] Local contexts and local consequences all offer variations on the experience of the global paradigm. In fact, the abstract concept of a truly globalised experience is a construct of advertising alone. All our experiences of global culture, whether through community life, media or travel, are tempered by the local context of ourselves and others.

Furthermore, instead of creating homogeneity, it can be argued that globalisation promotes and sustains difference and plurality in everyday experience. Anthropologist Arjun Appadurai has described this as a series of imaginary landscapes, where our view depends upon our location within that landscape.[46] These landscapes are formed by ethnicity, by technology, by finance, media and ideologies. Popular culture (as the primary form of contemporary expression) feeds off the intrusion of different cultural forms. Pop music, with its borrowing, sampling and recycling, is the best example of how imported tastes are indigenised, creating new and different forms. The new global cultural economy, according to Appadurai, 'has to be seen as a complex, overlapping, disjunctive order'.

The interweaving of global and local contexts is made more possible by developing networks of data and communication. The expansion of telecommunications means that different kinds of information can be transported across the globe in an instant (voices, text, pictures, sounds and moving images). These means of communication are also increasingly more cheaply available to a wider range of people. Contact between communities of people, between families, ethnic groups, shared-interest groups and so on can be maintained on a daily basis.

This can even mean the creation of 'virtual' communities. As people become more mobile and migratory while staying in contact across distances, there is a greater tendency to view the world as a single place. This shift to a global perspective has been called 'space–time compression'[47] and results in nation-state borders and institutions becoming less significant in people's worldview.

Rather than talk of a global culture, it is therefore more appropriate to talk of global flows and global relations – suggesting the fluidity and diversity that globalisation encompasses. However, this should not be taken as a utopian view. The late twentieth century has witnessed the rise of religious fundamentalism alongside the decline of nation-state frameworks. Social mobility and the migration of populations are more often enforced or reluctant than the result of personal choice. The kinds of compression that result from mobility and technology are not available to everybody – economic and educational factors restrict this to those who have the means to exploit them.

Just as globalisation has prompted new social formations and encounters, so has it affected the production and distribution of goods around the world. Again, this is crucial to an understanding of how branding operates. Few truly global corporations exist. The idea of a multinational company without a preferred geographical locus is hard to imagine. Many companies that operate globally still exhibit the signs of a latent national or cultural specificity. Coca-Cola is inseparable from its carefully nurtured image of the American 'good life' as global exemplar. Microsoft,

whose branded interfaces appear on most desktops in the world, is synonymous with its founder, Bill Gates, and spends much legal time fighting allegations of monopolisation on home territory. National legislative controls are used to curb the global freedoms of transnational companies.

There are also few truly global products. Again, both state legislation and cultural differences mean that goods tend to be 'adapted' to suit local conditions. Consumables are produced in localised sites (bottling plants, packaging and assembly sites). There are technical restrictions on producing a homogenised product (think of the difficulties in getting electrical products to work when travelling without adapters). There are language and cultural barriers to instructions and ingredients, as well as sometimes problems with the name of a product. Despite the claims of a few companies, such as the Italian fashion and lifestyle business Diesel, advertising is more likely to be tailored to local conditions than a global advertising campaign used. In the case of multinational advertising agencies, 'there is no tendency towards globalisation in the production and transmission of the ads themselves'.[48] There are far too many different possible readings both between and within social and cultural groupings (consider how assertions of sexuality and female individuality are not acceptable in Muslim cultures).

The only constant, it appears, is the brand itself. Product names and specifications may vary, but the brands of Ford, Unilever, General Motors, Toyota and Sony are global standards. Protecting the value and image of that brand, then, becomes paramount. It is the vehicle for the placing of goods in certain market contexts and niches, and the means of differentiating the product in the absence of a 'home-grown' context. However, as both company and consumer behaviour indicates, brand image is a vulnerable concept, susceptible to social and local interpretation, which can be good or bad for the value of the brand.

The vulnerability of brands means that brand owners invest considerably in consumer research. Patterns, behaviours and preferences are minuted in an attempt to anticipate our purchasing habits.

Unsolicited mail shots are targeted by postal or zip codes, and also by subscriptions and mail ordering. Our choices of newspaper, magazine, bank and supermarket all apparently indicate other kinds of consumer preference, such as the shampoo, washing powder or holiday we might buy. With the advent of digital and pay-per-view television, we are likely to find in the future that TV advertising is tailored more directly to us as individuals. A preference for watching animal programmes and sports channels may mean that the ads that appear most frequently on our screens are for cat food and sportswear.

Our identity as consumers appears to be our chief mode of existence. State and cultural services, government, education and even the law see us as citizen–consumers.[49] Consumer rights organisations, television programmes, advice lines and charters are all signs that the right to purchase is now seen as the means by which we gain representation. Those who can not or choose not to engage with consumer culture might appear disenfranchised.

Yet, as Gareth Williams shows in 'The Point of Purchase', consumption is also politicised. Consumer protests and boycotts, acts of consumer terrorism and subversion, the appropriation of branded goods to convey alternative messages are all powerful ways of communicating political messages to a world primarily focused on consumption. Similarly, there are environments for the exchange of goods that are mediated by the consumer, rather than the brand owner. Barter and labour exchange, second-hand networks, car-boot and jumble sales, children's toy libraries, all form part of an alternative system for exchange and consumption.

Within this map of company and individual allegiances and behaviours the brand acts as chief navigator. It is the vehicle for both corporate messages and personal appropriation, and we go on now to explore the wide diversity of both brand behaviours and consumer interventions. The object of this journey is to assess the cultural significance of branding and look at some of the ways in which brands have been fetishised, eulogised and demonised in recent years.

# "The signature is part of the identity of a product or brand."

**PAOLA ANTONELLI**

# Signature value

**Below left and right:** Michael Graves Design™ Collection blender and Collection toaster, both Target Stores, 1999.
**Opposite:** Good Goods by Starck.
**Following pages:** Frank Gehry, Guggenheim Museum, Bilbao.

Among all the promises that brands make to consumers, the 'signature' of the designer is seen as a particular mark of distinction. Signature and editioned goods are promoted as an alternative to the 'mass market', as they target closely identified audiences and lifestyles. The value of the signature is such that it can represent a contract between the named designer and the consumer, and an endorsement of the goods on sale. The signature is part of the identity of a product or brand.

The development of corporate identities in the twentieth century has involved the creation of distinctive visual devices, logos and colours that can be applied across a wide range of products, packages and locations. In this way designers were being used to create the company signature, rather than 'sign' the goods themselves. Some of the oldest successful examples of corporate-image design like AEG, Olivetti and Campari are European. The integrated designs by Peter Behrens for AEG, which comprised products, buildings and advertising campaigns, spoke the supernational language of neoclassicism. By hiring such artists as the Futurist Fortunato Depero, Campari became a patron of the arts, and its campaigns became awaited cultural events. Olivetti employed renowned Swiss designers of the century as art directors and created a top executive position that dealt with the company's influence on the arts. These three companies, which

remain shining examples of corporate communications skills, could invariably count on a smaller and homogeneously sophisticated audience.

Rather than targeting such distinctive audiences, many American designers aimed to create brands identified with universal appeal. Raymond Loewy, for example, engineered identities for some of the most distinctive brands of the century. Loewy's Lucky Strike and Shell brands, much as other designers' Coca-Cola, McDonald's and Levi's, are branding masterpieces, as well as live organisms that to this day employ thousands of designers striving to keep them current and powerful. Branding has also been the key to success for a host of American non-denominational designed goods: those traditional low-cost, everyday objects that carry a brand, like Swingline, Tupperware or Black and Decker, but do not need an established author's name to enter the firmament of good design. At least not in the past.

The demands of consumerism, however, have also changed. Increasingly, brands offer differentiated products designed to particular lifestyle groups. The democratic ideal of the universal product is disappearing. The star system of designers and architects that has emerged in recent years has been particularly noticeable in the American market. The popularity of names of influential twentieth-century figures such as Charles and Ray Eames and Frank Lloyd Wright generates a myriad of merchandising opportunities for, among others, museums. The star system has also encouraged more mainstream manufacturers and retailers to call on the services of living 'celebrity' designers.

In the late 1990s, large American retail companies such as Target, K-mart and 7-11 have revamped their image by signing on celebrities to provide

'quality' products at affordable prices. Philippe Starck, for instance, has designed a range of basic items for the Japanese division of the 7-11 chain, including stationery and personal products, such as toothbrushes and hairbrushes, that retail for less than $10. Martha Stewart, a woman who made her name into a commercial empire, has been involved with K-mart since 1987 as a lifestyle consultant. Two years ago she initiated 'Martha's World', a store within K-mart featuring 'Martha Stewart Everyday' and based on her unmistakable concept of quality and ability to provide her public with an attainable status promotion through their purchases. In 1997, the sales of bath towels alone were forecast at $500 million.

Similarly, the Minnesota-based Target has produced a range of more than 200 products, ranging in price between $3.99 and $479.95, for the home, designed by architect Michael Graves. They were introduced in September 1998 under the slogan 'Michael Graves Targets Everyman'. The common denominator – be it lower or higher – are coquettish petlike shapes and sweet knobs and handles. The collection flew off the shelves. Architects, too, have become brand signatures as exemplified by the use of Richard Meier by the Getty Museum and Frank Gehry by the Guggenheim Museum.

Once again, Americans are succeeding at the game, this time by personalising it. Through a person's eyes, the public learns to notice objects and architecture for what they are – carriers of function, beauty and meaning, personal choices that define each person's universe. Ultimately, the shrewd commercial operation has a positive outcome in our contemporary world, the opposite of a suffocating standard for everyday living. With or without a signature.

**JONATHAN WOODHAM**

# A brand new Britain?

During the 1990s both commercial and state-sponsored organisations looked to the idea of branding to create a 'New Britain'. In Mark Leonard's Britain™ *Renewing Our Identity*, a report commissioned by Demos, a left-wing independent think-tank, funded by the British Design Council and published in 1997, the conclusion reached was that Britain's national identity was for most people largely associated with history, heritage and tradition. It was sorely in need of radical rejuvenation.

For much of the twentieth century, official projections of Britain's national identity embraced the past, usually with a strong English inflection. In 1932, writer Stephen Tallents identified Oxford, Bond Street, the English Countryside, the English Home, English servants, gardening and tailoring as essential ingredients of identity. Such retrospection was echoed in many of the displays in British Pavilions at international exhibitions. It was not until Expo '67 in Montreal that much official space was given to the portrayal of dynamic contemporary British culture. Designer James Gardner created an evocation of '60s Britain, featuring a BMC Mini against a Carnaby Street-influenced display of urban chic that was peopled by mannequins dressed in clothes from Mary Quant and Biba.

By the 1990s a number of British companies had found that overt identification with 'Britishness' was rarely advantageous in the global marketplace. British Telecom, which re-branded itself as BT after privatisation in 1984, found that the 'British' label had ceased to be associated with technological expertise. However, not all internationally oriented British companies found the position so straightforward. The most notable commercial re-branding exercise was that of British Airways, which invested in a

£60-million corporate facelift in June 1997. Cast aside was the red, white and blue of the 1984 Landor Associates' Union Jack aircraft tail-fins in favour of a series of eye-catching artworks that represented the cultural diversity of the airline's global passengers, ranging from Celtic illumination to Aboriginal designs. The aim was to commission more than 50 world images from artists and designers to appear on 300 aircraft, thus promoting the idea of British Airways as a 'citizen of the world'. However, such global aspirations found little favour with the nationalism of the British public. Indeed, domestic chauvinism asserted itself so strongly that after a mere two years, it was announced in June 1999 that British Airways would once again fly the national flag.

After New Labour swept to power in 1997, an updated version of 'Swinging London' was championed by the new administration. Cultural patriotism assumed a fashionable guise with the advent of 'Cool Britannia,' and the promotion of cutting-edge and popular British fashion, design, arts and music. Indeed, the origins of 'Cool Britannia' may be seen to derive from the 1967 song from the Bonzo Dog Doo-Dah Band's *Gorilla* album ('Cool Britannia/Britannia you are cool/ Take a trip/Britons ever, ever, ever shall be hip'). Britain's then Prime Minister Harold Wilson lost favour with some in the 1960s when he invited the Beatles to his official residence at No. 10 Downing Street. Tony Blair's receptions for media celebrities were similarly criticised as showing a preoccupation with style rather than substance. Not helped by the 1998 launch of Ben & Jerry's 'Cool Britannia' brand of ice cream, New Labour soon began to

**Above: Traditional Britain: the Country Set display in the British exhibition at Expo '67, Montreal, designed by James Gardner, figures by Astrid Zydower.**
**Below: Rebranding Britain in the 1960s – 'Swinging London': the Carnaby Street display in the British exhibition at Expo '67, Montreal, designed by James Gardner.**
**Opposite: The 1997 re-branding of British Airways.**

distance itself from the associations with over-hyped notions of 'Cool Britannia'.

'Cool Britannia' notwithstanding, the Blair government continued in its efforts to re-brand Britain as a dynamic and diverse economy with a wealth of creative talent in design, fashion, science and technology. The powerhouse::uk exhibition in London in 1998, housed in an inflatable pavilion designed by Nigel Coates, was a showcase for creative Britain, including fashion designer Alexander McQueen and products by Tom Dixon and Jasper Morrison among others. Simultaneously the Foreign Office launched Panel 2000, which comprised people 'at the cutting edge of industry, design, the media and the Government itself' whose 'creativity and energy show what modern Britain is about'. The creative industries are still an essential ingredient of a re-branded Britain. Embracing design, fashion, publishing, digital technology, the performing arts and music, this sector was estimated to be worth £60 billion per year, generating £7.5 billion in annual exports and 1.4 million jobs. Millennium Products, another scheme launched by Blair in September 1997, sought to identify and promote ground-breaking products and services created in Britain and feature them in exhibitions and publications around the world until the year 2000 and beyond. The Millennium Dome is perhaps the finale to this reinvention of Britain through design.

The extent to which these and many other initiatives to 're-brand' Britain will succeed remains to be seen. As the new Millennium unfolds it will soon become clear whether such projections of a creative, dynamic and exciting new Britain will influence those in the global marketplaces or whether the weight of history, heritage and tradition will remain the most potent brand of 'Britishness'.

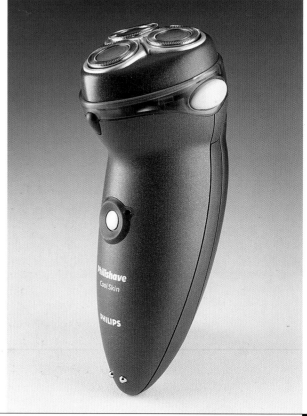

**STEFANO MARZANO Philips Design**

# Branding = Distinctive authenticity

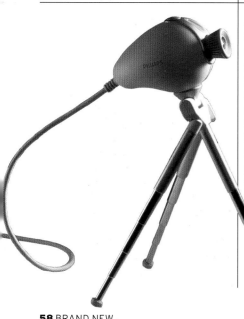

A successful brand is ultimately a question of authenticity. It needs to reflect transparently the values of the company behind it. In this respect, it is not unlike an individual. My name, indeed any name, calls up in the minds of those who know me a certain set of qualities or values. Those associations have been built up over time, abstracted from the totality of their experience with me. If I promise to do something that is in line with those values, they will trust me to carry it out. If it clashes with those values, they will be sceptical.

It is not easy, either as a brand or an individual, to make sure you are authentic in this sense. As individuals, our personalities are composed of a number of

values that determine our ethical framework - our self. When these core values govern our behaviour, we are behaving authentically. When one of our sub-personalities gets the upper hand, however, we behave 'out of character'. This unbalanced state can occur by accident, but it can also be deliberately induced, as when we put up a façade, behaving in accord with values that do not belong to our core. Such situations become untenable.

**People**

How does the company make sure that there is a perfect match between values and behaviour? Products, buildings and machines - even ideas - can be copied, but the only unique elements in a company are its people. They constitute

the soul of the brand. The first step to creating brand authenticity is therefore to ensure that its core values are clear and have been fully internalised by those who work within the company. That is not to say everyone has to be identical - that would be impossible and undesirable. But there should be certain values that they share as part of their own core values.

**Role of Design**

Our primary role at Philips Design is to create the aesthetic of the values behind the Philips brand. Given the enormous range of products that bear the name and the many countries around the world where they are sold, we can only do our task if we have properly internalised the company's core values. Of course, we can - and do - try to lay down guidelines for

PHILIPS

2574   2g/3kg

PHILIPS

"A successful
brand is ultimately
a question of
authenticity."

designing packaging, say, to make sure that wherever they are produced they reflect the right values. But rules only take us so far: general principles are better, and internalised ones are better still, because they ensure the right decisions are taken automatically in new situations. Such principles or values give us a touchstone to help us produce any brand expressions that are consistent and authentically reflect those values. This applies at all levels, from decisions on product features and form language, to packaging, advertising and displays – everything, in fact, that brings the brand into contact with the consumer.

The role of design in representing the brand is greater than ever before. Technologies are increasingly shared

among companies, so that the real differentiating factor is the way technology is shaped. This is more than a question of styling. To design is to shape the future. The Italian for design is *progetto*, or *architettura* – project, or architecture. These expressions clearly convey how design gives physical shape to ideas that will affect people's lives. Viewed in this way, design is a continuous attempt to create future civilisation – no small undertaking.

**Continuity**

The set of values that forms the self takes shape over time. The same applies to a company: its values do so as a result of the values of the individuals who work there, particularly those who guide it. In the autobiography of Frits Philips, the son

of one of the founders and a former chairman, the personal principles of the Philips family can be clearly discerned – from their refusal to buy black market food during the German occupation to their support of the first collective labour agreement with the unions. And then to the inclusion (decades before others got round to it) of a statement of the company's responsibility to society in its articles of association – what is now called 'stewardship'.

In many respects, Frits Philips was very much a 'people's industrialist'. His values were the universal ones of civilisation. Although they remain constant, the way in which they are applied at different periods and in different circumstances varies. In his day, during and after a

devastating war, the main needs of people were those relating to the lower rungs of Maslow's scale: food, shelter, work. Today, in our age of relative prosperity, Frits Philips would be a 'cultural industrialist', an agent of the future whose objective is to advance people's self-actualisation, to enhance their cultural well being, by creating ways of helping them towards the highest levels of Maslow's hierarchy.

This is what we at Philips Design are aiming at today, and I hope that by internalising core values we will be able to do so in the same spirit – though in different form – as our predecessors at the company. To me, this continuity of core values is what constitutes the essence of successful brand design.

# Brand associations through advertising

This page and opposite:
Levi's 'Original Levi's'
campaign, August–November
1996. Published in
magazines including *The
Face*, *i-D*, *Dazed & Confused*,
*Sky*, *Arena* and *FHM*.
Photographer: Nick Knight;
Stylist: Simon Foxton;
Casting: Jason Evans
and Stefan Ruiz; Concept
creators: Steve Hudson
and Victoria Fallon.

Brands that aim for mass-market appeal nevertheless also target more narrowly identified market sectors through localised campaigns. Such campaigns might employ a more unconventional brand image, but one that is still in keeping with the core values and image of the brand in question. In 1996 Steve Hudson and Victoria Fallon at the UK-based BBH advertising agency were given the role of concept creators for the British magazine advertising for Levi's original jeans. Their brief was a campaign that would authenticate the brand's 145-year heritage as the original workwear-jeans manufacturer and clearly distinguish Levi's from long-term market rivals and the growing number of new jeans brands. The aim of the campaign became to trade on the idea of 'age' and authenticity, using older models in the context of youth-oriented advertising. In broader terms, it was felt this idea held the potential to highlight attitudes to ageing within the fashion and advertising industry. Such a campaign would also create a more radical edge to Levi's well-established brand image.

British photographer Nick Knight was chosen to work on the campaign. Knight had not worked for a 'high street' brand before, and his commercial image making had been for the editorial pages of magazines and campaigns for fashion designers including Yohji Yamamoto and Jil Sander. Knight said in interview:

What I was getting frustrated about was that I work with my heart, using real feelings that take into account the world around me. There was a division between the work that I was producing of supposedly beautiful women in supposedly beautiful clothes doing supposedly beautiful things and real contemporary issues. The Levi's project was the first time that I was being paid to have a social agenda to my work.

While the setting for the ad played on the traditional associations of the Levi's brand with the American cowboy, the approach to the subject was highly unconventional for fashion advertising. The proposed campaign was not market tested by BBH, and as Hudson acknowledges: 'I think that if they had asked young kids they would have said, "I don't want to see some old people in Levi's," and blown the idea out.'

Jason Evans and Stefan Ruiz undertook the casting for the campaign over a six-week period in Colorado. Their search centred on the senior rodeo circuit. Ironically, the rodeo had been sponsored by Levi's competitor brand, Wranglers, since the early post-war period. Well aware that the American West had been a rich source for American photographers throughout the twentieth century, the team set out to reflect the grandeur of the Midwest in both the choice of models and setting. Knight wanted to explore some of the issues around the conventional representation of the American West. The significance of Afro-American cowboys, who made up one third of cowboys in the nineteenth century, but whose history has remained relatively hidden, was one area highlighted by the campaign.

The fashion shoot took place over a period of a week in Colorado. Simon Foxton, who has played an important role in the shaping of the identity of Levi's during the 1990s, styled the shoot with a minimal approach. The models brought their own clothing and props, which were mixed with items collected by him. Knight used a large-format camera positioned low with the models posed on a platform in front of a neutral white backdrop. In the printing process, this backdrop was given a stylised coloration of the high, flat plains of Colorado. Although the staging of the shoot was carefully planned, there were last-minute changes such as the inclusion

"In a society where we don't need another pair of jeans or trainers, there is very little chance to redress this unless you give your work a political angle."

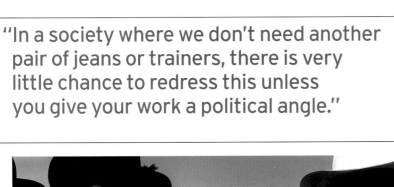

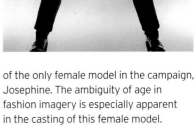

of the only female model in the campaign, Josephine. The ambiguity of age in fashion imagery is especially apparent in the casting of this female model.

The media response to the Levi's' original jeans campaign moved beyond the more typical appraisal of technical and aesthetic accomplishment to focus on the social issue that the campaign raised. It was flagged as the start of a re-evaluation of the way advertising portrays older people in light of an ageing and affluent population of consumers. It was also credited as the most influential mainstream fashion campaign to politicise its overt and central narrative. The campaign was produced within a climate of growing popular desire to see our commercial image making, our collective fantasies, reflect real social concerns. As Nick Knight says: "It felt like I was engaging with people. In a society where we don't need another pair of jeans or trainers, there is very little chance to redress this unless you give your work a political angle. Fashion photography is by its very definition shallow but in a good sense – it can be changed."

JANE PAVITT

# Diesel
## for successful branding?

The Italian fashion and lifestyle brand Diesel was launched in 1978. Beginning life as a jeans and clothing company, the Diesel brand has grown to include licensed fashion goods such as eyewear, footwear and scent, and a distinctive and subversive advertising campaign. Diesel is now a global brand, retailing in over 80 countries in Europe, Asia and the Americas. Here Renzo Rosso, its President and Founder, Wilbert Das, Creative Director and Head of Design, and Maurizio Marchiori, Advertising and Communications Director, discuss the value of the brand and the relationship between design and communication.

**RR**: Diesel means being international, innovative and fun. Our brand's values are our own just as much as the clothes we produce are those we like and wear. Every product has to have its own brand image and values built. For consumers, brands and brand values are a way to 'feel' the product as part of their own personalities. Consumers need more subtle motivations than ever to buy a certain brand. They have to identify themselves with the product they are buying, with its lifestyle, its attitude.

Being global is essential for a brand like ours: young people worldwide are more and more one group, disregarding their nationalities. They are furthermore divided into several 'tribes', centred round a particular kind of music, or habit or taste. During my travels I have the chance to meet kids from Tel Aviv to Los Angeles, from Helsinki to Tokyo, and I regularly find evidence of this. Global distribution is obviously a means and a necessary condition. Therefore we have a large international network of subsidiaries and distributors who

work extremely closely with us in order to project our brand consistently and accurately to the far corners of the world.

**WD**: Diesel is not made to be a local brand, by its very nature it is meant to be global. We believe that our ideas of design and communication are borderless and can be shared across all cultures, by like-minded people all over the world. Our design team is made up of young people who share a lot of the same ideas and sense of imagination. They blend together well, travelling the world constantly in pairs or small groups in search of new inspiration and ideas, which they bring back to our style office and share with the other designers. After all ideas are collected, the real design process starts. Although we produce a single worldwide product line, it is so large and diverse that it gives consumers abundant options to dress themselves. We offer them the possibility to define their own style within our range and this aspect tends to play well across all markets of the world.

One thing that consumers possess abundantly today is choice. They have countless options for everything they could possibly want, so that often the single reason a consumer will choose one item over another is the perceived values of the brand behind it. We therefore have to make Diesel goods 'different' from others, not just in consumer perception gained through branding and communications but also in product characteristics such as design, manufacture and distribution techniques. This is particularly important and relevant today because the tendency in fashion seems to be that branding and showing off logos and labels is diminishing. Consumers now want to have clothes that can stand out naturally, without being overtly

branded. This doesn't mean, of course, that the brand is not important, it still is, but the perception of consumers now is that you shouldn't have to 'shout' what brand you're wearing, others should be able to recognise it naturally.

**MM**: In the beginning the product in Diesel advertising played the same role that costume plays in movies. Brand awareness was key, but now product quality has become more important. We must give back to the product what has been neglected in the past for the sake of brand awareness and without forgetting the historical values of our brand. Our communication respects the brand's style and personality. In today's 'jungle of communications' it is more and more necessary to stick your head out and to walk close to the border sometimes. Consumers are free to explore the meaning of our ironic advertising campaigns.

The basic concept of the FOR SUCCESSFUL LIVING campaign is a kind of mockery of the idea that brands such as ours can 'sell' people better

lives. By playing the 'bad brand' or laughing at ourselves, we distance ourselves from big corporate brands and bring ourselves closer to the attitudes of young-minded consumers. Big brands try so hard to portray themselves as sincere and well-intentioned but it doesn't come across as real, and you can almost always feel the monstrous corporate structure behind it.

**RR**: For companies, brand image and brand values are priceless; they are increasingly the field upon which future battles for market survival will be fought. Every brand must have a mission, but what is more important is the company's added value. The more people realise that wearing is a way to communicate, to express their personality, the more companies must increase and protect their brand's awareness. During the '80s, brand logos were enormous, people liked uniforms and identifying oneself within a social group was so important. Nowadays people look for an individual and personal look and the world of fashion has [to] come to terms with this.

"For consumers, brands and brand values are a way to 'feel' the product as part of their own personalities."

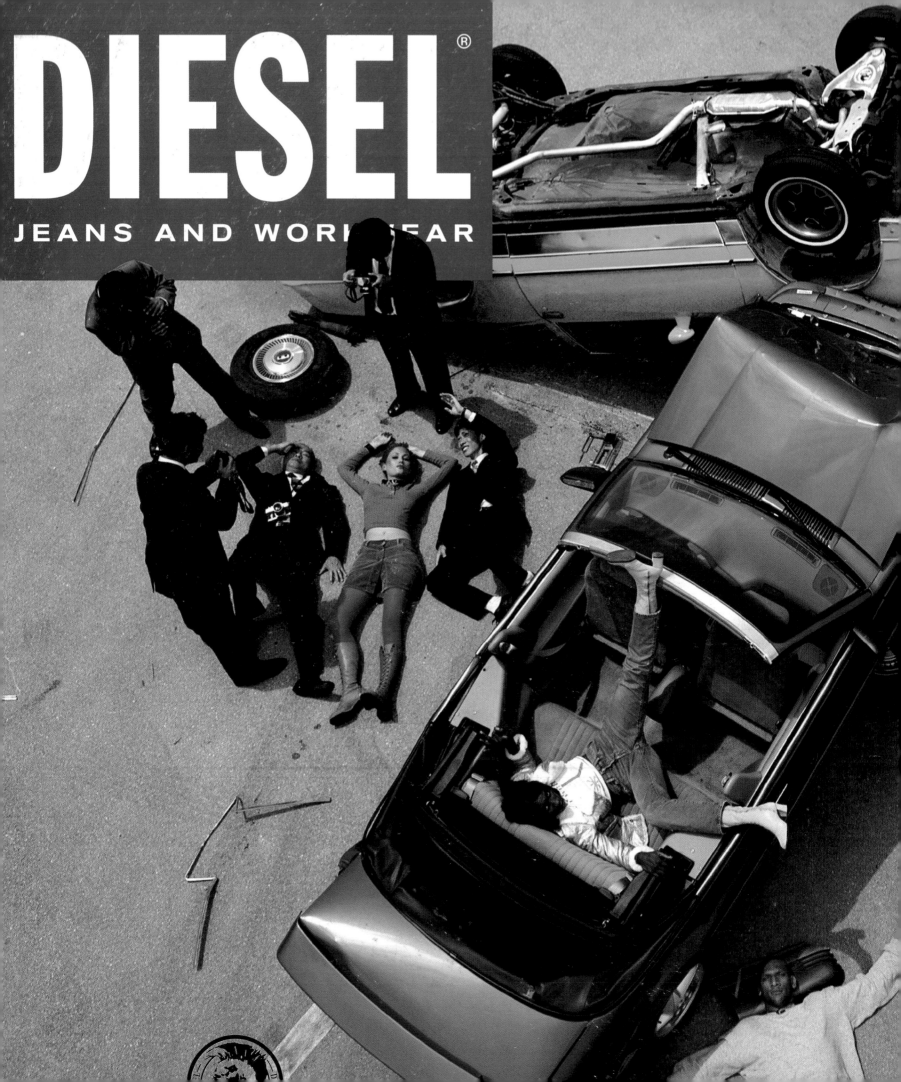

Left: Promotion for Iftar meal at McDonald's, Ankara, 1990s.
Below: Chinese New Year promotion at Singapore McDonald's, 1992.
Bottom: *Hongbao* envelope from Singapore McDonald's, 1992.

福祿壽禧賀新春
FOUR FESTIVE MONKEYS FOR THE NEW YEAR.

小福猴
LUCKY LUCY

小椿猴
HAPPY HARRY

小祿猴
RICH RICHIE

小壽猴
LONGEVITY LARRY

一年復始，萬象更新，麦当劳祝您猴年如意，事事顺利。
现在，买任何汉堡包，多付80¢，送一只贺年小猴。收齐四只，
把福祿壽禧，带回您家里！

Now when you buy any burger,
one of the four Festive Monkeys is yours
for just 80¢. Collect all four and greet
the New Year with Fortune, Prosperity,
Longevity and Happiness.

## RUSSELL W. BELK

# Wolf brands in sheep's clothing

RONALD McDONALD™

In the global marketplace competitions between local and multinational brands are often regarded as David and Goliath battles, with sympathies clearly on the side of the local brand hero. Such is the story that Daniel Miller (1997) tells about Trinidadian soft-drink brands fighting the multinational American and British giants. With local, national and even ethnic sentiment favouring the domestic, one countervailing strength of multinational brands is their ability to represent what is modern, hip, and (most likely) Western. But in the last quarter of the twentieth century multinationals found another way of defeating domestic offerings by clothing their brands in regional costumes. In so doing, they maintain their strengths as giant

multinationals while co-opting local sympathies by making the global brand appear to be immanently local. Their ingenuity in doing so is sufficient that a group of Japanese Boy Scouts travelling in the United States were amazed to find a McDonald's in Chicago (Safranek, 1986), while many young people in Hong Kong are also unaware of McDonald's foreign origin (Watson, 1997).

How are the disguises that help global brands pass as local created? In the case of McDonald's, conscious efforts are made for neighbourhood franchises to support popular community causes, to establish local Ronald McDonald houses for hospitalised children, to choose façades that fit the neighbourhood and employ decor that reflects sources of

pride in the vicinity. Menus often adapt to regional tastes in cuisine. As Watson discovered, McDonald's serves teriyaki burgers in East Asia, Maharaja Macs (mutton burgers) in India, McLaks (salmon burgers) in Norway, McHuevo (egg burgers) in Uruguay, pasta and espresso in Italy, and frankfurters and beer in Germany. McDonald's varies its menu as well for some occasions, as with free soup with Iftar (post-sundown) meals during Ramadan in Ankara in 1996. Not only are local cuisines incorporated into the menu, but rituals and holidays as well. During the celebration of the 1992 year of the Monkey in Singapore McDonald's offered for 80-cents Singapore, any of four plastic monkeys: Lucky Lucy, Longevity Larry, Rich Richie and Happy

"Multinationals have found some clever
ways of co-opting local sentiment. How
can we feel anything but warmth toward
a clown who promotes regional traditions?"

Harry. In these figures Chinese virtues combine with Western names in order to insinuate McDonald's into the local celebration. Singapore McDonald's also transformed traditional plain red *hongbao* (gift) envelopes for Chinese New Year into branded versions featuring Ronald McDonald, the Hamburglar and the Fry Babies. Ronald McDonald's observation of local rituals helps McDonald's become a part of local culture.

Coca-Cola, the quintessential global marketer, also forgoes totally global brand promotion in order to cultivate a local image. In southern Africa, its Sparletta Creme Soda is green and comes in a green can. On 1998 cans from the Namibia bottler much of the front of the can is taken up by a hip green hippopotamus dressed in a suit, hat and wingtips. On the back of the can he introduces himself: 'Hi, I'm Mr Big, the Hippo. I come from Manzini [in Swaziland] where everything is green. That is why Sparletta Creme Soda is my favourite drink. While I may wear a suit, underneath it all, I am a hippo and I haven't forgotten my roots.' The appeal to urbanised Africans with strong links to the villages from where they come could hardly be clearer.

Sometimes Coke must play conflicting roles in order to create a local identity. During the 1996 Atlanta Olympic summer games, the brand was billed in the USA as an 'official food service partner' and was widely seen as a sponsor of the US Olympic Team. But in their corporate museum at Circular Quay in Sydney, a booth invited proud Australians to 'send a [videotaped] message to our athletes in Atlanta'. One of the items for sale at Circular Quay, but not at the main Coke museum in Atlanta, is an advertisement featuring an outline of Australia draped in a Coke logo. These emblems try to evoke a strong nationalistic feeling that Coke is indigenous to Australia.

As these examples suggest, multinational brands have found some clever ways of co-opting local sentiment. How can we feel anything but warmth toward a clown who promotes regional traditions, helps community causes and waves national flags? It is increasingly common to see packages of global food products bearing promotions for local sports teams, theme parks, museums and entertainments. Sponsoring neighbourhood events, contributing to regional charities and hiring resident employees are among the other ways that global brands indigenise themselves. Rather than being seen as a corporate giant, such tactics help to make the global brand seem familiar, friendly and an integral part of local traditions.

# CHAPTER TWO

# TIES THAT
# BIND

PATRICK BARWISE, ANDREA DUNHAM AND MARK RITSON

# BRANDS, CONSUMERS
# AND BUSINESSES

Opposite: Branded shopper, London, 1999.
Top right: Ford logo
Bottom: The FA Premiership trophy, sponsored by the brewers Carling.

We live in what anthropologist John Sherry has called 'brandscapes', places in which brands are an integral part of our everyday existence.[1] Yet, the prevalence of brands goes almost unnoticed in today's world. Because there are so many of them around us, we rarely question their nature and function. They are simply there.

Such is the power and prevalence of branding that a variety of organisations are increasingly adopting the methods and language of brands to describe themselves and their activities. The recent successes of Manchester United have seen the football club 'brand' itself across a range of products from sports clothing to tomato ketchup. In an age of global media, celebrities from sports stars to opera singers are also increasingly packaged and managed as brands. We hear of political parties and even politicians being 're-branded'. We may even find that we brand people and things in our day-to-day personal life. The woman who chooses one boyfriend over another because the first is a real 'Armani man' and the other is 'man at C&A' is bringing the philosophy of brands to bear on her most intimate relationships.

Brands have been around for a long time,[2] though their nature has changed significantly. Traditionally the brand was a symbol of production. It represented the type of ingredients, the method of manufacture and the skill of the manufacturer to any prospective consumer.[3] Yet it is clear that many brands today represent more than just production qualities. Often a particular brand logo on a product or service can enhance the consumption experience.[4] The Nike brand worn by many says little about the nature of production, and few wearers could say where or how their clothing was made.

The primary reason why brands exist is economic.

Brand names and other trademarks are still used to identify a supplier's products or services, distinguishing them from those of its competitors. This, at the very least, makes life simpler and less risky for the consumer. Although their symbolic role plays an increasingly important role in consumers' lives, most brands are still sold on a straightforward set of benefits, such as familiarity, predictability and value. In image-rich categories like cosmetics and fashion, the brand image and associations may also, in themselves, be an important part of what the consumer is buying. Because a successful brand has value for the consumer, it allows the firm to sell more, or at a higher price, than if the product were unbranded. It therefore rewards the company for developing and promoting new products and services, and for their consistent quality and image.

What exactly is a brand? It is a word that is so over-used that we rarely stop to consider what it actually means. The brand concept is complex, and different people define brands in different ways. Some focus on the brand as trademark, such as David Aaker from the University of California, Berkeley, for whom it is: 'A distinguishing name and/or symbol (such as a logo, trademark, or package design) intended to identify the goods or services of either one seller or a group of sellers, and to differentiate those goods or services from those of competitors.'[5] Others, such as Jean-Noel Kapferer at the HEC School of Management in Paris, fix on what it means to the consumer: 'A brand is not a product. It is the product's essence, its meaning, and its direction, and it defines its identity in time and space.'[6] This is a view to a large extent supported by Stephen King from the J. Walter Thompson advertising agency: 'A product is something made in a factory; a brand is something bought by a customer. A product can be

copied by a competitor; a brand is unique. A product can be quickly outdated; a brand is timeless.'[7]

But a full definition of the brand surely encompasses both perspectives. It is a combination of a set of trademarks (brand name, logo etc) as well as consumers' perceptions and expectations of products or services branded with these trademarks. For example, Coca-Cola Inc owns a range of trademarks and registered designs, including the shape of the traditional Coke bottle, and employs intellectual property lawyers, whose job is to ensure that no one else can use any of these symbols except – with permission and by paying a royalty – under licence. But the underlying reason why the Coca-Cola brand is so valuable is because of the perceptions and expectations about Coke that consumers carry in their heads. In the words of one Coca-Cola executive:[8]

"If Coca-Cola were to lose all of its production-related assets in a disaster, the company would [survive]. By contrast, if all consumers were to have a sudden lapse of memory and forget everything related to Coca-Cola the company would go out of business."

Because millions of consumers have built up positive perceptions and expectations about Coca-Cola over a period of time, most will choose it instead of another brand if they are both on the same shop shelf, even if the other one is cheaper (and often partly because it is cheaper). Customers' perceptions and expectations are sometimes called 'brand equity'. If these are strong and positive for large numbers of valuable customers, the brand is said to be 'strong' or to have 'strong brand equity'. A strong brand like Coca-Cola, Sony or Mercedes-Benz can have huge financial value because it can support profitable sales of both existing and future products. Unlike most of the tangible assets owned by a company, such as factories and computers, brands can have indefinite lives. In fact, increased usage of a brand – over time and over different products – can raise its value, if properly managed. Sony (the company) is constantly launching new products to replace its existing ones, but the Sony brand lives on, potentially strengthened by every new product.

A striking feature of brands is their potential longevity. Except in industries such as personal-computer software, where the whole product category is only about 25 years old, most big brands are at least 50 to 100 years old. Coca-Cola was launched in 1886, Gillette in 1902, Kodak in 1888, Shell in 1897, Sony in 1958.[9] A brand like Coca-Cola is older than not only the physical plant and equipment used to produce it but also the consumers who carry its value in their heads. A crucial feature of the business of brands is to manage these potentially valuable intangible assets for the long term and nurture their relationship to successive generations of consumers.

Paradoxically, to understand what a brand is it is helpful to consider what it is not. Commodities are like faceless brands – products or services that achieve their primary functional aim but do so without any distinctive characteristics or identifiable differences. Flour is a commodity. Beer is a commodity. A plane journey is a commodity. To understand what a brand is we must juxtapose Coca-Cola (a brand) against a carbonated-caffeinated beverage (a commodity). When this juxtaposition is performed it is possible to grasp the added value that brands confer on the consumer. This consists of the symbolic associations that the consumer attributes to the branded good – attributes they may not associate with a rival or store brand. People may buy cola because they are thirsty, but some may choose a Coca-Cola because they see it as the 'real thing'. When we talk of brand equity, we are really talking about the differential associations between a brand and a commodity.

Where does this equity come from and what does it consist of? Kevin Keller, a leading expert on brands and branding, breaks brand equity down into two dimensions: awareness and image.[10] Awareness represents the ability of a customer to recognise a particular brand. Most people when asked for some examples of brands will immediately recall a list of

Changes to the design of the
Coca-Cola bottle, 1899–1994.
The classic contour design,
which is still current today,
was first used commercially
in 1916.

Below: 'My Kinda Town',
October 1999. Television
advertising campaign for
McDonald's featuring Alan
Shearer.
Opposite: Saab
advertisment, 1999.

famous brand names, which, typically, might include Coke, McDonald's, Disney or Microsoft. On a day-to-day level, brand awareness is usually prompted by need. Thus when a consumer realises that they have run out of washing powder or when they decide to grab some fast-food while out shopping, they will usually recall between one and three brands for which they have high brand awareness. For most manufacturers this 'top of mind' position is an important place to be. Using advertising, sponsorships, huge zeppelin-style balloons, store designs and so on, the managers of brands fight an ongoing battle to reinforce their brand in the consumers' consciousness.

More complex is the second dimension image, which can include any association that a consumer has for a brand. Coke may make us think of America, The Real Thing, red and white. Microsoft suggests Windows, Bill Gates, or their slogan, 'Where do you want to go today™?' These brand images can take any number of forms. At their simplest level they come from the products and services with which a brand is associated. McDonald's main brand image is simply their restaurants and their burgers. A successful advertising campaign may add the images featured in the ads to the brand image. A 1999 British TV advertising campaign for the fast-food chain featured soccer star Alan Shearer visiting his local McDonald's. The 'values' attributed to Shearer – English football hero, down to earth, Northern, working class – are equated in the consumer's mind with McDonald's, and so its image becomes more 'local' than global. But this is not all

one-way traffic. Ideally the manufacturer could simply flick switches in each consumer's mind and have them associate the brand with whatever was its most positive brand image. But unintended and negative images can be linked with a brand and may even be prompted by a particular ad. Not everyone likes Alan Shearer, England, football, the North or the working class.

One of the biggest challenges of brand management is to control and channel the image. With the help of advertising, PR and marketing, most major organisations attempt to do just this. They monitor the current brand images that exist in the minds of different types or 'segments' of consumers and try to highlight some and sideline others, while continuously introducing new, positive associations. A key challenge is to find brand images that are different from those of competitors' brands. Many successful brands have been built around a unique connection with a particular place, individual or process, and this distinctive image has become the cornerstone of their business. Saab created a successful brand image around the world for its cars partly by exploiting its brand associations with aircraft manufacturing. Saab cars were imbued with associations such as safety, precision, speed and technological advance because these links already existed with aircraft manufacture.

Three key concepts contribute to the brand equity of any particular brand. Irrespective of the kind of target market, the nature of the product or service, or the origins of the manufacturing company - all brands depend upon trust, familiarity and difference. A brand is a badge of trust. Consider the difference between an unbranded packet of headache tablets and a well-known brand such as Nurofen. The presence of a visible and recognised brand name is likely to engender confidence in the mind of the consumer.

It is one thing to describe the brand concept, but quite another to explain its prevalence and popularity. For consumers a brand plays several interrelated roles, from familiarity and reassurance through to a range of symbolic devices.[11] The business of branding

Above: Shopping centre
signage, London, 1999.
Below right: Discount
clothing store, London, 1999.
Opposite: Unbranded goods
on sale, London, 1999.

is to position the brand favourably in one or more of these roles. To do this, understanding brands from a consumer perspective is essential. Familiarity is vital to success, and regular exposure to brand names over a period of time will go some way to fixing them in the consumer's mind.[12] A brand provides a source of identification. In doing so it is able to transform a unique act, such as going for a meal, into a familiar one: going to McDonald's.

It also acts as a guarantee of quality. The brand represents a connection, or a promise, from the manufacturer to you. The absence of such association in non-branded items partially explains why branded goods almost always cost more. With purchases such as gifts for others, or for highly symbolic products such as clothing, this visible signal of quality can be particularly important.

A brand offers insurance against many different kinds of risk that we, as consumers, try to avoid. Perhaps the most obvious one is functional risk: the fear that a new product might not meet our expectations. A trusted brand name might be enough to reassure most of us. This is important when consumers do not know much about a product, where experience of the brand in other contexts may reassure them. Then there is physical risk, an even more basic fear that a purchase will result in a threat to the consumer's (or their family's) health or wellbeing. Again, brands can offer assurance, a familiar airline being the classic example of this. Some consumers will prefer to pay a premium to fly with a well-known branded air carrier than risk a lesser-known operator (or one with a tarnished reputation). The planes, journeys and on-flight services may be exactly the same, but the brands are different, and this and its impact on risk perception is enough to persuade people to pay more for a known brand.

Financial risk is the fear that what is being purchased is not actually worth its price. Again brands reassure us here with their associations of trustworthiness. Faced with an unknown product, we have no reference point against which to calculate whether the price is good value or not. A branded

product, however, offers us reassurance that we will get what we are paying for. We can even check this by comparing the price of the same brand across different stores to make sure that the price is constant or nearly so. Paradoxically, this price may be considerably more than we would pay for a non-branded product. Yet many consumers would prefer to spend more, assuming that they are getting value for money by buying a familiar brand.

Finally, social risk describes the threat of enduring social contempt or rejection as a result of a particular purchase. In a world in which we increasingly form opinions of others based on what we buy, this form of risk is becoming more prevalent, particularly among the young. In many cases brands today offer us a reassurance that what we purchase will be accepted by others. Indeed, in especially intense social contexts, such as the school playground, this need to avoid social risk is heightened to the degree where a child feels it has to have a specific brand or face public humiliation. Psychologist Judith Harris argues that peers are an even stronger influence on children and teenagers than has traditionally been assumed.[13] If so, we are likely to see even more brands targeting the young, often with imagery that consciously excludes adult consumers. Demographic trends will encourage many other brands to target the fast-growing segment of well-off, active over-50s.

Brands do not just have a role to play in the expensive, fashion-conscious buy. Most purchases we make are mundane, repetitive and not at all interesting to us. Yet we still want to make sure that we get the best product to meet our particular needs. The consumer behaves like a 'cognitive miser': they

want the best without having to commit to the thinking energy associated with buying a car or a new suit. It is here that brands can again play a useful role in the consumer's life. Rather than reading every package and comparing every price in the supermarket, we simply look for the brand that we want. Because of the other roles that brands play in our lives (identification of source, quality assurance, risk reduction) we can make a cognitive short cut and simply pick the one we like. This 'brand preference' is actually a complex gestalt reflecting many different factors such as advertising, past experiences and word of mouth. It allows us to make a choice quickly. In many cases the wheels of our shopping trolley hardly stop while we do so. We may be tempted to assume that brands are popular because of their symbolic value, their luxury and their ability to communicate to others who we are. All these factors play a role, but ultimately the main reason we populate our houses with familiar brands is because they are easier to buy. Brands simplify our lives.

The final and most complex role for brands in the consumer's life, however, is the symbolic role. They are often used as a signal or measure of personality. We might assess others on first meeting by the car they drive or the clothes they wear. We do the same interpretative job on our own sense of self. We go through life trying to find answers to existential questions: What does it mean to be young? What does it mean to be a mother? Respected? Professional? Increasingly as a culture we have used brands to help us answer these questions. Wearing Diesel jeans rather than Levi's emphasises my youth. Buying a Volvo rather that an Alfa-Romeo reinforces my identity as a father. When we consume a product or service we do not just consume its physical properties. We also consume it on a symbolic level.

Brands are important in this cultural sense because they stand for things – often for things that are arbitrary and unnatural yet we accept them. Consider Häagen-Dazs ice cream, one of the more sexually suggestive brands you can buy. The meanings of adultness and sensuality that have been associated with it have been developed through a decade-long advertising campaign and can now come to mind when we consume the product. Anthropologist Grant McCracken calls this process the 'meaning flow'.[14] In essence meanings and symbols are created by advertising, then transferred to the product that is featured and finally celebrated through its consumption by the consumer. Brands are used symbolically in two different directions: inward and outward. Outwardly, to communicate to others the kind of person we are. Inwardly, to bolster our sense of self. These twin roles are perhaps the most influential factors in explaining the increasing numbers and popularity of brands within the last two decades. All of us are now all fluent in the language of brands. In addition, we are defined, and we define ourselves, as much by the brands we do not buy as by the ones that we do.

These are the building blocks of brand equity from a consumer viewpoint. From a business perspective, however, a brand only has value to the extent that it influences customer purchases, by making more people buy (and more often) at a given price, or the same people pay a higher price, than if the product or service were sold under an unknown brand. Although there is an extraordinary number of brands on the market, really valuable ones are relatively few. For individuals, only a proportion of these will be relevant, and even the most brand-aware consumer knows only a few hundred.

What we buy and use is not a brand and a product/service but a combination of the two, neither of which is clearly separate from the other in our minds. When Coca-Cola launched 'New Coke' to compete with Pepsi in 1985, it forgot the value of Coke's own reputation as the original and unique cola. Coke drinkers did not want this changed.[15]

Following pages:
Advertisement for BMW M5,
1999.

In the event, it was able to retain and eventually increase its market share, but at enormous expense. The financial value of the brand and of the total corporation ('shareholder value') were reduced and, without the remedial action taken at the time, might have been even more so.[16]

The functional price-performance of the physical product is usually only part of what customers are buying. When computing was dominated by mainframes, IBM's competitors would often launch models with 15 or 20 per cent better price-performance. But none could match IBM's service reputation or its range of compatible hardware and software. Nor was it easy to recruit staff to program or operate systems that were not IBM-compatible. Nor was there any risk of IBM pulling out of the business as General Electric, Xerox and other major players did. No wonder 'No one ever got fired for buying IBM', despite the higher price.[17]

Maintaining the reputable associations of a brand is of huge importance as these are the predominant source of brand value. Think, for example, of what the BMW brand tends to bring to mind. What associations do you make? Typical links with BMW might be: German; one or more of its car models, or perhaps a general idea of upscale, fast saloons ('sedans' in America); good engineering; driven by successful yuppies. You might also recall the blue-and-white four-quadrant logo, although perhaps not

as readily as Mercedes-Benz's even better known three-pointed star. Interestingly, with a strong, global brand like BMW, millions of consumers around the world would have these same associations in their heads. Most of them might not be able to afford a new BMW. Even among those who could buy a BMW if they wanted, most may never do so because they prefer other marques or because they dislike Germany or fast cars or yuppies or the particular styling of BMWs. They may not wish to associate themselves with the BMW brand. But many will do so – BMW is a large and growing brand – and this will be partly because of the mixture of functional and emotional associations of the BMW brand in their heads.

BMW (the company) does not own these associations, but its shareholders are richer because they exist. Most of the value of the BMW brand derives from its strong brand equity (in consumers' heads), not from its trademark *per se*. This is an interesting situation, because BMW (the company) owns the trademarks but not the brand equity. It could, if it wished, sell the trademarks, but the extent to which it could sell the brand equity is unclear – and would depend greatly on which firm was the buyer. If a manufacturer of cheap, volume cars bought BMW and used the BMW marque to rebuild its own sportier saloon models, consumers would not suddenly start thinking of these cars as BMWs. More likely, they would see the change as mere 'badge engineering' probably weakening their perceptions of the BMW brand as a whole. With a well-known brand like BMW, each individual may have many more associations than the listed core ones. Someone interested in cars or brands may know more details about BMW: its history, design and engineering. Most consumers will also have personal ties with the brand, for instance, people they have known who drove a BMW.

Consumers buy branded products and services; they do not buy trademarks. A trademark is a symbol, and its value derives from what it symbolises. If consumers' beliefs about that underlying reality change, so may the value of the trademark. An extreme case of this occurs if the consumer believes

'Beckham Delivery, Guaranteed Anytime - Anywhere'. The celebrity footballer David Beckham is shown as a brand, in this poster campaign for adidas, 1999.

that the seller is trying to 'pass off' an inauthentic product such as a fake Rolex watch.

A less extreme example occurred in the late 1980s when Mars started a policy of standardising on a limited portfolio of global brand names. In spring 1990 the well-established Marathon trademark was dropped and replaced by the global Snickers trademark in the UK (at that time almost unknown there). Before the change, the strapline 'Internationally known as Snickers' was printed in smaller type below the Marathon trademark. Again, for some months after the change, the strapline 'The new name for Marathon' was printed below the Snickers trademark, and another strapline 'All that's changed is the name' printed on the packaging along the side of the bar. Also, the overall 'look and feel' of the before and after packaging was very similar. Mars slightly increased its advertising for the brand and made it a priority for the sales force selling to the retailers. The result was that, far from losing sales, the brand actually increased its market share. Changing the brand name from Marathon to Snickers had no significant effect on consumers' perceptions of the brand: in their minds it still exists, under a new name. This is a clear illustration of the fact that the concept of brand-as-trademark (name, logo etc) fails to capture the full concept of what brands mean

to consumers and therefore to businesses.[18]

From a company perspective, we are moving into an age in which management is increasingly about 'intangibles'. Companies no longer look at their tangible assets (cash, factories, machinery, inventory and land) as the markers of their success. Instead, they now view the intangible aspects of their business as the central indicators of the value of their firm. Brands represent an important example of this shift to 'weightless' assets. The 'weightless' part of a modern economy includes not only other intellectual property (patents, copyrights) but also knowledge and know-how, libraries and databases, information and communication systems, research and so on.[19] Many would include employee, customer and supplier loyalty.

Successful brand management starts with a deep understanding of what the brand means to customers and what drives choice. It then becomes clear that the role of the brand is to raise expectations in consumers' minds of specific benefits. These must be delivered on a consistent basis in order to build a franchise of satisfied loyal customers – the translation of brand choice into predictable and steady income for the firm, year in and year out. Since firms are valued by shareholders on the basis of their predictable income over a five- to ten-year period, the role of the brand in driving customer choice can be central to a corporation's strategies for increasing 'shareholder value', that is the financial value of the company to its shareholders.

Businesses survive, grow and make money by profitably meeting customers' needs better than the competition. More precisely, customers buy products and services because they are seeking functional and emotional benefits that they expect a category of products or services to provide. The main benefits promised and provided by the brand provide the key to management decisions about the firm: competitive strategy, innovation and technology and marketing.

Valuable brands reflect the development of positive brand perceptions, usually over a long time period. Firms seek to establish a virtuous cycle whereby people choose the brand and use it, and the benefits delivered by usage lead to high customer satisfaction. This in turn leads to both positive word-of-mouth recommendations to other potential customers (especially important for infrequently purchased products and services) and positive brand perceptions in the mind of the consumer. In the case of frequently brought items like groceries or fast food, it is these positive brand perceptions leading to repeat purchase of the same brand that establish it with long-term value. Repeat-buying constitutes a positive feedback loop, in which brand choice and usage lead to satisfaction, which feeds through to reinforced commitment to the category, brand preference and brand choice. Repeat-buying also reinforces top-of-mind awareness, which, as already noted, has a direct link with brand preference, and is, itself, a predictor of brand choice and therefore stable revenue streams. At this stage, repeat-buying becomes more of a habit than a conscious choice. This type of repeat-buying is what is normally meant by brand loyalty.

Big brands enjoy two advantages over small ones: in any given time period, more consumers buy big brands and do so more often. This type of pattern was first observed in a study of radio announcers by Columbia University sociologist William McPhee in 1963 and labelled the Law of Double Jeopardy (from the perspective of the less popular brand, which

suffers twice over).[20] It has also been found in a wide number of other contexts.[21]

For high-involvement, infrequently purchased goods such as cars or holidays, and to a lesser extent new products and brands, customer satisfaction can also be communicated by word-of-mouth. This is the most trusted source of information about brand benefits, apart from the consumer's own direct experience, because, unlike advertising or promotion, it is not seen as commercially self-serving. Customer dissatisfaction is even more potent for service businesses: such customers seldom complain, but often tell their friends and acquaintances, other potential buyers, about their bad experience.

Perhaps the single most important role for brands within an organisation is their ability to spawn loyalty; this is akin to a long-term relationship between brand and consumer. Because the brand identifies itself and because it is able to stand for certain meanings, it is sometimes able to impact upon a consumer over several purchases to form both a practical and symbolic part of that consumer's life. At its most extreme a brand-loyal consumer will specifically ask for the brand by name if it does not appear on a grocery shelf and will defer their purchase until it becomes available.

In the UK one example of long-term brand loyalty is the relationship between British consumers and MG sports cars. When the new MGF was launched in the mid-1990s, some people had to wait months before their car was available. Yet wait they did. Indeed, such was the power of the MG brand that for several years after its launch, the second-hand price of an MGF was significantly higher than its original list price. Such loyalty is rare, especially in today's markets where the consumer is seen as increasingly fickle. However, the more fickle the consumer becomes in general, the more valuable brand loyalty becomes in particular. In a fascinating study of nostalgia and brand loyalty Barbara Olsen[22] suggests that the latter may exist for several lifetimes. She described one Italian-American family who 'inherited' their brand loyalty for the household brands Gold Medal flour and Domino sugar from their mother whom, in turn, had adopted it from her mother. The value to the firm of such loyalty patterns is enormous. If manufacturers can build brand loyalty at an early stage in the consumer's development they may reap a lifetime's benefits.

Marketers increasingly try to demonstrate not only how much of the total market they currently service but also how much of each single consumer they will service in a lifetime. The key is to win over the consumer while they are still developing their preferences and then try to ensure that they will remain loyal. This strategy has proved successful for many high-street banks that specifically target new students with attractive packages to draw them in at the start of their financial lives. This is equally the case with Sony's range of goods produced for children: 'My First Sony'.

Brand strategy is about managing the manufacturing, distribution, communication and economic mix to develop consistent perceptions of the brand among certain customer segments, so as to maximise how often it is chosen at a price that pays. This involves choosing the most profitable target market and making sure that these customers see the brand as likely to provide more core benefits than competing brands. It also means ensuring that the brand (or strictly the combination of brand and product/service) is priced and distributed to maximise long-term sales and profits. In a competitive environment, brand perceptions, prices and 'availability' (how and where the product can be bought) are always relative to the competition, not absolute.

Relatively small differences in brand preference – if shared widely among consumers – can therefore lead to large differences in brand choice and therefore in the value of brand equity to the firm. That is, a brand need not be 'powerful' (in the sense that consumers believe it dramatically superior and refuse all substitutes) to be extremely valuable to the business.

There are large systematic variations between the branding strategies of different industries. Most industries (industrial products, industrial services, consumer services, infrequently bought consumer products) market largely under a single corporate/umbrella brand, often with sub-brands

**Right: 'My First Sony', 1992.**

Advertising hoarding in
a London car park, 1999.

THE NEW PRIMERA.
UR CAR WASN'T SO BORING TO DRIVE.
YOU WOULDN'T BE READING THIS.'

NISSAN

Above: Supermarket
shelving, Tesco, West
Kensington, London, 1999.
Below: Harrods carrier bag.

and other detailed product descriptors. The main exception to this is with anything that is bought infrequently, in which case the same firm may market two or more distinct product lines/ranges at very different price levels. Portfolios of brands may cover a range of products within a single category, such as whisky, marketed to different social groups and purses.[23] In this case, a separate brand name may be used for each of these. General Motors was established after the First World War with a portfolio of five main brands at different price points and other positionings or attributes, such as sportiness: Chevrolet, Buick, Oldsmobile, Pontiac and Cadillac.[24] These brands, and their relative market profiles, continue today.

Toyota, Nissan and Honda have all launched luxury-car ranges under separate brand names from their volume-car brands. GM and Ford have acquired European manufacturers such as Saab and Jaguar, and a large part of their motive for doing so appears to be to gain control of the brands that are valued for luxury or style. Part of BMW's rationale for buying Rover was the latter's portfolio of mostly dormant classic British car marques, such as Morris, Triumph, Riley, Wolsley and especially MG. Until BMW pulled

out of Rover in 2000, the main reason for the takeover was for BMW to acquire Land Rover, the only serious 4x4 manufacturer in Europe with a very strong brand name. Another current example of a car-brand portfolio is VW's four-brand strategy (Audi, VW, Seat, Skoda) using a limited number of platforms shared across the brands.

One of the most obvious aspects of brand strategy is advertising, which can have many roles in building and maintaining brand equity.[25] It can be used to create awareness of a new brand or product; to encourage trial purchase (for a low-ticket item) or a request for more information (for example brochures and a test drive for a car); to reinforce repeat-buying of a familiar, frequently purchased product, perhaps just by reminding or 'nudging' the consumer; or to strengthen and develop consumers' positive long-term perception of the brand.[26]

Advertising is pervasive, but perhaps less powerful than many people believe. Quite a widespread attitude is that it influences – even manipulates – other people, but not oneself. The evidence is that it is both less powerful and less sinister than this. Most advertising focuses on trying to influence consumers' choice of brand, such as Ariel versus Persil, not on trying to persuade them to buy more of the product category.[27] This is not clear-cut. For a dominant brand in a growth market, such as BSkyB in pay TV or Coca-Cola in the Chinese soft-drinks market, advertising may be as much aimed at bringing new consumers into the market (and encouraging existing consumers to buy more) as at capturing or protecting market share from other brands. Again, if the product category is defined very narrowly, brand advertising will tend to increase category sales, by 'capturing' consumers from other brands.

Even at the brand-choice level, advertising is a weaker force than many people believe, and firms' investment in it more of an act of faith. Most major advertisers can roughly measure the impact of their advertising on short-to-medium-term brand sales – up to two or maybe three years. This sales impact varies greatly between brands and advertising campaigns, but it is rarely big enough to cover the

## THE WORLD'S MOST VALUABLE BRANDS

| | Brand name | Country of origin | Brand value $US billion | Company value $US billion | Brand value as % of co-value |
|---|---|---|---|---|---|
| 1. | Coca-Cola | US | 84 | 142 | 59 |
| 2. | Microsoft | US | 57 | 272 | 21 |
| 3. | IBM | US | 44 | 158 | 28 |
| 4. | General Electric | US | 34 | 328 | 10 |
| 5. | Ford | US | 33 | 57 | 58 |
| 6. | Disney | US | 32 | 53 | 61 |
| 7. | Intel | US | 30 | 144 | 21 |
| 8. | McDonald's | US | 26 | 41 | 64 |
| 9. | AT&T | US | 24 | 102 | 23 |
| 10. | Marlboro | US | 21 | 112 | 19 |
| 11. | Nokia | Finland | 21 | 47 | 44 |
| 12. | Mercedes | Germany | 18 | 48 | 37 |
| 13. | Nescafé | Switzerland | 18 | 77 | 23 |
| 14. | Hewlett-Packard | US | 17 | 55 | 31 |
| 15. | Gillette | US | 16 | 43 | 37 |
| 16. | Kodak | US | 15 | 25 | 60 |
| 17. | Ericsson | Sweden | 15 | 46 | 32 |
| 18. | Sony | Japan | 14 | 29 | 49 |
| 19. | Amex | US | 13 | 35 | 35 |
| 20. | Toyota | Japan | 12 | 86 | 14 |

cost – or even half the cost – of the advertising. Most of the mass-media advertising for established products and brands is therefore defensive, which is to say that it is aimed at maintaining brand equity. However, firms' ability to measure how much this actually works is limited because the effects are not strong, and there are so many other influences on brand choice: product improvements, price, promotions, retail presence, the state of the economy and, especially, competitor activity. To decide the long-term value of advertising, there would need to be an estimate of what sales might have been without it. This is rarely possible.[28]

Nor is advertising essential to the development of brand equity. The customer franchise of brands like Microsoft, IBM, Mercedes-Benz, Boots or Harrods has little to do with advertising in a traditional sense. A market such as petrol is dominated by the number, location and quality of outlets with price a secondary factor and branding probably only third. Similarly, with infrequently bought items such as cars or white goods, the product itself, its price and availability, and the firm's general reputation ('corporate brand equity') are considered to be more important than advertising.

As a result of some significant corporate takeovers during the 1980s, the concept of brands on the balance sheet came very much to the fore in UK corporate finance.[29] Brands had always been an important topic within the marketing departments of manufacturing organisations. Very rapidly they became crucial for the financial departments of these organisations, too, as the value of a particular company became as much associated with its intangible brand assets as with its more tangible ones, such as plant and machinery. Perhaps the best example of this sea change in British business was the Rowntree takeover. In early 1988 the stock market valued British confectionery company Rowntree at a little over £1 billion. Much of this stock-market valuation was based on the perceived value of Rowntree's familiar and well-loved brands (Kit-Kat, Aero, Lion Bar, Rolo etc). The tangible assets of the company (land, plant and equipment) were worth well under half of the overall market value of the firm – about £0.4 billion. During this period, Swiss company Jacobs Suchard made a 'dawn raid' on Rowntree, buying its shares at an inflated price in a race to gain control of it over their larger Swiss rival, Nestlé. During the next few frenzied weeks of competitive bidding, the price of Rowntree's shares more than doubled. Nestlé eventually paid £2.3 billion for Rowntree. Most of this was to secure (and stop Jacobs Suchard from getting a hold over) Rowntree's strong established brands. Nestlé believed not only that Rowntree's brands were strong and valuable but also that they would be even more so under their ownership, because of the strength of their international distribution. This example – from a solid, dependable, Swiss company – highlights the important financial value of strong brands in today's business environment.

According to brand consultancy Interbrand, the most valuable brand in the world is Coca-Cola, which they valued at $84 billion in 1999, over half the total $142-billion financial market value of the Coca-Cola Corporation. As the table on the previous page shows, the top 20 most valuable brands in 1999 are dominated by global US brands.

Brand valuation is controversial. For instance, Interbrand has arguably overvalued technology brands like Microsoft, Intel and Nokia, whose brand equity has shallow roots in fast-paced markets in which this year's winner may be a loser in two years. But these huge values nevertheless reflect an important truth for businesses today. Brands can represent enormously important assets that need to be carefully nurtured and exploited.

Now we have entered the new millennium what will become of brands? Their story is a long one. It has also taken some recent twists. In particular, the growing awareness of the financial value of brands stands out as one of the most important changes in recent business history, and their strategic management has emerged as one of the most important challenges for companies in the twenty-first century. Recent technological advances, and in particular the emergence of electronic or 'e-commerce', are already changing the way in which businesses operate and consumers make their decisions and purchases.

Inevitably we will witness new major brands emerging in the first few years of the new century. Nobody yet knows who will be the next Amazon or Microsoft, but its emergence is certain. Equally likely is the fact that some of the power brands of the twentieth century will fall by the wayside. Those that have not been updated and made to move with the times will suffer and perhaps even die. The recent problems of Levi's, Marks & Spencer and even Coca-Cola emphasise how rapidly the once mighty can stumble in the modern marketplace. Obviously the market context of the twenty-first century will be different. As consumers, we are already beginning to glimpse the kind of markets that e-commerce is creating for us. These are without national boundaries and have unlimited information, markets that provide us with an almost limitless array of choices from which to select with a simple 'click'.

Yet within these brave new markets the part that brands will play in the life of the consumer is unlikely to change fundamentally. Consider the consumer roles for brands discussed earlier: identification of source, signal of quality, risk reducer, search-cost reducer and symbolic device. These will continue because they concern issues that consumers will always need to address, regardless of the particular purchase in which they are involved or the market and technology context in which that decision has to be made. For example, the identification of the source of a product that brands can provide for consumers and the familiarity that this confers will prove vital as we begin to make decisions in on-line markets with an even greater menu of options. The more we are faced with familiar choices, the stronger the attraction for the brands that we know and trust.

Similarly, the role brands play in assigning responsibility and signalling quality will remain equally important in the next century. Consumers will be faced with online decisions in which their choices increase, but where direct, tangible access to the

# Microsoft®

Where do you want to go today?®

products from which they must choose will decrease. We shall buy bananas that we will not be able to squeeze or smell before we click them into our baskets. In situations like this the role of brands in guaranteeing quality will only serve to increase our dependence on them and their importance to us.

One implication of e-commerce is that new markets will offer more choices than ever before. While this may be a positive result for the consumer, many of the purchases will remain mundane. Once more, the role of brands in reducing search costs will prove crucial in ensuring their worth in the next century. Finally, and perhaps most importantly, no matter how we select and purchase goods and services in the future we will continue to consume many of them conspicuously. The role of brands as symbolic devices that feed our self-concept and our lines of communication to others will continue through the age of e-commerce and into whatever age may follow it.

While brands continue to exert a significant influence on consumer decision-making in the digital age, it is clear that online shopping offers the consumer a unique and unprecedented combination of features.[30] First, until now, most category and brand choice has been at a retail outlet – supermarket, travel agent or car showroom. Firms with big, strong established brands have had a huge advantage in making their products easily available to consumers – and sometimes ensuring that new competitors are excluded from the best retail outlets. But on the Internet, a one-person business can make its electronic shop window available to as many online consumers as Sony or The Gap.

Second, the Internet knows almost no boundaries of time and space. A website can be accessed at low cost at any hour and from anywhere. We are still at an early stage of assessing the future impact of what financial journalist Frances Cairncross has called 'the death of distance'.[31] Third, online shopping combines the real-time interactivity of the telephone with some of the best features of catalogue shopping. It lets the consumer evaluate and compare competing brands using pictures and text. Finally, online

technology allows the consumer not only to compare brands easily (as with a catalogue) but also, and increasingly, to use the power of the computer to do the hard work of searching for alternative supplies of a brand, comparing features and prices, highlighting special offers and so on. Bill Gates, Chairman of Microsoft, has suggested that we are moving towards a 'shopper's heaven'.[32]

The reverse of this coin is potentially a 'shopper's hell'. Firms too are able to use competing power to optimise their relationships with consumers, especially those about whom they have a stream of data from loyalty-card transactions, online interactions and so on. In principle, this will also aid consumers, since it will enable suppliers to tailor their products, services and communications to each individual to the benefit of both parties.[33] In practice, this kind of 'one-to-one' marketing (or 'mass customisation') is hard to do well – most consumers feel they now receive more junk mail than ever – and also raises other societal issues: the invasion of privacy, the tendency to focus only on the better-off, increasing social exclusion and so on.[34]

Digital technology is of course especially well suited to producing and distributing information products and services. Nicholas Negroponte, Director of the MediaLab at MIT, regards the distinction between 'bits' (information) and 'atoms' (physical products and services) as the key to understanding the digital age.[35] Some information products such as classified advertising and encyclopaedias, are especially well suited to digital media. Others, such as television programmes, newspapers and novels, are less so. But it is clear that digital technology will have a huge impact on some product categories, for example the travel-agency business.[36]

What impact will all this have on brands? As with everything to do with the Internet, the short-term impact on most consumer markets (as opposed to businesses selling to other businesses) has been over hyped. Although it is true that any online consumer in the world can access a one-person-business website, with no brand equity it will remain largely unvisited.

This is why all the Internet start-up businesses, often known as 'dot coms', are spending millions on advertising to create brand equity, mostly on traditional print and broadcast media. In practice, most e-commerce is being done by established brands – although there are many exceptions to this pattern. Some Internet-pioneer companies set the pace and have held it in their category, such as Amazon.com in the book market, but older brands, the venerable American book store Barnes & Noble for example, now online, are starting to catch up fast.

This is not to say that reputable businesses can be complacent. Almost every company is at risk from nimbler competitors finding new ways to reach the customer using this technology. The empowered consumer, helped by increasingly powerful software, will be more likely to find the best buy – or at least, the cheapest place to purchase the preferred brand – so price competition will intensify in many markets. But the fundamental reasons why brands exist will not disappear. In fact, in an information-laden society, their role in saving time and assuring quality will be as great as ever, as will their symbolic role. We may even have to extend our definition of brand equity to include information held in computer memory as well as human memory: if I and my computer are both geared to buy groceries online from Waitrose@work, our brand loyalty to that retailer will be higher than ever.

In addition to the influence of technology, brands will need to adapt to other consumer and societal trends. Some of these, such as the age profile of the population – with a higher proportion of retired people, many of them active, healthy and with high disposable income – are relatively predictable. Others are less so. For instance, US economists in the 1960s worried about how people would spend all their extra leisure time in the 1990s. In the event, Americans today – especially women of working age – have less leisure than then, not more.[37]

Now we are in the twenty-first century, the forces that have made brands such a feature of modern society and business – market economies and consumerism, globalisation, consumers who are money-rich and time-poor, information overload – seem set to continue. Even those who advocate a 'third way' – neither communism nor free-market capitalism – stress the importance of competitive markets and consumer power.[38] On this basis, we might expect the role of brands to become even greater during this century.

If present trends continue, huge populations in today's emerging markets – Asia, Latin America, Eastern Europe – will be able to afford branded products on an unprecedented scale. The evidence is that they will become enthusiastic consumers of brands, including global ones. In the developed world, as Gareth Williams confirms in 'The Point of Purchase', a small minority is saying, 'Enough.'[39] There are also signs of ethical considerations influencing brand choice, at least among a minority of consumers. Body Shop, one of the few global British brands launched in the last 50 years, has built its brand positioning in consumers' minds on its moral principles for developing and sourcing products.[40] Recently, Nike, McDonald's, Shell, Monsanto and Wal-Mart[41] have all been subject to aggressive campaigns by groups critical of the wider societal impact of their corporate policies.[42]

Campaigns along these lines seem likely to continue and, at least in some cases, will have enough influence on brand equity and therefore brand choice to persuade firms to adapt their policies. One prediction, therefore, is that the ethical dimension of brands will become more important to consumers and therefore to businesses. But this development should not be overstated: a trend, not a revolution, in the world of brands.

Many categories of the twentieth century have been dominated by the same brands for more than 50 years with remarkably little change in the competitors and their relative popularity with consumers. Some of the power brands that we encounter daily will disappear as competitive forces and market changes take their toll. Brands may well be promoted using innovative, as yet unheralded, techniques, but as long as people feel the need to produce things and to consume them, brands will remain with us.

# Why do we buy counterfeits?

From breakfast cereals to luxury hotels, what we like to hear about our favourite brands is that they keep their promises. Strong brands tell us what to expect from them and then deliver on those expectations. No brand can keep its promises all the time but building a strong brand image takes time, commitment and not a small amount of money.

So it is hardly surprising that some companies do not even try to keep their promises – instead, they pretend to keep somebody else's. Customers will be lured into buying inferior products by the illegal use of another company's well-established logo, packaging and reputation. This practice is about as ethical as using someone else's credentials to get a job, and in most countries it is illegal.

Counterfeiters earn millions every year selling not only the familiar fake watches and knock-off handbags but also bogus children's toys, sporting goods, car parts, even pharmaceutical products.

Because legitimate manufacturers

want customers to spend these millions on the real thing instead, companies will often hunt down and prosecute those who manufacture counterfeits. But while those who make and distribute counterfeit goods frequently are blamed for creating the market for fakes, it is important to recognise that this market is kept alive by supply *and* demand. So it is useful to ask why do we buy counterfeits?

Perhaps when people buy fake goods they are really being fooled by a clever imitation and believe they are purchasing the genuine article. Some counterfeiters are so effective that only an expert might notice the difference – the only dissimilarity between some Cuban cigars and their counterfeits, for example, is the way the paper is folded at the ends. On the other hand, even when a fake looks like the original, the way in which it is sold will be entirely different – usually by street vendors or temporary discount stores. The customer might be wary, but such goods are usually traded cheaply with the justification that 'They're factory seconds' or even 'They fell off the back of a truck.' Most customers, however, do not ask for an explanation and will happily buy knowing that the goods are fake.

Are these customers just good bargain hunters? Do they buy counterfeits because they believe they are getting the same quality for a lower price? A 1993 American study, by Bloch, Bush and Campbell, explored people's perceptions of fake versus real goods. Setting up a table in a shopping area, the researchers sold three types of shirt, all of the same quality and colour. The first shirt had a designer logo on the pocket, and customers were told it was a genuine designer shirt. Price: $45. The second shirt also had a designer logo, and customers were told it was a counterfeit. Price: $18. The third shirt had no designer

logo, but the label inside showed it to be from a well-known retailer. Customers were told it was genuine. Price: $18. By the end of the study 38 per cent of the consumers had bought the counterfeit. In a similar survey in Britain, 40 per cent of those asked said they too would knowingly buy a counterfeit if the price and quality were acceptable.

After the customers in the first survey had bought their counterfeit shirts, they were taken aside and asked to rate the quality of the three types on offer. Although all the shirts were of the same quality, those buying the counterfeit rated it lower than the 'real' designer shirt, but higher than the retailer's. It is clear that the 'designer' shirt was rated highest, because customers generally believe a fake to be of lower quality than the real thing. But why did people rate the supposed counterfeit higher than the shirt without the logo, even though it was said to be from a reputable retailer? Seemingly, even the counterfeit logo sends an unconscious message of quality. The customers know they are getting a fake, but the logo on the pocket, with its carefully cultivated brand image, offers subtle reassurances. If that is the case, then even customers knowing they are getting a fake are being deceived.

Not only that, but these customers may also be engaging in a deception of their own. They recognise the logo gives them fashion value and a certain status in the eyes of others. But for many, this value only remains as long as the customers keep quiet about the origin of their goods. Admitting to purchasing a fake 'bargain' affects the status of both the product and the wearer.

So maybe we buy counterfeits because we are fooled by a clever imitation – though in many cases we might instead be trying to fool others, or even ourselves.

"When people buy
counterfeit goods,
are they really
being fooled by a
clever imitation?"

# Consumer proactivity

**Right:** Defaced poster, Baker
Street Underground Station,
London, 1999.
**Opposite:** Dike T-shirt, Pride
March, New York City, 1997.

To consume or not to consume? Is that the question? When we find ourselves drawn into a shop by a particularly enticing window display, we are being consumers. When we buy a new brand of toothpaste because the packet informs us that it will whiten our teeth, we are being consumers. When we show our spouse an advertisement for walking holidays in India from the Sunday paper, we are being consumers. The act of consumption has been characterised as the flow of goods from producers to consumers. Consumption is what we do in response to the activity of retailers, manufacturers and advertisers. Consumption begins with the actions of the organisation and ends with some impact on people.

Of course there is an alternative. We can choose not to consume. We can dismiss the temptations of the window display and keep walking. We can scoff at the claims of the new brand of toothpaste and return it to the supermarket shelf. We can decide not to read any of the advertisements in the Sunday papers. In these instances we see ourselves as non-consumers. We may even derive as much satisfaction from these acts of non-consumption as we do from consuming; we may feel we have resisted temptation, or that we have acted with discernment. Of course, even in these acts of non-consumption we are still reacting. By choosing not to buy a product, not to enter a store or not to read an ad, we are still responding to the marketing efforts of organisations.

To consume or not to consume appear to be our only choices. Yet, when we dichotomise consumer behaviour in this way we assume that the only available option is consumption reactivity. But there is a third way, which represents the activities of people who attempt to reverse the classic causality of

> "Rather than examining the impact of brands on people, we have to examine the impact of people on brands."

consumption. This can be called consumer proactivity, and under its banner appear any acts that originate with people and are targeted at marketing organisations. Consumer proactivity questions our traditional assumptions about consumption. Thus, instead of asking what advertising does to people, we have to ask what people are doing to advertising. Rather than examining the impact of brands on people, we have to examine the impact of people on brands. The consumer becomes the active player in this new relationship, and the organisation is faced with the question of how they will respond.

Consumer proactivity is by no means a singular activity. Like the standard consumption behaviours that flow in the opposite direction, it can take many forms and exhibit varying levels of involvement. At its most superficial level it exists as a sudden, almost instinctive desire to break free from the passivity that most people experience on a day-to-day basis in their roles as consumers. Consider exhibit 1. An anonymous commuter waiting in the underground for their train is offended and angered by the explicit promotion of smoking as 'sexy' in a poster ad on the walls of the station. The traditional consumer dichotomy of consuming or non-consuming does not, in this case, present our commuter with an acceptable response. Instead, they turn to proactivity and deface the ad. It is a crude gesture, but one that illustrates the power of the consumer as proactive. The ad is now for ever changed. What's more its message is not weakened by the fact that it originally represented a medium of traditional consumption. Indeed, the very power of this new message derives from this origin and its subsequent transformation. The ad was designed to have an impact on people.

Now a person has had an impact on the ad, and its original intent, message and effect have been superseded by an act of consumer proactivity.

Consider exhibit 2. We see a familiar brand, Nike, transformed. A brand that looks the same yet now communicates the word 'Dike' – or dyke, a slang word for lesbian. Nike is a brand that is popular among all sections of the population and includes a significant number of lesbian consumers. Unlike some of the rest of the mass market, however, Nike do not explicitly acknowledge this group. There are no ads featuring a lesbian couple working out in Nike sports gear, there are no lesbian celebrity endorsers for Nike, Nike does not sponsor specifically homosexual events and activities such as the Gay Games. Yet the Nike brand is as

popular with these consumers as it is with the rest of society. The dichotomy of being a consumer or non-consumer is again insufficient for some gay women. They like Nike products; they use and consume them. However, they do not like the way in which their relationship with this brand is ignored by its manufacturer. As a result, some resort to consumer proactivity to allow them to redress the lack of explicit representation that they experience at the hand of Nike. Rather than letting the brand impact upon this market, the market is impacting itself upon the brand. Once again, the power inherent in this act of consumer proactivity derives from the transformation of a traditional, expected medium of consumption, and thus altered, its purpose is subverted.

Most buying will continue to be represented by a singular arrow of causality that flows from organisations to consumers and non-consumers. Yet, in these early days of the twenty-first century it is possible to glimpse more and different examples of consumer proactivity taking place. In this post-modern age of reflexivity and playfulness all the cultural indicators suggest that as consumers we will become increasingly predisposed to it. Standard consumption media such as advertising, branding and retail spaces that have typically assumed consumer passivity may need to evolve greater degrees of interactivity in order to enable them to engage with increasingly proactive markets. Only time will tell exactly how creative, constructive and subversive we shall become.

Barcode tattoo.

"I wanna get rich"

"Sell"

SHARON KINSELLA

# Japanese high-school girl brand

In the 1990s a new brand appeared not on the shelves but on the streets of Japan: *joshi kōsei*, the schoolgirl brand. It brought to the consumer the essence of authentic spontaneity and youthful naivety. It was all part of an idea that was current in the media of the time that Japanese schoolgirls had become brand-name goods in their own right (Miyadai, 1994). Time spent in their company had become a commodity that men could buy. What was purchased was not always sex but the elixir of youth. For producers, editors and intellectuals, who were aware of the trends, the company of these girls became a voguish and risqué entertainment that could be flaunted or presented as a gift.

## BURUSERA

News attention began in 1993 when the media became aware of the idea that schoolgirls were selling their school uniforms, knickers, even gobs of their saliva, to the proprietors of makeshift shops. *Burusera* or 'bloomer sailor' shops catered to men with a sexual fixation on the paraphernalia of schoolgirl uniforms (Miyadai, 1994). Titillating TV documentaries brought the *burusera* issue to the attention of the Japanese public. Images of Japanese schoolgirls began to be sold on-line to men in other parts of the world.

## URI

Buying, acquiring and selling became referred to at that time by two extremely fashionable words: *getto* ('get') and *uri* ('sell') These words derived their pleasing frisson from the fact that they explicitly blurred any distinction between shopping for goods and shopping for people. 'Getto' can mean 'being good at flirting' and 'getting a boyfriend' as well as 'acquiring something'. Both terms seemed to symbolise exciting elemental forces uniting as one all human and financial activity. An immense electronic stage-play acted out by high-school girls was being conducted across the interface of the media. Media workers and intellectuals struggled to write the script for a story about a people threatened with disappearing into the interstices of financial exchange.

## ENKŌ

In 1994 the *burusera* phenomenon bled into a new and greater scandal. Not only were schoolgirls selling off their uniforms, but apparently they were also throwing themselves into a new kind of amateur prostitution. This was called 'assisted dating' – *enjo kōsai* – but it was widely referred to by the cuter abbreviation '*enkō*' (Kuronuma, 1996). For the media and for schoolgirls *enkō* became a keyword of the mid-90s. The media featured images of schoolgirls on the streets; using their PHS handsets or borrowed mobile phones and dialling in to *terekura* (telephone chat lines) to find male customers for their dates.

Such stories were frequently featured on television for the next three years.

"I'm looking for an assisted date"

> "Schoolgirls seemed to merge physically with the technology of the electronic screen and telephone network. They became the *joshi kōsai* brand."

Schoolgirls in uniform peopled the news, documentary and educational programmes, chat and game shows. One journalist reported in the *Japan Times* on 22 October 1997 that 40 per cent more print space was devoted to discussing schoolchildren in Shibuya than to all domestic and international affairs combined. Their faces and voices were frequently disguised with screen pixelation and voice synthesisers so that the girls appeared as vague and shifting impressions of bodies with squeaky, computerised voices. Schoolgirls seemed to merge physically with the technology of the electronic screen and telephone network. They became the *joshi kōsei* brand. Time spent with them could be bought by men.

It was said that money raised from dates was used by schoolgirls to fulfil their only desire – to own brand-name goods, namely designer clothing and accessories. Journalists stood in theatrical awe of the ignorant gluttony of the girls. They were filmed clutching 10,000 yen notes. The viewing public were enthralled with the spectacle of an open, amoral and limitless pursuit of the symbols of corporate wealth.

KOGAL
The phenomenon of the schoolgirl-sex industry had influenced the style and mannerisms of ordinary schoolgirls, who customised their school uniforms in a sexually provocative manner. Known as *kogal*, these girls rolled up the waistband of their school skirts to turn them into miniskirts, and instead of regulation school socks *kogal* wore 'loose socks' crumpled around their shins. Their dishevelled style resembled the images of semi-naked schoolgirls featured in *burusera* pornography for men. *Kogal* played games with the dominant and fetishistic image of the schoolgirl as a sex object.

CHŌ-KAWAII
Beyond school uniforms *kogal* had another style, variably identified as *chō-kawaii* (super-cute), *shitagi-kei* (lingerie-style), *ō'share* (showy) and kitsch. *Kogal* wore cheap imitations of silk, fur and leather, such as silky acrylic shirts in prints reminiscent of Hermès silk-scarf designs and full-length coats with fur collars. Their gaudy look was accessorised with salon suntans, elaborate manicures and hair heavily streaked with whitish-blonde flashes. New fashion magazines were launched, aimed specifically at *kogal* culture. Utilising cameras, mirrors and accessories, *kogal* made heavy-handed performances of vanity and preening on the streets. The conspicuously staged materialism that was part of *kogal* style mimics the media images, in what was almost a parody of the notion of 'consumer lifestyle' itself.

JANE PAVITT

# At home with the Joneses

Next time you make a cup of instant coffee or feed the cat, think about how you do it and why. You never know who may be watching. Bar-code scanning, credit-card usage, the prevalence of CCTV and surveillance technology are all used for monitoring the social and demographic nature of consumption. The means of analysing contemporary consumer behaviour are literally embedded into the fabric of our technological society. An understanding of how consumers' preferences are formed and articulated provides vital information for marketers and brand owners. Major corporations have used market research and the observation of consumer behaviour as a means of understanding our responses to brands

since, at least, the 1930s. Current brand research also now demands an even more intimate access to our personalised choices and private behaviours around brands. The London-based advertising agency BMP DDB has an experimental consumer-research department called Culture Lab, run by Siamack Salari. Working with householders and shoppers, Salari builds profiles of consumers that focus on their habits, routines and personalised use of products. Salari explains:

> Culture Lab is a context-based observation research unit. Our premise is that no action or occasion can be understood in isolation or as a discrete event. Context is the unexplored frontier in marketing services. Consumers

are increasingly unpredictable and less likely to be persuaded by advertisers' messages. Their responses to brands are more likely to be based on how they relate to family and friends, and the contexts in which they encounter goods. By gathering this data, we can tell our clients how their brands fit into people's lives, and how their brand values are interpreted.

Our method is to set up relationships with individuals and households, documenting the random and inconsequential instances of their daily lives, to build up a picture of them as consumers. Subjects are also given cameras and encouraged to film themselves. Because we do not describe our findings as objective, they are made as transparent as possible to both client and subject. Households are actively involved in the

"Brands are like chess pieces – the moves we make with them are an indication of our relationship to others."

research process, and the researcher becomes a participant in the process of discovery. The emphasis with observational research is to keep the subjects as animated and comfortable as possible. Their behaviour is affected by the presence of the observers, but the way we explore decision-making processes is by telling households, at opportune moments, about our own habits and traits.

The home is where most things happen. We cook, write shopping lists, save vouchers sent by post, plan our finances, read magazines, watch television and discuss the near and distant future with our families and friends. The home, therefore, is a decision-making backdrop against which most buying choices can be understood. It is impossible to explain a mode of behaviour,

without understanding its context.

A tired parent may choose a frozen or ready meal to prepare for the family after a hard day. Only, before she places it in the oven, she adds her own grated cheese, some extra pepper, onion or tomato. By the time the pizza is ready, the preparation time is the same as it would have been to make it from scratch. The reality of the scenario is that her choice took her less thinking time, but her actions personalised the family meal.

Home is also where we organise our relationship with brands, and each household has a nerve centre for the management of this – by the phone, on a pin board, where the bills and money-off vouchers are kept. It is where we choose to read or throw away junk mail. Whatever the location, it is here

we can discover an individual's brand preferences and observe decisions being made that the buyer may not be conscious of when acting on them.

Sometimes the most insightful data comes in the form of stories that we are told concerning a particular subject. These can be sad, funny, angry ones or even lies. They reveal an enormous amount about an individual and his or her realities; the way we perceive the world around us. We observe activities and naturally occurring conversations in order to decode everyday behaviour and understand how brands fit into people's lives. Brands are like chess pieces – the moves we make with them are an indication of our relationship to others.

# CHAPTER THREE

# ALL THE WORLD'S A
## STORE

AARON BETSKY

## THE SPACES OF SHOPPING

The world is not just a stage, but also our shopping mall. We put together our identities by buying bits and pieces of consumer culture. We identify ourselves and others by how we dress, what music we listen to, which brands we sport. The places in which we do this are our temples of consumption, where we learn some of the rituals of belonging. These are the locations of desire and the home of branding. The shopping mall is our church and our palace, our mirror and our agora.

The question we need to ask is to what degree both we as consumers, and the brands we buy, are connected to and affected by the nature of the spaces in which that buying and selling takes place. At a time when marketers want their customers' buying experiences to be 'seamless', from the first time they see the advertising to the day they purchase the product, how well do the forms of the selling space reflect this desire?

The architecture of contemporary selling spaces is difficult to pin down. We expect buildings to reflect the abstract values we hold, in structures that are both literal and metaphoric. The architecture of the shopping environment, however, disappears into the background as much as it can. Retail environment design is dominated by engineers of various sorts. Retail consultants, store planners, security specialists as well as designers all work together to create the spaces in which we encounter brands. Their task is to make the building, as a physical form, as invisible as possible. All the shopper should find is the products and the brands – appearing as if by magic and floating free from constraints – in a space that we can inhabit by reference to them. We are never supposed to be aware of the systems that make all of this possible. This would open our eyes to an order that is larger than us, something that by implication we cannot purchase. The logic of shopping is that we are fully able to make, and control, our own world.

This is the importance of the shopping environment. The store and the mall offer an alternative to many traditional types of architecture that have largely led to dead ends. Traditional architecture was concerned with the central institutions of a society, whether temples or palaces, offices or museums. Architects set out to build fragments of perfection that stood out against the realities of everyday life. These moments of order always represented the values of those in control. Architecture in such cases became the concrete expression of an abstract and alien order, to which we, the common consumers, could only aspire.

An architecture that appears to remove itself from the arena of power offers an alternative to such a traditional vision. This would be an architecture that allows us to assemble the fragments of everyday life into a continually changing collage. As sociologist Anthony Giddens says:

> The self established a trajectory which can only become coherent through the reflexive use of the broader social environment. The impetus towards control, geared to reflexivity, thrusts the self into the outer world in ways which have no clear parallel in previous times. The disembedding mechanisms intrude into the heart of self-identity; but they do not 'empty out' the self any more than they simply remove prior supports on which self-identity was based. Rather, they allow the self (in principle) to achieve much greater mastery over the social relations and social contexts reflexively incorporated into the forging of self-identity than was previously possible.

By weaving together a tapestry of forms, we can cloak ourselves in a pleasing and ever flexible representation of our reality. To a certain extent we have always done this with our interiors, where furniture, mementoes and other fragments of our lives come together to form a highly personal and always changing composition. We can also find a momentary sense of this 'collage' environment at festivals, concerts and other expressions of collective enjoyment and exploration. Such a woven architecture also exists in our memory, which we are constantly reordering so as to make sense of our current situation. Conversely, we also project our sense of a flexible and modular reality into the future, imagining a better world in which we may some day live.

Superficially, the places where we shop seem

to provide us with just such a free space. The displays change constantly. We can see ourselves reflected not only in the scenes and mannequins the stores show us but also in the shop windows themselves. These thus become tools for social connection and seduction. We gather in malls and stores to promenade, socialise and construct a social sphere. The architecture of these places reconstructs the past in pastiches of bygone eras, as well as presenting the future; and the very absence of fixed form seems to liberate us to make anything we want of this world. As Margaret Crawford has said: 'In a city of endless atomisation, infinite individual ecologies are available.'[2]

But it is all a fiction. We are not truly free in our shopping environment. We have to buy into this world – literally. Many of us cannot even enter this scene, either because social or economic disadvantages exclude us, or because we do not possess what has been called the 'artefactual literacy' required to interpret and enjoy it.[3] We may also exclude ourselves by choice, if we recognise how our behaviour is being manipulated. For those who

can enter, however, it appears to be a beautiful world, and one that appears to set us free to create our own scenarios. This is the central paradox of the shopping environment: it is both a place of freedom and the ultimate expression of a society in which we are all composite constructions controlled by the laws of ownership, production and demand.

To understand the potential and the dangers of our contemporary retail architecture and brandscape, we must look closely at the new shopping spaces. This is not something we usually do, since we consider the store, the mall or the market to be a place that offers little to hold our attention apart from the things we want to buy. Yet this very lack of imposed order can make these spaces liberating.

What is more, the vestiges of the physical frame that these spaces provide can actively help to prevent the goods on sale from disappearing into the background. Without this spatial influence, what we are buying would vanish into a seamless continuum: a collection of properties that can only assemble themselves as branded products through the production and consumption processes. As the

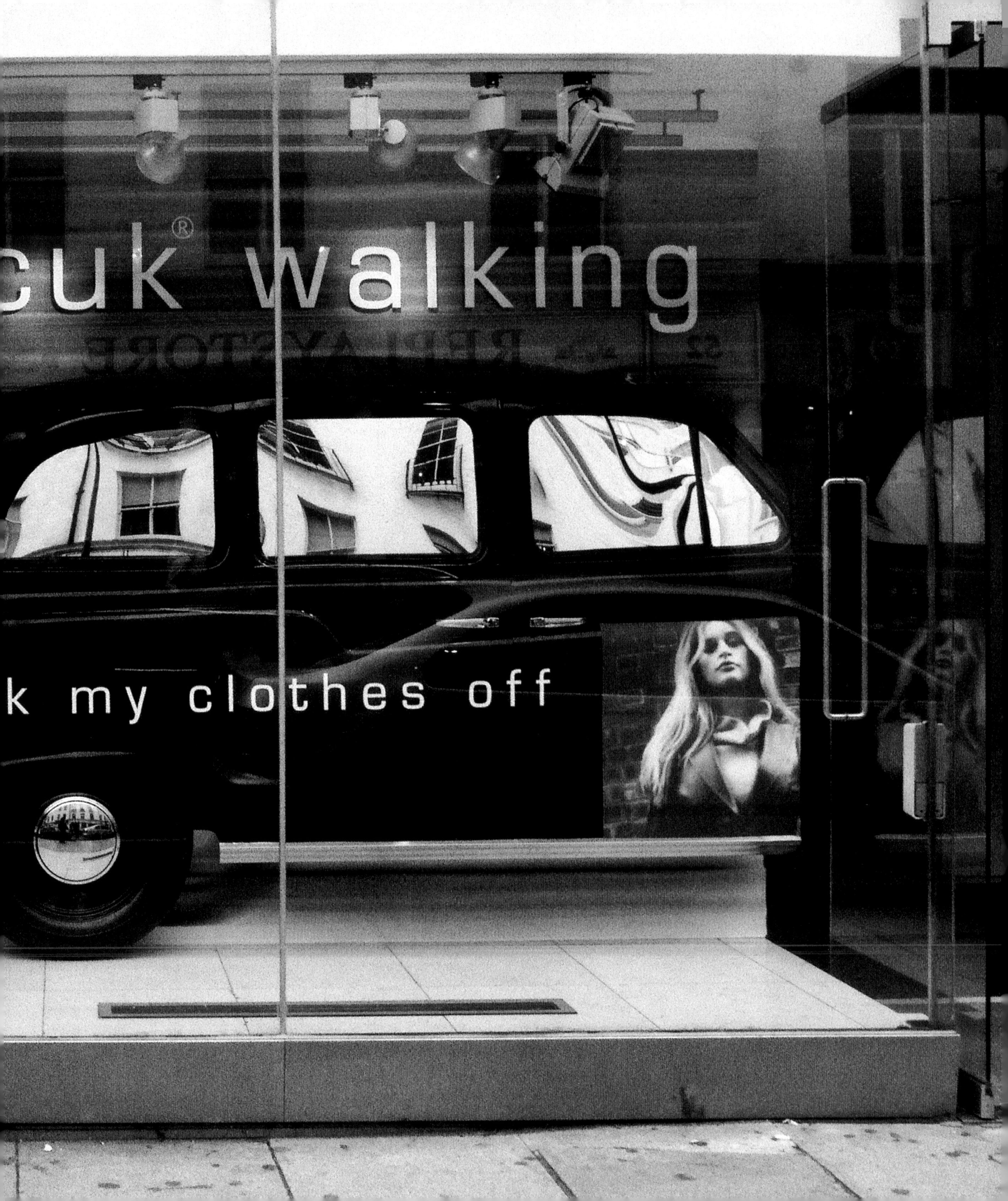
cuk® walking
k my clothes off

things we buy turn into brands *into which* we buy, the physical distance to the goods, the social space in which we buy them, and the difference between the physical thing and its projected appearance all disappear. We can no longer understand the spaces of shopping as places that assemble the riches of the world into a collage of colours and materials, within a choreography of spatial sequences amid the rituals of buying. With a *swoosh*, the spaces themselves disappear into brands.[4]

This situation is deeply rooted in the past. The history of retail spaces is one in which the presentation of goods is always thinly framed. Yet in the past, this structure always offered a 'third scene' – an alternative prospect both of the goods themselves and to the civic structures in which they were being sold. Brands mediate between object and ideology, while architecture offers a cut, a division or a critical break between them. The architecture of shopping is always characterised by openness, opening up within the city and around the product.

Democracy began in the agora, an outdoor market.[5] In much the same way, even the Roman Forum was originally a place to shop, rather than a place to adore ancestors or debate matters of state. The open space at the heart of any city was, and still is, an empty void that implies order and control. But it is only of use when it is filled with cafés, stalls and other accoutrements of commercial life.[6] Cities congealed not just around defensive points but also around crossroads, river crossings and harbours: places where goods arrived, were displayed and bought.[7] As Jane Jacobs has pointed out, the city starts as an open space where we display our artefacts, the products we create from the raw materials that surround us. It is from trading in such things that culture arises.[8]

The logic of the open-air market provides us with the first order of commercial architecture. The formalisation of the selling space offers a rhythm, a hierarchy and an increasingly complex form of organisation. Each stall is one small part of a scaffold, constructed from simple materials. It gives us a defined area, shelter from rain or sun, and an arena for social interaction. Midway between the tent that

was our first and moveable home, and the rigid walls of our houses, the open-air market suggests a notion of order that is still sufficiently flexible to contain the changing displays of the products and allow them to offer themselves to us.[9]

As time passes, these stalls are arranged into rows or other geometric forms that imply a stronger rhythm. As proto-streets, these sequences of stalls blend into each other to form a concatenation of sticks, cloth or whatever material we can string together into a sequence. We observe each stall in order, and yet each has a relationship to the other. This is the space of appearance of those goods that mediate our relationship with the larger world; and their display is halfway between an abstract order (the rows of stalls) and the collage of individual forms with which, for example, we dress ourselves.

In a larger sense, the marketplace is also a spectacle. This is where we have traditionally acted out alternatives to the official reality, where we gather to dramatise innovative realities and viewpoints that we would not otherwise see. Here we find the comedies and tragedies, the Punch-and-Judy shows, the carnival acts, the grotesques and the magic tricks, mixing in with the real goods we purchase to provide the unorthodox alternatives, the ob-scene to the scenes of everyday life. The marketplace is the stage for freedom of ideas and expression. Here law and order dissolves, licentiousness appears, tricks are played on the unsuspecting, property is bought, sold or liberated by sleight of hand, and we give and take freely of our commentary on each other.[10]

The architecture here is almost invisible. The appearance of the marketplace stands midway between forest or field and the formality of the city. In Greece and Rome, where it was at the heart of the urban scene, the marketplace was an opening that recalled the countryside outside the walls. In medieval Europe, where the fairs first knitted together an economy that was to conquer the world, the great cities were as often as not generated around a clearing or crossroads.

In other cultures the shopping space was darker and less open. The souk or bazaar was a labyrinth that

# XIV.
## Der Metzger oder Fleiſcher.

Nächſt dem Brod iſt auch das Fleiſch des Rindviehes, der Kälber, Schafe und Schweine eins der erſten Bedürfniſſe unſrer Tiſche. Der Metzger oder Fleiſcher kauft dieſes Vieh von den Landleuten, die ſich mit der Viehzucht beſchäftigen, ſchlachtet ſolches und verkauft das Fleiſch wieder, entweder in ſeinem Wohnhauſe, oder an einem öffentlichen Ort, welcher die Fleiſchbank genannt wird. Unſre Tafel ſtellet eine ſolche Fleiſchbank vor, wo die Frau eines Metzgers Fleiſch an eine Köchin auswiegt. — Es iſt ein wichtiger Artickel für eine weiſe Polizey, dahin zu ſehen daß kein anders als gutes und geſundes Fleiſch zu Markte gebracht, und die Fleiſchbänke möglichſt reinlich gehalten werden. Die Stadt Nürnberg übt dieſe nützliche Polizeyanſtalt in demjenigen Grad der Vollkommenheit aus, daß ſelbſt auswärtige Tadler ihr in dieſem Stücke einen nahmhaften Vorzug vor andern groſſen Städten einräumen müſſen.

intensified the dense order of the city. It wormed its way between houses and removed itself from the stark contrasts of light and shade where palaces, temples and the city skyline itself stood against the landscape. The bazaar is a place of shadow and shade. It is a nebulous in-between where edges bleed, where there is no beginning or end, where order breaks down because the architectural structure becomes invisible. The medieval streets of Europe, where guilds banded together in linear sequences devoted to the sale of one product or service, were analogous to souks. Here a nascent community of makers and sellers created a rhythm all of their own in the shadows of the church and the castle.[11]

For centuries, we took such spaces for granted. They offered an alternative to places where order prevailed and ideas and appearances were rigid. These were the points in between the growing official order, where things actually happened – where public life actively involved its participants. It was only when the centralised state acted to control such arenas that we realised they were actual distinct places, possessing their own nature and order. As central spaces became straight-edged squares, as fairs were exiled from the heart of the city, and as policing became more rigorous, the freedom of the marketplace disappeared.

At first the marketplace vanished into the regularised environment of the covered market, such as those of eighteenth-century England and France. Here the grids were regularised, and an equality between goods and vendors established. In the emerging world of brands, what mattered was the provision of services in an efficient manner. Similarly, store interiors and exteriors became increasingly dominated by signs, product containers and the formal organisation of the goods themselves.

The once fluid selling space became crystallised in the formality of the arcade. The stalls only made their appearance on certain days. Other stores spread throughout the city, becoming fragmented visions of commercial activity. The only unified visions were to be found in the stockpiles of the warehouse, or, translated into interior decoration, in the furnishings

of palaces. Shopping and the vernacular experience become one and the same – as, to many people, they still are today.[12]

At the very moment that this was happening, the first consciously constructed palaces of consumption appeared. These were the arcades that cut through the cities of Europe in the late eighteenth and nineteenth centuries. Starting with the Palais Royal in Paris in 1781, which reached its final form just before the Revolution, the new arcades presented alternatives to the closed orders of the old regime. They gathered together various kinds of commercial enterprises into much lighter versions of the then prevailing column arcades. The developers who were laying out these internal-shopping streets also used new materials such as plate glass and iron. These new constructions bathed products in light and did away with the heavy frames that had previously contained them. The new shopping spaces provided a series of scenes that were in contrast to the grids of streets then replacing the historic cores of great European cities.[13]

These places became the haunts of the *flâneurs*, the prostitutes and the new middle classes. There was something promiscuous about the presentation of the goods that was matched with the availability of human bodies, and all of it could be surveyed by those men and women who were fortunate enough to have time for leisure. Everything – goods, bodies and buildings – were but fleeting images and reflections, held together by the brand of the building, the product or the person, each of which was vouchsafed by style, fashion and advertising. Here a group of people, whose very identity depended on the abstracting of values from goods and services, could find a place. In these arcades, an endless parade of products from around the world, and representative of different times and cultures, fuelled the construction of interiors and clothes that had little to do with the conventional orders. People could define themselves by what they owned, and they could find such definitions in the new stores that gathered multifarious objects all together in the space of the arcades.[14] It was a new world, one which Walter Benjamin described in 1927:[15]

Above: Le Passage Choiseul,
Paris, c. 1900.
Following pages: Delivery
Carts at the Bon Marché,
Paris, c. 1900.

In the Avenue Champs-Elysées among new hotels with Anglo-Saxon names, arcades were opened recently as the newest Parisian passage. A monstrous orchestra in uniform played at its opening among flowerbeds and flowing fountains. People groaned as they pressed together to cross over the sandstone thresholds and pass along mirrored walls; they viewed artificial rain falling on the copper innards of the latest automobiles as proof of the quality of the material, observed gears oscillating in oil, and read on black placards in street letters the prices of leather goods, gramophone records and embroidered kimonos. In the diffused light that came from above, they glided over tile floors.

Even more than the arcade, the department store came to embody the urban experience of the bourgeoisie. The first department store, the Bon Marché in Paris, was larger than most of the cultural buildings that had until then formed the focal point of the city. In the 1850s and 1860s Aristide Boucicaut developed the Bon Marché from a *magasin de nouveautés* or draper's shop into a true department store.[16] Its architectural transformation began in 1869, with the laying of the foundation stone for a new building on the site of the old. The architect of the building was L. A. Boileau, and its engineer was Gustave Eiffel. Both of these men were pioneers in the new architecture of iron and glass. The scale of the new building project was vast, and by the 1880s visitors to the store could browse through departments of ready-to-wear clothing, home furnishings, oriental rugs, umbrellas, ribbons, hair accessories, stationery, trinkets, travel goods and a perfumery. Here was a new gathering place for the

Below: The grand staircase
of the Bon Marché, Paris,
*c.* 1870, engraving by
Karl Fichot.

middle classes, where they were surrounded by the goods that defined them.

Department stores became increasingly elaborate and developed their own spatial order. The sequences of counters mimicked the old stalls, while the atrium became the void at the heart of this activity. The grand stairs offered performance stages on which the shoppers stood in for the actors. The dressing rooms became places of liberation and transformation in which mirrors reflected a new self being born, while the tea rooms and restaurants became sites for the construction of a new set of social relations. The

stores even introduced many people to such technical innovations as the elevator. Here was a whole new world in one building.[17]

The new stores also brought a sense of uncertainty as new forms of social order that replaced the concerns of the individual with those of the mass. The freedom of entry meant that in theory the department store was accessible to all sectors of society; although in practice some were excluded or at least discouraged. The department store was more than likely to be seen as a middle-class, feminised space.[18] During the much publicised opening of Selfridges in

Right: *The Dedication of a Great House: A Day Well Spent is Passed at Selfridges*, 1909, print, for Selfridges & Co, London.
Far right: *Selfridges by Night*, 1909, print, for Selfridges & Co, London.

London in 1909, for example, the store was declared as 'dedicated to woman's service first of all'.

While the great department stores that arose at the beginning of the twentieth century helped reform and renovate cities, they also lost their power to amaze and liberate.[19] Although certain of them remained Meccas, such as Harrods or Selfridges in London, Bloomingdales or Macy's in New York, the march of advertising and branding meant that goods were also available everywhere – even by mail order. The diffusion of the buying public into the suburbs created an audience that depended on advertising more than the physical framework of the store to convince them to buy. As a result, stores became integrated once more into the fabric of the city. Occasionally, architects would use commercial environments as places to build a vision of the new – one thinks of German architect Erich Mendelsohn's Schocken department stores, such as in Stuttgart (1928) and Chemnitz (1929). But in general, the store became just a place to buy goods. It now existed in urban environments that were so thoroughly dominated by middle-class structures and advertising that there was little sense of memory or aspiration for

the architecture to embody.

It was only when the middle class began leaving the city and making a place for itself on the fringes of the city that stores regained their function. They became focal points in the new, artificial landscape the middle classes were making for themselves. The suburb, that place between the city and nature where the middle class constructed its meandering, uncertain and technologically driven homeland, found its heart in the shopping mall. Movement – roads, railroad lines – dominates the suburb, which has no clear order and is always changing as people shift within it or develop it. This is the logic of suburban spaces, which demand reinvestment of capital as quickly as possible for the purposes of further speculation and profit.

The basis for the suburban shopping space was the market stall. In this case, however, the new retail spaces were designed to service the automobile culture, and so they banded together to provide an aggregation of goods for the shopper on the move. They provided plenty of parking, thus creating a void that extended the street, and added large and prominent signs that could be read by people moving at speed. These soon overwhelmed the architecture.

Previous pages and above:
Macy's, New York, 1920s,
decorated for the Christmas
season.

These new, auto-friendly selling spaces also became the focal point of their community:[20]

> The drive-in was oriented not to recreational paths, but to routine ones of area residents. If enough people living within about a one-mile radius drove by the site on a regular basis, a respectable business could be sustained and, just as in more densely settled districts, other retail outlets might be attracted to the vicinity. The drive-in market thus helped to pioneer business locations within an urban context rather than standing as an outpost that would long remain isolated in more or less open surroundings... When the drive-in market was a catalyst for commercial development, the resulting aggregation often lacked the centralised structure of a neighbourhood business district, having no clear hierarchy of sites or functions. At a pivotal point in the metropolitan area's growth, when business owners were beginning to understand the implications of a mass motoring populace, the drive-in market demonstrated how even a place catering to mundane shopping needs could be an attraction in itself.

The supermarket grew directly out of these small strips, the first being opened in Memphis, Tennessee, in 1916 (it was called Piggly-Wiggly). Supermarkets were formalised in 1928 in Los Angeles by the store brand Ralphs. Here the model was not so much the interior market halls – it was the open world of the seasonal market made permanent: 'Ralphs created a new kind of space that was lofty, imposing, yet non-hierarchical and conductive to perambulation, allowing consumers to choose their own paths of movement as well as their own goods. In no previous instance had so large a retail space seemed so perceptually open and so liberating.'[21] After the Second World War, these techniques were adopted both by British retailers such as Tesco, and by the French with the growth of hypermarkets such as Carrefour. The latter became a supermarket blown up to a scale at which even the American chains could only wonder.

The real monument to suburbia, and the final scene where we see goods transformed into brands that float in an abstract retail environment, was the

Right: Display of household goods, Woolworths, Great Britain, 1960s.

shopping mall. The first of this new breed was Southdale , outside of Minneapolis, designed in 1954-6 by the Los Angeles-based architect Victor Gruen. Southdale was a meandering collection of modernist pavilions that fragmented and popularised the interlocking compositions demonstrated in both the buildings and the teachings of the German modernist design school, the Bauhaus. It was also a thoroughly American building that exalted space and movement. The shopping mall was, like rock'n'roll and the skyscraper, an American invention that spread to the rest of the world with the globalisation of commerce.

Leaving the parking on the outside, the shopping mall created a new version of the city street that ran between the stores themselves. The mall became an abstract version of the city that the middle class had left behind. It had gateways, streets, alleys, service areas, central squares and gathering spaces. What it did not have was a hierarchy. The biggest stores became anchors, rather than focal points. These big, windowless boxes signalled the beginning of a journey into the commercial world. They had few features that would distinguish them from other retail establishments. Those stores then marched

around whatever pattern the planners established in such a way as to get the shopper lost.[22]

The key moment in the shopping mall experience was the 'Gruen transfer'. This was where shoppers, who may have arrived intending to purchase a particular product, would become distracted by something else, deviate from their path and start wandering. Before long shoppers would be lost in a maze from which the only escape was to expose themselves to more chances to buy. One had to become lost in the world of artefacts to find one's self. The bazaar had merged with the marketplace stalls and the arcade to form a perfect shopping environment.

As shopping malls grew in size and importance, they became community focal points. This was where housewives and children gathered, where old people strolled, and where community activities took place. Since the mall was often the largest building in the landscape, it became the signpost by which the suburban resident could identify different parts of an amorphous and changing world. Ironically, the mall lost most of the crystalline nature of the marketplace, the arcade or even the strip mall. It became a featureless box whose interior was as often as not

**Right: Northland Shoppping Center, Detroit 1954. Architect: Victor Gruen. Gruen's plans for both Northland and Southdale Center (1954-6) defined the American shopping experience of the 1950s.**

inarticulate. The core of the suburban experience was a place that did not offer visual hierarchies. It displaced the columned fronts and articulated facades of courthouses, city halls and banks that had previously been the focal point of communities. As a result, civic traditions were no longer embodied in its architecture.[23]

The shopping mall that evolved in the three decades after 1945 was the endpoint for the development of the marketplace. From a temporary construction of stalls that appeared as needed, it had become a closed box that defined a completely artificial realm of shopping. The commercial scene now excluded the ob-scene, the informal and vulgar culture, as much as it could. As brands and store chains gained importance over the goods, even the reality of the object of desire dissolved into nothing but signs of seduction. Since at least the second half of the nineteenth century, advertising had striven to create a sense of cohesion across time and space by breaking through the physical barrier of the store. The end result was that the rise of branding had reduced the chaotic variety of commercial images to a set of singular and iconic graphic identifiers. The panoply of merchandising devices that recalled the advertising campaign could then disappear from the selling space. The store environment needed fewer and fewer features, just as the goods themselves became more and more abstract carriers of meaning.

Malls have become the same all over the world, with only minor regional variations.[24] In Asia, many are underground, and are part of large railroad or subway stations. Here the lack of exterior becomes literal. In Europe, they have tended to be smaller and often integrated more carefully into existing urban situations. While some projects are also underground and part of large railroad or subway stations – for example, Les Halles in Paris – others are more complex and seamless parts of the city. The model here is the Lijnbaan, the 1954 mixed-use project in Rotterdam, designed by Bijvoet and Duiker. The Lijnbaan plays off open-air shopping arcades against housing slabs set in small parks, and an anchor department store designed by Marcel Breuer. As both

developers and designers have increased their global reach, however, regional distinctions that might extend from their organization to differences in colour schemes and signage have disappeared.

Similarly, as the science of shopping and its finance have gone global, the organisation of malls has developed into a series of quite closely matched variations. The most common malls are still those that connect two or three anchor stores with a dominant corridor and several smaller cross-corridors. Food courts and cinemas are usually located either at the heart of the building or on a higher level. They form a public square within the maze of corridors. The entry is not usually taken as an opportunity to make a major statement: the developers do not want shoppers hanging around admiring the architecture, when they should be progressing into the active shopping environment as quickly as possible.[25]

Though tastes and architectural styles have changed, the overall structure of the elements within the mall's spatial organisation has not.[26] Stores are very narrow (usually no more than 20 to 30 feet) and long, so that as many stores as possible can announce themselves to shoppers. The storefronts are almost completely glass, with frames that are meant to validate the merchandise: wood for a bookstore, marble for a jewellery store. Lighting is bright.

Signage – or 'way-finding systems', as the experts like to call them – dominates these spaces. These signs create a rhythm akin to that of trees, they establish focal points, and they combine the images that tell us what to do (road signs) and what to want (commercial advertising) into singular structures. In recent years, these systems have come to dominate the malls so completely that they have merged with the architecture. They form continual arcades, strips along the centre of the mall and frameworks for planting, seating or other decoration.

There are few right-angled turns or orthogonal grids in shopping malls. This is not so much because designers wish to make a statement, as because developers want the experience of shopping to be seamless. All barriers and all possible

stumbling-blocks have to be removed. Shops rarely have visible doors and corridors angle into each other; even the lines between soffits and ceilings dissolve to where a skylight or the coving hints at nothing but a nebulous other realm. A good example of this 'classic' shopping mall design is the Beverly Center in Los Angeles, designed by Welton Becket & Associates in 1982.

In recent years, the stalls that sparked all this have reappeared as carts – 'incubators' where individual retailers can try out their merchandising ideas before they invest in a store or are taken over by a large chain. They give the mall a sense of reality and diversity, though they are only temporary way-stations that lead us to the mall proper. Just as any architectural style quickly disappears into the fabric of the mall, so these expressions of commercial innovation soon fade into the background.

By the mid-1980s, the mall had become stagnant. In their perpetual need to entice shoppers into the next experience, developers had created ever larger malls ever further removed from urban centres. Some developers turned to tricks such as opening up malls to the outdoors again whenever possible, or

propelling them vertically upwards in the centres of city in their willingness to try anything that might upgrade the appearance of their buildings. However, they were caught out by the fact that the mall had become utterly formulaic, dominated by chain stores and a gloomy sense of familiarity. It was felt that there was little room for growth. After the Reagan recession, retail developers began looking at ways out of the tomb they had built for themselves.[27]

In the last two decades, the shopping mall has begun to fall apart. It has dissolved into mini-malls and convenience centres, Big Box retail centres, hybrid entertainment and shopping environments, and quasi-malls that have become reintegrated into the city. Each of these new types points the way toward a potential re-deployment of the marketplace into a form that might be either more liberating or even more constricting. The appearance of the electronic mall, whether on the World Wide Web or through television shopping and catalogues, further extends these possibilities.

The mini-mall condenses its big brother into a form that both minimises its importance and reintegrates into our daily lives. It was a type that emerged in the south-western states of America in the mid-1980s, when environmental regulations and rising gas and real-estate prices conspired to put many urban gas stations out of business. Their corner lots became the sites for L-shaped commercial developments. These mini-malls combined the auto-oriented configuration of the strip mall with the contours of the urban grid. They made use of the rhythm of the city, determined by traffic lights and pedestrian crossings, to form nodes of shopping. Though the original malls were one-storey tall, a few two- and even three-storey variations have emerged.

Some developers have tried to turn their mini-malls into giant signs or have adopted stylistic devices such as colonnades to distinguish them. But the vast majority of these buildings are indistinguishable from their surroundings, to such an extent that it is difficult to identify any particular architectural element. Beyond the number of storeys, these malls exhibit other variables such as the inclusion of a fast-food outlet or drive-through box (either for a bank or for services such as dry cleaning, photo developing or coffee). Other variations include the way in which signage is incorporated into the building or vertical circulation appears as exposed and articulated.

There is little to say about such structures as buildings. They are no more and no less than the intensification of those parts of the city's fabric in which shopping has become practically the only element in the public realm. This is true to such an extent that we now equate vast stretches of empty road only as the space between commercial developments. And yet they are somehow unnoticed: it is only when something calamitous happens, as it did following the civil unrest after the Rodney King verdict in 1992, that these commercial nodes become visible: during the riots, it was the mini-malls that burned.

The Asian variation provides us with the vertical mini-malls found all over Japan, Korea and other developed nations. Here an open sliver of circulation leads up, and down, to floor after floor of stores and restaurants. As in the West, there is little to distinguish these developments from the overall texture of the city. Just as the traditional shopping malls of Japan are underground expanses spreading out from railway stations, so the mini-malls are invisible intensifications of an immensely dense urban grid.

Right: Mini-Mall, Atlanta, USA, 2000.

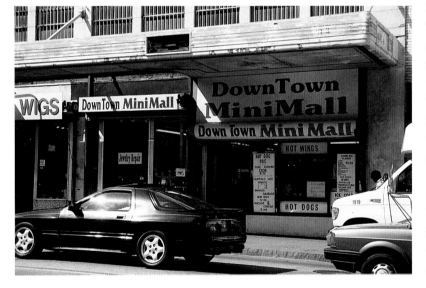

The other interesting point about mini-malls is purely economic: they serve as points of entry for small entrepreneurs into the mainstream economy. Many of the shop owners belong to ethnic minorities, and these relatively cheap stores give them a chance to establish their own commercial ventures. The presence of many different cultures and languages further fragments the appearance of these shopping spaces. An assortment of typefaces, signs from a variety of ethnic visual traditions, and different approaches to what makes a store an attractive space are all in vigorous competition. From brightly lit interiors to an explosion of advertising signs, everything undercuts the homogeneity the shopping mall has imposed on the commercial environment during the last few decades.

A European variant on the mini-mall is the small-scale 'local shopping centre'. British versions of these small strips of around ten to twelve stores, built on what was previously unused space at the edge of traditional High Street shopping areas, have become adept incubators for entrepreneurial immigrant store owners.

Big Box retail centres go the other way. They are huge structures, often further removed from population centres than traditional malls. They are constructed to house collections of large chain stores that specialise in bringing a series of related goods together under one immense roof: Home Depot, Ikea, Maxis and Toys'R'Us are good examples. The mall becomes a collection of immense boxes standing in vast expanses of parking. There is no room here for the Gruen Transfer – only for the piling up of more and more goods in ever greater bulk. There are no public spaces, other than an occasional food court, and no sense of a promenade. Here the space of shopping has become larger, more directed and less a part of the fabric of everyday life.

Ironically, this has given architecture an opportunity to get back into the picture. The big blocks give designers a chance to create grand monuments to shopping. Though their clients usually restrict their freedom, designers have occasionally created some rather striking structures.

A good example is the intensely coloured, almost surreal landscape Ricardo Legoretta created for the Tustin Center in Southern California. The architect made good use of the fact that here the parking lot and approaches do not surround a singular object, but comprise a more complex landscape that connects an assortment of nodal points. Lines of palm trees, tilted rock planes and geometric fragments take the place of way-finding systems and give the development a strong sense of place.

In Europe, the mode for Big Box retailing started with the enlargement of supermarkets such as Maxis and Carrefour. These grew to such gigantic proportions that they began to take on the character of an enclosed market, offering a wide variety of goods and acting as a regional centre. Ikea made its forms recognisable by turning their stores into abstract blue sculptures, and providing day care and decent food in their interiors. Here the Big Boxes became abstracted and interiorised versions of the agora.

The interiors of the Big Boxes can be overwhelming. Except in the case of companies like Ikea, which has divided up half of each of its stores into environments of domestic vignettes, almost all of these retailers present their spaces to the viewer without any modulation. The spaces are high, the aisles repetitive and the structure on which the goods present themselves are evident. These are places that resemble the vast archives of which the architects of the Enlightenment dreamed. All is clear, available and at hand. Machinery for stocking and moving goods mixes with both the scaffolding for construction and display, and with the human beings making use of these technologies. So they resemble the kind of city architects Fred Koetter and Colin Rowe called for in their seminal Collage City.[28] This is about as modern as architecture can be. There is no decoration, no hint at hierarchy and no sense of the real world. In this artificial world, the shopping environment has become a total experience.

A variation on these Big Box retail centres is the outlet mall. Here stores present their goods in warehouse-like settings, the size of which

approaches that of the Big Box retailers but the arrangement of which borrows from aspects of the traditional mall. Most of them are outdoors, and thus they also have some of the direct nature of the older strip centres. The emphasis on cheap construction (not only to save the developer money but also to give the customer the sense of a bargain environment) again allows designers to experiment with forms less reserved than those permitted in a traditional mall. Though the quality of the graphics and the materials used for the stores is often rather harsh, the primitive quality of the concrete, block or stucco construction has given some designers an excuse to experiment with forceful forms.

Shopping in these spaces is divorced so completely from the experiences of everyday life that it has little connection with the tradition of the marketplace. These are destination points that resemble a strange hybrid of the cathedral of commerce and democratic versions of the king's or priest's warehouse of wealth. They are placeless spaces where technology reveals itself in all its naked glory, alongside the abandonment of packaging and other forms of seduction that habitually enclose objects at the core of our consumer society. Their scale approaches the point at which people become almost insignificant – a utopia of which some architects have always dreamed – while any chance of experiencing the hidden, the secret or the oppositional space has completely disappeared. Here shopping, architecture, storage and space have come together to create ex-urban magnets that seem to have no particular meaning.

When the branded goods, stacked high in eerily immense spaces, do not speak for themselves, architecture provides its own brand that dissolves the product brand from the outside in. The opposite of such stripping down of form, in which shopping becomes an experience of the goods in an abstract landscape, is the entertainment architecture of the themed malls. The prototypes for these spaces were the urban renovations performed by the Rouse Corporation in Boston (Faneuil Hall), Baltimore (Harborplace) and New York (South Street Seaport),

as well as by John Jerde, whose San Diego Horton Plaza was the first and in many ways remains the most sophisticated themed environment. The precedents, however, were Disneyland and its Florida cousin, Disneyworld. These gave birth to the idea that one could go somewhere for an experience that was neither religious nor transforming, but merely enjoyable – and then further merged this with the evocation of other times and places. The fair became permanent, and the experience consumable.

In the earliest themed-shopping environments, the mall re-invigorated itself by turning back to its own history. Faneuil Hall was a marketplace repackaged as a mall, which was meant to resemble a marketplace. It also used a historic structure that made people feel as if they were coming to that quaint place of memory, the city. The location of almost all of these early re-developments was at such edges of the old city as the docks. Here the old order used to break down and the freedom of the open seas crept into the city's mores along with the wares that arrived there. These locations reinforced the artificial sense that the new selling space was a place of freedom. The themed environment offered the ability to capture the past and then to use it as a place of liberation from the control of the present.

Architects such as John Jerde justified their work by claiming that they were providing the public with a space that rediscovered the values of community, dense housing and public space – elements for which the renovation movement of the 1970s had fought so hard. Jerde borrowed the forms of the Italian Renaissance to dignify his malls, then gave them bright colours and abstracted their outlines in the manner of Charles Moore. The results were stage-sets, the operatic overtones of which became more evident because of the combination of their large scale and flimsiness. It took a while for the retail establishments to catch up with the visual pandemonium Jerde produced, but soon the balance between the architectural and retail packaging was restored. What remained was the scale of Jerde's gestures; their evocation of a language that was primitive in its cartoon pastiche of a child's idea of home or official building, yet still able to indicate some form of public space.[29]

Jerde also mastered the use of the curve as an alternative to the corridor. In an era in which the importance of department stores was waning, fragmenting the retail experience along with most other elements of the economy, Jerde and his followers came up with a simple gesture. The curved

BORDEN MAIN STREET ICE CREAM PARLOR
MAGIC KINGDOM-WALT DISNEY WORLD

Above: Ontario Mills,
California, 1997. One of
a series of retail sites
selling discounted brands,
developed by the Mills
Corporation. Designer:
Communication Arts Inc.
Following pages: Bluewater,
Kent, England, 2000.

paths and fragments of paths, leading to and from nowhere in particular, let shoppers promenade past the retail establishments without seeing any hierarchy in what they encountered. Food courts and cinemas, plazas and cul-de-sacs interrupted these fluid lines as places for gathering, rest and reflection, where shoppers would find themselves completely surrounded by signs and symbols of retail.

Many of these themed environments were also open to the outside, so that they began to resemble something like a 'real' city. Other architects made this reference even more clear by adopting closer approximations of classical architecture. They might sometimes create storefronts to make the mall appear like a New England, French provincial or vaguely Spanish street. British examples such as Bluewater, on the edge of London, wear their theming rather lightly and concentrate on creating an overwhelming, festive environment in which we can become completely immersed.[30]

Only a few architects chose themes outside of the more-or-less traditional urban repertoire. In the Orient especially, a few high-tech environments appeared, as they did in Renzo Piano's Bercy shopping mall in Paris. Only in airports, which soon began to rival malls as locations for mass retailing,

did the language of glass and steel connections, streamlined into vaguely futuristic fragments of angular geometries by the likes of Helmut Jahn, become truly popular.

Disney and its theme-park imitators took the themed shopping environment to its logical extension by creating complete villages that were both tourist destinations and stores. Disney's original stores were recreations of a mythical American Midwestern small town constructed at 5/8th scale. When they became more adventurous they designed French, British and even 'Japanese' villages. In Hollywood, Universal Studios worked so hard to recreate the eclectic architecture of a Los Angeles located only a few miles away, that one executive exclaimed: 'If I have to get bums to make it seem more like a real city, I'll just call central casting.'[31]

Though some critics predicted that such theming would come to dominate all retail environments, most developers chose not to be too specific.[32] Instead of definite references, designers chose to evoke a generic past that was also modern enough to promise a better future through acquisition. As a result, many themed environments began to blend with their more conventional predecessors. They offered just a hint of a specific atmosphere, just enough to distinguish one

Opposite: Canal City Hakata,
Fukuoka, Japan, 1996.
Architect: Jerde Partnership
International, Inc.
Right: Bellagio, The Resort,
Las Vegas. Architect:
Jerde Partnership
International, Inc.

mall from another. It was the way-finding systems that became the principal repository of such themes. The master of such binding elements is Communication Arts. This Colorado-based firm, headed by Henry Beer, a former employee of Charles and Ray Eames, manages to give each of the malls in which they are involved a specific flavour without making them too specific. The Ontario Mills project, for instance, pays homage to local agricultural traditions, a Hispanic heritage and a vague notion of California modernism – all without offering literal references to any of these.[33] Companies such as Jerde and Communications Arts are becoming brands in themselves, and imposing their themed abstractions on cities everywhere: Jerde's design for a 'shopping ditch' in Rotterdam has essentially the same form and elements as his giant Canal City in Fukuoka.

The only time when theming dominates is when shopping becomes part of an overall entertainment experience. Here New York-based architect David Rockwell, designer of restaurants for the likes of Planet Hollywood and Nobu, as well as of the Foxwood Casino in Connecticut, excels at creating a place in which customers are made to feel they are simultaneously on, behind and in front of the stage. These fairy-tale lands invite participation not only through consuming but also by playing games or taking rides. Though most of the theming concentrates on such restaurant franchises as the Rainforest Café, in certain places it does seep into

the more traditional retail environment. The most obvious example of this is in Las Vegas, where the Forum Shops – the most successful shopping mall in the United States in terms of per-square-foot sales – intensifies the theme of the Caesar's Casino. The Bellagio pretends to be a village on Lake Como, the Venetian offers gondola rides past the stores, and the Parisian focuses on a scale model of the Eiffel Tower.[34] In Tokyo, planners are trying to imitate the Forum Shops with a new mixed-use development in Tokyo Bay.

One innovation that the theming movement has given the development of the mall is a more complete divorce of appearance and space. In Disneyland, though all the shops look separate, they are in fact one large department store. Behind small storefronts, the shops actually sprawl out and interconnect. The Limited, an Ohio-based brand, has picked up on this idea of an alternative to the department store. It lines up its various 'products' (or brands) in sections of malls. There is The Limited, The Limited Too, Victoria's Secret, Bath and Body Works and Compagnie Aérospatiale, all of which seem to be distinct stores, each with its own theme. In fact each is selling differently targeted versions of the same merchandise. The most amusing of The Limited's subdivisions is Structure, a store aimed at young men themed around architecture. Market research informed them that their target audience considered architects their role model, so these sections of the quasi-department store display quotes from Mies van der Rohe and Louis Sullivan, and are furnished and furbished with Le Corbusier 'cube' chairs and fake metal beams. Here, retail

Above: Rainforest Café
Interior, Trafford Centre,
Manchester, 1999.
Right: The Changing Sky,
Forum Shops at Caesar's,
Las Vegas.

architecture has disappeared into its own theme.

In other instances architecture has vanished into the fabric of the city. Many of the world's traditional shopping streets have become de facto malls. The same stores line up along Fifth Avenue in New York, the rue du Faubourg-Saint-Honoré in Paris or Bond Street in London. The theming here is more related to the economic class to which these streets have usually catered; the forms take and adapt whatever architecture is at hand. As in the traditional mall, it is the way-finding system that makes sense of it all. Business Improvement Districts (BIDs) create a graphic identity for shopping areas that extends from street signs to the uniforms of the private security guards they hire. Here the vestigial hierarchy of the department store disappears in the tumult of urban form, while the artificial public spaces again become one with the public street. Ironically, however, the city becomes a facsimile of itself. The BIDs clean up the storefronts, regulators control the appearance of buildings, and those aspects of the city that are not for sale disappear around the corner. The city itself is now for sale.

Today even suburbs, influenced by the New Urbanists theorists and the success of BIDs, are creating imitation urban centres. Existing village streets that had lost their stores to highway-convenient strips are revitalised, and retail villages are created on the same 'cornfield sites' that once sprouted malls. Behind the stores, parking structures offer convenient access. The anchors for such retail villages are, as is now the case in most malls, cinema complexes combined with restaurants and clubs for night-time attraction and bookstores with their own cafés to cater for the daytime crowd. Once again, it seems we can only establish a community in our culture if we focus not on shared institutions, but on the things we can buy.

Both The Limited's strategy and the reintegration of the mall into the city point to the place into which the architecture has actually disappeared: into the brand itself. Henry Beer has said that he wants 'the experience of the shopper from the moment they see the Nike commercial on TV to the point where they are wearing the shoes when they come out of the store to be completely seamless'.[35] In some of the projects he designs he has come close to achieving this ideal. The walls have become so thin and abstract as to be almost invisible; and way-finding systems have merged with the stores' individual signs. In urban malls today, Big Box retail, the department store and the advertising environment all merge into such 'superstores' as NikeTown or Old Navy. Here commercials and projected images assault the viewer, while the logo ties all manner of otherwise only lightly related products together. The most extreme example of this is the emergence of stores such as those devoted to Microsoft, which has few tangible goods to sell.

But to most shoppers, even such a concentrated statement of the brands they buy is usually not necessary. Increasingly, they seem to base their retail decisions on the advertising that sells a particular lifestyle to a 'cohort group' through a logo the company extends into its packaging. To these logos it adds narrative images that show the kind of scene in which they hope their customers would like to be actors. Brands are the uniforms for the tribal nomads, who buy them at whichever caravanserai they find themselves.

The obvious extension of this movement is the disappearance of shopping into the ethereal realm of the electrosphere. The tremendous growth of catalogue shopping around the world has already increased the retail space to the point where it almost completely infiltrates both home and office. In the 1980s, catalogues branched out on to television through such cable channels as the Home Shopping Network. Now the Internet promises to make it ever easier to acquire goods without even the luxury of a catalogue framework or a disembodied salesvoice at the other end of a toll-free number. With a drag and a click, the object of desire is yours.

While the space of retail thus shrinks to the thickness of a screen, new spaces appear. These are mainly located in the area of distribution. Immense new warehouses and trans-shipping centres are growing up in strategic locations. One of the largest of these in the western United States ironically dwarfs Ontario Mills, one of California's largest shopping malls, which sits just across the freeway. Indeed, it is many years since the landscape critic J. B. Jackson pointed out how the architecture of delivery services has shaped our cities.[36] Now the needs of large and small trucks, the warehouses and the control centres continue to erode what we think of as traditional architectural form. The appearance of double-stacked containers has required the rebuilding of thousands of bridges and roads all over the United States to create the necessary clearance for trucks and trains. The warehouses and the clerical centres that service the invisible shopping networks are often the largest buildings on the ex-urban landscape.

The new landscape of shopping is one of completely anonymous volumes, which can house either goods or people. The only articulate elements we can distinguish are the containers, *their* containers (ships, trains and automobiles) and the methods of loading and unloading them. Logos (FedEx, UPS) tie together these eternally moving components. The back of the store has not only survived the disappearance of the shop as a physical artefact but also completely overwhelmed its original *raison d'être*.[37]

There is a logic to the architecture of the electrosphere. I asked Jim Bezos, founder of Amazon.com, why the 'splash page' for the firm's 'store' appears to be so chaotic. He pointed out that every square inch of that page, when viewed on a 13-inch monitor, was worth about $1 million in revenues through advertising and product placement.[38] Each element the viewer sees on the screen has an active and continually changing relationship to the viewer's desires and actions. The site appears as a collage changing in space and time as compositions and messages arrange themselves on pages and across the screen. They are animated by Java-activated programs to become ever changing images. The only thing that remains constant (more or less) is the scaffolding of the site or virtual store. This structure consists of a relationship of typography, fields of colour and abstracted forms.[39] Here the space of

retailing, the company carrying out the retailing, the packaging of the goods and the logo all become one. The only thing missing from this merger is the product itself. Indeed, some science-fiction writers would have us believe it is only a matter of time and miniaturisation (or incorporation of technology into the body) before this final step takes place.[40]

We should be careful not to overestimate the scope of the electrosphere. Though boosters claim huge growth in this sector, in reality it is still only a very small part of the retailing experience. Most people, it seems, continue to prefer to visit a physical location when they want to shop. They go to such sites because they can discover a direct relationship between themselves and the goods they consume in a social setting defined by a certain kind of architecture. They still go to the marketplace because it is still the scene of their social activity.[41]

If it is true that our most profound work as human beings is to construct ourselves to appear on a stage of our choosing, then the activity of acquiring the costumes and props, building the stage-sets and acting out our roles is not just a secondary one.[42] We need brands, and the spaces in which they and we appear now seem to be melded together. We may not like the fact that the engine behind all these developments is a form of capitalism that both creates and (though never quite fully) fulfils desires, but that is the situation, and one that we cannot ignore. We can only try to understand its mechanisms – the ways in which it operates through the appearances of product, brand and architecture in the selling spaces in which we act – so that we can enlarge our own roles and take control of our destiny. As retail environments become places of fantasy and convenience, be they bare-bones bulks or fancy forums for commercial creativity, they present us with a varied set of scenes that can help us understand our desire to live through objects and appearances, and integrate this with some notion, however momentary and however mercenarily conceived, of a public space. We may not want to shop till we drop; but we can construct meaning in, and through, the retail environment.

Following pages: 'Wal-Mart' goods train, USA, 2000.
Below: Amazon.com website.

HELEN JONES

# Packaging
## petroleum

As we drive along our highways, the petrol station is one example of what American architect Charles Jencks describes as '60-mile-an-hour architecture' – its aim to signal the presence of the station to a driver travelling at speed. Roadside architecture is an architecture of branding. The marketing priority of the station is to inform the driver of not merely its existence but also the particular brand on offer. The gas station has attracted the attention of American architects other than Jencks: for Robert Venturi 'its buildings are small and cheap, the signs are big and expensive', while Hitchcock and Johnson sum it up as: 'Dominating roof plane over transparent screen wall. Colors: Brilliant red and white for advertisement. A design easy to standardise'. This was in 1932.

Indeed the methods of branding petroleum have changed only slightly in the last 100 years. The corporate identities of the major oil companies have remained remarkably consistent during this time ('You can be sure of Shell'). Petrol stations have become a unique building type, evolved through the interface between architecture, engineering and industrial design, together with signage and advertising graphics. In its totality it is a giant-scale advertisement. Global brands, such as Shell and Texaco, take a monolithic approach to their global presence, using, according to Wolff Olins (1980), 'one simple name and one visual look wherever they go'. By standardising their image across the globe, oil companies are also reinforcing the brand promise of consistent quality and reliability.

Increasingly the 'brand experience' is supplemented with the offer of consumable services: fast food, supermarket shopping, news agencies and car valeting. The future of the world's most powerful oil companies lies not so much in their oil products but in the success of their branding strategies. After all, petrol is petrol, but a brand must promise much more.

**Top: Esso, Birchanger, England, 1999.**
**Left: Texaco, Route 271, PA, USA, 1999.**
**Opposite: Shell, Yakima Valley, WA, USA, 1999.**
**Following spread: Total, Stansted, Mount Fitchet, England, 1999.**

"Petrol is petrol, but a brand must promise much more."

BENTFIELD ROAD

# TOTAL

| premium unleaded *per litre* | 69·9 |
| 4 star *per litre* | 77·9 |
| diesel *per litre* | 72·9 |

**Alldays** *your local store*

4 Business · energy · OVERDRIVE · ALL STAR

Dial card · Diners Club International · DELTA

EUROCARD MasterCard · SWITCH · VISA

TOTAL Shop

No-one TOPS our rewards

FREE ...OKE ...CAR WASH

Now there's an easier, smarter way to collect TOPS Points

RECRUITING NOW ASK INSIDE FOR DETAILS

CAMBRIDGE ROAD

AUTO POI...

**GUY JULIER**

# From object to experience

**Left: 'Skegness is SO Bracing', UK. First published in 1908 by Great Northern Railway; reissued by LNER, c. 1925.**
**Below: Legoland, Windsor, England, main entrance, August 1997.**

Cadbury World, Legoland, Heron City, Center Parcs, Warner Village. These are all places to relax, enjoy yourself, spend time with friends and family. But they are also products. We have been parting with our hard-earned cash to have a good time in increasing amounts since before the Industrial Revolution, but the way we do it has changed dramatically.

In the nineteenth century, the growth of railways provided easy access to the tourist destinations of the seaside and spas. Subsequently, entire industrial towns would close their factories for specific fortnights, known as 'the wakes', while its workers and their families headed *en masse* for Blackpool, Bridlington or Bognor. Seaside entertainment - music hall, amusement parks and piers - developed to cater for the concentrated demand for pleasure that they brought with them. Just as work became increasingly rationalised and regulated by industrialisation, so, then, did leisure.

Holiday resorts would compete with each other by promoting their attractions - the length of their piers, the quality of the air - often through advertising. In this way, leisure spaces began to be conceived of as brands. The seaside resort of Bridlington, for example, was marketed as 'Bright, Breezy, Bracing'. The Butlins holiday camps, established in 1936, were, then, a more tightly orchestrated commercialisation under a single brand of what seaside towns had been doing for a century.

The growth of the Spanish costas in the 1960s and the development of charter-flight operations ensured a more flexible attitude to when and where holidays could be taken. In this system, the basic offer of sun, sea and sand was the same for most resorts. Tour operators had then to compete on price and the strength of their brand. The greater flexibility of tourist demand in choosing destinations and activities is thus met by the development of 'off the peg' tailored holidays.

In *Capitalism and Leisure Theory*, published in 1985, sociologist Chris Rojek identified four key features of contemporary leisure. First, it is a more privatised affair increasingly focussed on the home, rather than the public sphere. No doubt this has been encouraged by the development of radio and television, then teletext, video, Internet and computer games. Thus it is the job of leisure entrepreneurs not only to get people out of their homes but also to give their leisure spaces the same security, exclusivity and, paradoxically, 'buzz'. Second, leisure is more individuated; more subject to personalisation. Leisure spaces must deliver a menu of choice without destabilising the core values of the brand. Third, Rojek believes that leisure has become more commercialised, evolving into a major industry in itself. Currently more money is spent on leisure and tourism in the UK than on food, rent and rates. Finally, leisure is more pacified: it entails more complex and encultured expression through activities that require learning, practice and mastery. Whether it is appreciating high cuisine or trying out a new sport, leisure activities are, in fact, more restrained and regulated than ever.

As work patterns in the late twentieth century have become more fragmented and varied, so has leisure. While there has been an overall decline in the length of the working week, for those in employment the total amount of leisure time - that is hours spent in unproductive activities - has paradoxically diminished. Leisure entrepreneurs increasingly take seriously the notion of 'time-squeeze': in a consumer-research survey by the Henley Centre, a London-based British

## "The distinction between leisure and retail is increasingly blurred."

consultancy, which was published in 1998, 59 per cent of respondents agreed that 'I have never had enough time to get things done.' This is particularly so among women who work, who report only 13.5 hours per week free as against the 60 hours average. This time-squeeze has given rise to the development of one-stop leisure complexes, or so-called E-zones (for entertainment), which incorporate a variety of leisure activities into one branded site. This allows consumers the most efficient use of their precious leisure time as they move from cinema

to pizza restaurant to bowling alley or from swimming pool to tennis court to health spa. Much design-consultancy work is dedicated to achieving the right 'fit' between the retail and leisure brands situated within a single branded space.

If this makes such centres sound like shopping malls then it underlines the point that the distinction between leisure and retail is increasingly blurred, as in so-called 'retail-tainment' sites. Thus Tesco Extra at Pitsea in Essex offers a fast-food and takeaway area, mooing cows and roller-skating customer-services

assistants. Specific brands have also extended into the leisure sphere: the Volkswagen Autostadt in Wolfsberg, Legoland in Windsor or Cadbury World in Bournville, NikeTown in New York and London all provide visitor attractions that subsequently reinforce their brand identity, whether that is based on technological innovation, play or heritage. Significantly, investment for these 'brandlands' comes from global advertising budgets rather than capital-revenue.

In bringing together a range of

activities and identities in leisure spaces, content has to be arranged to build a narrative flow, to give the visitor a sense of moving through a set of activities or sensations to make up a complete story. Small wonder, then, that designers increasingly talk of 'scripting' leisure spaces. They ascertain the message and effect of its overall structure before mustering design components around this that will frame the desired consumer response. The emphasis thereby switches from the design of objects to the creation of experiences.

**Above: Cadbury World.
Right: Center Parcs,
Longleat, England, forest
subtropical swimming
paradise, 1990s.**

Left and right: Branded street signs, Hong Kong, 1999.
Below: Li-Ning Trainers, 1999, V&A Museum.

**ANDREW BOLTON**

# Great mall of the people

In China today people are faced with an inexhaustible supply of consumer products from around the world. But what are they buying and what are their aspirations? Some answers to these questions can be found in an analysis of the range of goods on sale in department stores and shopping malls in major cities throughout China. Limiting my field of enquiry to the arena of fashion, I will focus on the mammoth Sun Dong An Plaza in Wangfujing, one of Beijing's most popular shopping districts.

The Sun Dong An Plaza, which opened in 1998, offers a diverse range of fashion, by which I mean world or cosmopolitan fashion, everyday dress that is often referred to as 'western' but is in fact worn by people in both the eastern and western hemispheres (Eicher, 1995). Customers to the Plaza can choose from an assortment of tailored suits, jackets, trousers, skirts, shirts, blouses, jeans and T-shirts. Sold in boutique-style shops arranged over seven floors, customers have access to a wide range of fashion labels, both international and local. The type of labels available is significant and a close look at their scope and profile provides subtle and revealing insights into current consumer trends in modern day Beijing.

A large proportion of those on offer are local (about 70 per cent), which would seem to suggest a lower demand for international labels among customers to the Plaza. Quantity, however, is not necessarily a reliable indicator of taste.

Neither is it a particularly accurate reflection of the preferences and aspirations of shoppers. Indeed, an examination of the building's infra-structural rhetoric indicates a definite hierarchy of fashion labels. Shops selling international western labels are given a much higher profile on the ground and first floors of the building, while those selling local Chinese labels are less prestigiously situated on the remaining five floors. Arguably, it is the prominent placement of the former rather than the profusion of the latter.

It is not just any western label that shoppers aspire to wear. Generally speaking, people living in Beijing dress in a relatively conservative manner and favour international labels that

many westerners might consider conventional. The British label Burberry, for example, is popular among professional men and women. Considered an 'exclusive label', the shop is situated on the ground floor with its own off-street entrance. To satisfy the conservative taste of its customers, Burberry limits its product line to the Burberry Traditional collection. The more avant-garde Preview or Prorsum collections, designed by Robert Menichetti and popular in Europe and America, are entirely absent. Nike is extremely popular among younger customers to the Plaza. Its high-profile status is confirmed by its prime location on the ground floor, again with its own off-street entance. Almost all (about

Above: Sun Dong An Plaza,
Wangfujing, Beijing, 1999.
Right: 'Pye' fashion brochure,
Hong Kong, 1999.

"It is not just any western label that shoppers aspire to wear."

99 per cent) of Nike shoes are manufactured in Asia, with a large proportion made in China by independent firms (Skoggard, 1998). Other major western sports companies that produce their shoes in China include Adidas, Puma and Reebok. Nike, however, is the preferred choice among many Chinese. Its popularity can be explained less by the localisation of its merchandise than by its image, since Nike often uses Chinese sports personalities to front its advertising campaigns, such as the football hero Cheng Siu Chung. In fact, so popular is Nike that the Chinese sports company Li-Ning, has appropriated and slightly adapted its Swoosh logo. Perhaps because of this brand association,

Li-Ning has become one of the most popular Chinese sports companies in China.

As well as western labels, customers to the Plaza also aspire to wear those from Hong Kong, which, on the whole, are also located on the ground and first floors. Pye is one of the most popular among professional men and women. Part of the Esquel Group founded by Y. L. Yang in 1978, Pye is one of the few Hong Kong labels with an instantly recognisable, albeit westernised, Chinese logo π. Popular among a younger audience are Bossini and Baleno. Similar in style to the Gap, their clothes often display no visible logo. This invisibility explains why Bossini and Baleno appeal to the brand-

conscious youth of Hong Kong. The absence of any logo means they can be mixed with more prestigious in their own right western labels such as Calvin Klein and DKNY to give the overall impression of an internationally designed ensemble. While some young people in Beijing may buy Bossini and Baleno for similar reasons, the majority look upon labels from Hong Kong as prestigious.

There are, of course, several Chinese labels that are considered desirable among customers to the Plaza. Popular among professional men are Ying Weng and Lan Bao situated on the ground floor and among professional women Yingdak and Sanong, located on the first floor. On the whole, though, customers to the Sun Dong An Plaza prefer wearing western

labels and those from Hong Kong. The internal dynamics of other department stores and shopping malls in major cities throughout China reflect similar hierarchies of labels, such as Parkson in Shanghai. Until Chinese labels are successful in penetrating the international fashion market this trend is likely to continue. The Hong Kong label Episode, which belongs to the Toppy Group, has managed this successfully. For a Chinese label to do so, Chinese consumers need to develop more confidence in their own brands, which, by necessity, would have to entail a mental shift away from the superiority of international western fashion labels to those that are locally produced and consumed in China.

# Supermarket futures

In 1962 the British trade journal *The Grocer* published a centenary number, which included a fanciful feature on 'The Grocery Shop of the Future?'. The accompanying illustration, a black-and-white drawing, shows mother, daughter and dog returning from the supermarket in their flying saucer-shaped helicopter. Outside a ranch-style suburban dwelling, father and son stand waving a welcome in the distance. This private helicopter fantasy had some currency at the time: in France, René Uhrich, in a book also published in 1962, imagines that in the United States at least, 'the civilisation of the automobile', will soon give way to 'the civilisation of the helicopter'.

In *The Grocer*, author Howard Fox runs through possible prospects for stores that in the 1970s will move from rectangular to circular designs, perhaps with 'a series of little personal shops' round the perimeter. The customer stands on moving aisles, getting off whenever she wishes. In the dim distance that can be glimpsed beyond the 1970s, the shoppers have come to a complete standstill as the goods circulate to offer themselves for inspection: 'Eventually, the entire perimeter of a store may be arranged in lounges, with the shopping area a huge revolving island. The housewife would sit, talk with her friends

## "We all have our special trolleys now, thoughtfully provided to meet our aisle-cruising needs from Pampers to eternity."

Above: Woolworths fruit and vegetables display, *c.* 1960. Below: 'Back from a trip to the grocers! Future stores will be designed to accommodate new trends in transport. "The Grocery Shop of the Future"', *The Grocer*, 1962. Opposite: Tesco supermarket, West Kensington, London, 1999.

and pick items as they pass by.'

This passage is quoted from an American source in another trade journal, on which the whole article is based; characteristically, the future of supermarket shopping is imagined in an American mode. And in numerous respects, the piece returns us to earlier histories, of supermarkets themselves, of their antecedents and of the first projections of their futures. With those little shops round the edge, the old High Street is back, now inside the single store. Shopping, we learn, is to be 'a pleasure rather than a chore', the same term that generations of store operators had imagined from the start of the century.

From the perspective of 1990s Britain, these 1960s fantasies, in their own time echoing futures past, become strange in another way, comfortably and uncomfortably familiar in their partial anticipation of our own present. There is the out-of-town site reached by private transport; the deli and fresh fish and bakery counters round the edge to signify service alongside self-service, the best of all worlds under one roof; the place to sit and talk. Supermarkets may not have changed their structure, to transform themselves into circles with moving aisles. But in certain ways, they have almost gone further than Fox's projections. It is as though they were turning the wheels of retailing revolutions full circle, coming to be all shops to all people, to recapitulate all the phases of retailing history under one roof.

Evoking the fonder memories of the high street and the market they have supplanted, supermarkets parade their counters with personal service - the baker, the fishmonger, the butcher, the dry cleaner, and even the Post Office. In the wake of their general up-marketing, as they come to sell more and more expensive, recherché lines, they loudly proclaim their fidelity to their cheap origins, still piling it high and selling it low with ranges of minimally priced own-brand goods. At the same time, like the grand department stores, they now sell fashion as well as cheapness. Where the department stores collected the exotic products of the colonies, supermarkets sell 'ethnic' cuisine and plant out the

former colonies to supply them with esoteric tropical vegetables. And where they were once associated solely or primarily with the selling of food, supermarkets as superstores have extended their range of non-food lines so far that they have come to resemble the department stores in contents as well as in forms. The introduction of cafés, inviting the slower time of an outing, puts an end to the identification of food shopping as a definite task to be completed as quickly as possible. Now, you can be doing the shopping and going shopping, getting the basics and enjoying yourself, all in one place and one time.

Or indeed, it might seem, at all times and everywhere. For supermarkets in Britain have risen in the 1990s to a position of unprecedented prominence in that blur between media representations and actual behaviour that makes up the fabric of our daily life. They seem to be occupying every possible space and time, from daytime and prime-time TV advertising to Sunday morning family shopping, in the wake of the relaxation of the laws on opening hours in 1994, and now all-night shopping as well. In their metamorphosis into out-of-town superstores, they have become the focus for a new environmental argument about the decline of urban centres and the growth of a car-dependent culture. The 1960s image of the supermarket shopper as a female zombie has given way to a much less identifiable figure, anyman, anywoman and especially anybaby – for we all have our special trolleys now, thoughtfully provided to meet our aisle-cruising needs from Pampers to eternity. The future of supermarkets in the twenty-first century is in one sense anybody's guess, anybody's choice. Yet it sometimes appears that the future itself is envisaged in the image of a great supermarket in which citizen-consumers move about making their more or less informed and random individual choices. Whether that image draws on a hope or a fear depends on the persuasions of the speaker. But it is perhaps not irrelevant that in the UK stores are often designed so that customers start with the fresh fruit and vegetables on the left and exit, after the drinks, on the right.

# BRANDING

# CHAPTER FOUR

## THE
JANE PAVITT
## INDIVIDUAL

# "It's a marketing given by now that the consumer defines the brand. But the brand also defines the consumer. We are what we wear, what we eat, what we drive. Each of us in this room is a walking compendium of brands."[1]

This observation by Sir Michael Perry, Director of Unilever, may sound sinister. Is it true that brands define us? We are often told that as consumers our 'rights to choose' are paramount, and that the success or failure of brands is in our hands. Yet we also know that a vast economy is devoted to the investigation of consumer preferences, so that brand promises and advertisements may closely match (and fuel) our fears and aspirations. We use branded goods in a myriad of different ways. At times, these will be the same as or close to those suggested by brand owners. What we wear might make us feel powerful, happy or reassured. At other times, they may be different from those anticipated or implied by brand owners – and more personal, localised or closely connected to family or social situations.

Anthropologists Mary Douglas and Baron Isherwood have proposed, 'the most general objective of the consumer can only be to construct an intelligible universe with the goods he chooses.'[2] We can use goods to locate ourselves and establish a sense of belonging. We might also employ them to individuate ourselves, both in terms of how we see ourselves and how others see us. This means that branded goods can be simultaneously our anchors and our springboards.

Most often, shopping is a relatively mundane activity, but there is a difference between 'going shopping' and 'doing the shopping'.[3] We may enter a store to buy something several times a day, without attaching a great deal of significance to the purchases we make or the reasons for them. 'Doing the shopping' means provisioning for the household, buying food, visiting the supermarket, stocking up on staple household goods. We say we are 'going shopping' when we mean we are out for pleasure, browsing or making special purchases. Going

shopping might be an adventure, doing the shopping a chore. We attach much more significance to the purchases we make when we are shopping for leisure; these are the goods that may give us identity or bring to us a sense of belonging. A third kind of shopping – 'shopping around' – is implied by the kinds of purchases that involve time, research and planning, such as buying a car or a house.

Of course, brands are involved in all of these activities. Sometimes, choosing a particular one can be a way of not having to think hard about the purchase. Selecting or rejecting brands can also be part of the process of defining our lifestyles and of presenting an identity to the world. Some are selected to make a statement to others about ourselves as a form of communication, and branded goods are specifically designed to speak to us on an emotional and associational level. In turn, we use them to speak for us.

Sociologist Zygmunt Bauman has argued that the consumer is involved in 'self construction by a process of acquiring commodities of distinction and difference'.[4] Buying an identity, the idea of the 'commodity self', is a useful way of looking at the relationship between people and things. 'Is that me?' is a question often addressed to not only certain types of goods, particularly clothing, but also leisure and entertainment activities, such as choosing a restaurant, a film or a holiday. Goods can be a means of differentiating oneself in order to belong. Bauman also argues that consumption has become the primary means of formulating and expressing personal identity, arguing that: 'the same central role which was played by work, by job, occupation, profession, in modern society, is now performed in contemporary society, by consumer choice.'[5]

The image of the consumer is fraught with anxiety

Previous spread: Adidas wearer, London, 1999. Below: Waitrose supermarket, promotion of washing powders with washing machines, supplied by Caleys of Windsor, Slough, England, c.1958-63. Opposite: Shopper, London, 1999.

and contradiction. For most of this century consumption has been associated with not individuality or the 'authentic' self but mass culture and a loss of self. A substantial literature of the twentieth century has been devoted to a critique of the consumer as victim, who willingly succumbed to the persuasive messages of advertiser and marketer. The packaged delights of mass culture, from lipstick to tinned salmon, were frequently derided by inter-war cultural observers. The leisure pursuits of the majority, such as cinema-going, popular fiction and theatre, and, of course, shopping, were seen as tawdry and unfulfilling. Even now some critics persist in arguing that we are purely the products of media manipulation. One recent 'exposé' pronounced: 'It was advertising that taught us to define ourselves by what we consumed ... and we would never have been so sheep-like compliant if it had not been for television.'[6]

Class and gender prejudices tended to lie at the heart of these criticisms. The irrational or imaginative consumer so often depicted is feminine, irresponsible with money or the spender rather than the begetter of wealth. Although leisure shopping is usually defined as a feminine activity, the female consumer was also likely to be portrayed as the frugal or careful shopper, holding the purse strings and stretching her husband's wage to cover household expenses. Supermarket choices, the evaluation of one brand of soap powder over another and the search for bargains are usually skills assigned to women.[7] Consumer culture plays a role in the creation, maintenance and occasionally the subversion of assigned gender roles, just as it does with class or with definitions of sexuality. Take this example of the male writer's characterisation of women's spending and leisure activities in 1938, from a piece by the Irish writer Louis MacNeice: 'Suburb-dwellers, spinsters, schoolteachers, women secretaries, proprietresses of teashops, all those, whether bored with their jobs or idleness, go to the theatre for their regular dream-hour off. The same instinct leads them which makes many hospital nurses spend all their savings on cosmetics, cigarettes and expensive underclothes.'[8]

Much more recently, however, a more celebratory image of the consumer has predominated. Instead of a victim, the consumer has been depicted as a free-thinking creative individual, who constructs a sense of self out of their consuming culture, in ways that are regardless of such 'limitations' as class, gender or even geography. Modern consumer society has been depicted as a spectacle of goods and experiences, an exciting and adventurous terrain. Consumption is viewed in terms of fantasy and personal exploration rather than subjugation. The post-modern subject, it has been argued, constructs him or her self through the appropriation of goods, 'surfing' through style cultures and 'trying on' personal identities like clothing. The myth of the post-modern consumer is as unfettered global traveller, socially mobile and regarding material goods as the chief indicator of culture, ideology and status. In such a scenario,

Above: Passer-by,
posters, London, 1999.
Right: Billboards, London,
1999.

traditions of defining consumption. The idea of the 'rational' consumer does not allow space for an imaginative and emotional engagement with goods.[11] Many of us purchase for reasons that are not immediately rational, nor simply a response to the persuasions of a glossy advertisement or package.

Modern consumerism has been defined as when 'the individual's interest is primarily focused on the meanings and images which can be imputed to a product'.[12] In other words, we are not simply buying and using things because of functional or rational justifications but for the range of emotional and social meanings they can also embody for us. Furthermore, to want something for these reasons does not necessarily mean that the gratified wish will satisfy once the purchase is made, as such desires are relatively fluid and transient. Longing is an important part of our relationship to goods. This constant deferral of gratification is one of the hallmarks of modern consumerism and identity.

The consumer may at times be a pleasure seeker, but this is only one guise among many others.[13] We use different consuming strategies for different kinds of goods, occasions or locations. Sometimes we might be very self-conscious about the strategy we use (for example, if we choose to boycott a product or brand), other times we take a more passive and less time-consuming approach. Consuming choices are not made in isolation; even if we feel free to choose, they say much about our cultural and familial background. Identity, therefore, is much more than the sum total of an individual's possessions. Rather, the crucial building blocks of identity, such as gender and ethnicity, shape our attitudes to consumption.

The French philosopher Michel de Certeau has argued that, as consumers, we are also producers of meaning, because we make meaning with the goods we buy.[14] We might display a concept of personal identity through our association with particular goods, cultural preferences, leisure activities and, inevitably, brands. We call this 'style', which is, in the words of one critic, 'a tool for constructing personhood'.[15]

But how do we individualise ourselves through the

individuality is defined as having the freedom to pick and choose from a range of commodified lifestyles. The contemporary consumer is pictured as 'the isolated individual, juggling with assorted signs and symbols in a never-ending attempt to construct and maintain identity in a fragmented and ever-changing environment'.[9]

In short, the consumer has tended to be depicted as either pleasure seeker, motivated by hedonistic desire, or victim, manipulated by cynical advertisers and corporate interests. Consumption is either a tool for the 'invention' of self, or a process that strips away our individuality. Both of these views are problematic.[10] There are as many different types of consumption and consumer behaviour as there are

Right: Passage de L'Opéra
Debouchant, Boulevard des
Italiens, Bibliothèque de la
Ville de Paris, late 1800s.

mass of consumer goods and brands that are, in fact, widely available? After all, the nature of brands is to offer up images that are purchased 'off the peg' rather than bespoke. Mass-produced commodities are impersonal and may not appear even to offer the space for personalisation. As Celia Lury says in her contributions to this book, the pervasiveness of brands is such that there is less space left for us to 'think with things'.

The collective appeal of brands, however, is such that to identify with one is a way of identifying with a particular social group. These practices of self-definition through branded goods are more common among some age groups than others. Close identification with fashion and lifestyle brands is most often found among teenagers and young adults. Brands are useful because they also provide ways to belong. To take one example: 'I have to shop at Wal-Mart to buy clothes. I try my hardest to fit in but my clothes don't say Abercrombie & Fitch or Gap. They don't say anything.'[16] This is a comment from Nicole, a respondent to a website discussion forum about the American clothing company Abercrombie & Fitch in July 1999.[17] She explained how her family could not afford the brands with which she wanted to be associated. Nicole wants to align her own identity to the fashion brands she mentions rather than the discount store Wal-Mart. By not being able to do this, she does not feel a sense of belonging – she says elsewhere that 'my friends make fun of me'. Nicole sees clothing as a form of communication but feels that the clothes she can afford 'don't say anything'. The brands she wants are ubiquitous American ones, Abercrombie & Fitch and Gap, found in every mall in America and, increasingly, worldwide.

During the same period, the American boy band LFO had a hit both in Britain and the USA with a song ('Summer Girls') that included the chorus line: 'I like girls that wear Abercrombie & Fitch.' The band sang also of preferences for fast food, TV stars and other 'consumables'. The list, which included Coca-Cola and the former teen star and actor Michael J. Fox, echoes the preferences of many teenagers. Lists like these, of favourite brands and bands, are posted on

thousands of personal websites. Fashioned into a vocabulary of collective significance, they are meant to communicate to others and invite correspondence from those with similar tastes. In this way, brands are used as a means of expressing personal identity and identifying with a collective taste.

Differentiation and belonging are two of the main driving forces behind what has been termed 'conspicuous consumption'. At the end of the nineteenth century, the American theorist Thorstein Veblen identified social emulation as the impetus behind what he saw as most 'unnecessary' consumption. For Veblen, 'conspicuous consumption' meant the acquiring of goods in emulation of one's social 'betters'. Goods were markers of social status for the leisure classes; their symbolic function one of ostentatious display. The traditional codes of luxury and wealth in goods, for example, were used as a means of indicating one's status to others. Even now, brands use luxury and opulence, such as gold, silk or exotic references, to sell consumables like chocolate, coffee or cosmetics.

As well as material goods, leisure itself was evidence of one's economic status: [18]

> Goods are produced and consumed as a means to the fuller unfolding of human life; and their utility consists, in the first instance, in their efficiency as a means to this end. The end is, in the first instance, the fullness of life of the individual taken in absolute terms. But the human proclivity to emulation had seized upon the consumption of goods as a means to an invidious comparison, and had thereby invested consumable goods with a secondary utility as evidence of relative ability to pay.

Veblen's idea of emulative spending was one means of explaining the system of fashion in modern society. The competitive nature of the leisure classes, according to him, meant that fashions changed with increasing fluidity. The function of wealth in modern society was not only to emulate one's social superiors but also to differentiate oneself from one's social inferiors. In Veblen's view, the dynamic nature of fashion is due to the 'natural' process of society, which dictates that habits in food, leisure, dress and etiquette are formed by the aristocratic classes and from there filter down the social ranks. Veblen suggested that the symbolic purpose of goods was to demonstrate our place along that chain and perhaps to assist in moving us upwards. He also implied that certain tastes and fashions become debased after a time, as they become diffused throughout the social hierarchy. Although Veblen establishes the vital link between consumption and class, it is also clear that fashion does not simply work in the 'top-down' manner he describes. Rather, tastes and fashions circulate around class, age and cultural boundaries, being transformed from many different directions.

Veblen was writing at a time when modern consumerism appeared to be revolutionising America. The origins of such behaviour have been traced back to the seventeenth and eighteenth centuries in Europe[19] and even further.[20] However, many of the institutions and experiences that have shaped consumerism in the twentieth century originated in the nineteenth.[21] The character of

Above: Street stall,
London, 1999.
Right: Yves Saint Laurent
shop window, London, 1999.
Below: Shoppers in 'Peartree'
Stores, Welwyn Garden
City, England, c.1964.
Opposite: Closing-down sale,
London, 1999.

this consumer society was reflected in its desire to construct and consume symbolic meanings around goods, and to seek out personal fulfilment from things. The acquisition and display of material goods was one means of indicating social success and status. Investing in the construction of one's social self by consuming was a way for people to announce their membership of the bourgeoisie.[22] Whether or not such consumer practices and desires were new at this time is questionable, but for Veblen the idea of the conspicuous consumption of the bourgeoisie was the hallmark of his age. Others, too, identified the elusive nature of fashion as the sign of a society seeking social differentiation and 'betterment' through goods. 'The peculiarly piquant and suggestive attraction of fashion lies in the contrast between its extensive, all-embracing distribution and its rapid and complete disintegration,' wrote the German sociologist Georg Simmel in 1904.[23]

Veblen's theories were vital in establishing the idea of the value of goods as markers of social status. However, the uses of goods are far more varied that

his view implied. For instance, expensive luxury items gain their status because they are only affordable to a few, but other kinds of 'cult' goods will only appeal or even be known to a narrow band of consumers.[24] Social status is therefore dependent upon an ability to demonstrate not only wealth but also 'taste' to those of a similar lifestyle or social group.

According to some anthropologists, 'all material possessions carry social meanings,' and therefore we must think of goods as 'communicators'.[25] Material goods are often seen as insulation against one of the inherent dangers of the modern world: social embarrassment or exclusion. They are a way of representing social relationships, and they help us to 'pin down' values and meanings in society. As well as being used to communicate, consumer goods are used to regulate our lives, perhaps to compensate for any feelings of inferiority, even to confirm status or reward success. Wrapped up in the logo, the product, the ad and the name lies a promise of emotional satisfaction – branded goods are saturated with this meaning.

The ways in which we acquire goods and the places in which we shop can also be said to be 'socially meaningful'. Do we view shopping as pleasurable or routine? Do we think our approach to shopping is based on thrift and the search for 'bargains'? Do we choose to shop in local stores, second-hand markets and shops or large out-of-town shopping malls?[26] These kinds of decisions are not simply a matter of free choice, as they are clearly governed, if not solely determined, by economics. If there is little pleasure to be had from 'doing the shopping', for instance, then a large and convenient supermarket might be felt to

be an economical choice, in terms of time spent. In contrast, while shopping for second-hand goods is for many an economic necessity, others might view it a pleasurable and alternative (as well as cheaper) means of buying clothing, for example in the shops that advertise 'designer labels for less'. Buying counterfeit or imitation branded goods involves another complicated set of social relations – we might congratulate ourselves on buying a 'name' more cheaply, but do not want to be seen by others as having done so, as Kent Grayson observes in 'Why Do We Buy Counterfeits?'.

Below: Fruit and vegetable stall, London, 1999. Right: Boots from Timberland.

The ways in which we choose to shop as well as the goods we choose to buy (or not to buy) are an indication of the social groups to which we belong (as well as those with which we might choose to identify). Traditionally we might have viewed this as a straightforward distinction between classes or ethnic groups. However, working both within and against these residual hierarchies is the concept of lifestyle, another form of social differentiation. It can be defined as 'the ways in which people seek to display their individuality and their sense of style through the choice of a particular range of goods and their subsequent customising or personalising of these goods'.[27]

The formation of taste is a product of social patterns as much as it is of individual choices. Assuming that taste is a social as well as a personal mechanism, however, does not discount the role of the individual in asserting his or her independence from the taste-distinctions of his or her background. Social mobility, particularly since the Second World War, has tended to be made most visible in the changing taste and lifestyle patterns of different generations. The proliferation of a variety of lifestyles within the broader social divisions of class and ethnicity is another indication that consumption has become our primary mode of living. What appear to be rather arbitrary, subjective and even whimsical demonstrations of taste – a preference for one soap opera over another, or for particular cooking ingredients – are signs of social positioning.

In Britain, for example, an increasingly broad range of activities has been drawn into what we might term the 'fashion system'. Food – both eating out and cooking at home – is now more than ever a focus of the lifestyle industry. Interior design, sports, gardening and home entertaining are popular subjects for television and print journalism. Although it is true that all of these subjects have generated a consistently popular literature for at least a century or more – from Mrs Beeton to Delia Smith – they now appear to saturate our media more than ever. The popularity of a new or alternative sport, such as snowboarding or surfing, will result in the quick emergence of lifestyle goods, TV programmes and magazines devoted to that subject. These may even become popular with a segment of consumers who have no intention of taking up that particular sport, but identify with its associated media images and musical or fashion preferences.[28]

In his influential study of French tastes and cultural preferences in the late 1960s and 1970s,[29] sociologist Pierre Bourdieu argued that what we take for granted in terms of our own taste is actually an indication of our familial, educational and professional background. Bourdieu called this our 'habitus'. While we are generally unaware of its actions, habitus is embodied in all our daily lifestyle choices. It does not impose a straightjacket, for example making us replicate our parent's preferences, but is malleable according to other environmental factors. As new cultural forms emerge, whether in music, literature or fashion, our preferences will adjust. Whatever we prefer, however, our choice will be a means of differentiating ourselves from other groups and identifying with our own.

Our cultural preferences are thus indicators of a social hierarchy of taste. Tastes are not merely a sign of economic status but also of what Bourdieu terms 'cultural capital' – the expression of social difference through value judgements. A preference for fine art, classical music or repertory theatre, for example, demonstrates cultural capital and is a vital part of an individual's identity, as it marks them out socially. Social distinction is an important factor in our commodity preferences and patterns of consumption will reflect this. In his discussion of sports preferences and sports gear, Bourdieu considers the kinds of goods that are promoted as appealing to a particular social preference for country walking:[30]

> parkas, plus-fours, *authentic* Jacquard sweaters in real Shetland wool, *genuine* pullovers in *pure natural* wool, Canadian trappers' jackets, English fisherman's pullovers, U.S. Army raincoats, Swedish lumberjack shirts, fatigue pants, U.S. work shoes, rangers, Indian moccasins in supple leather, Irish work caps, Norwegian woollen caps, bush hats – not forgetting the whistles, altimeters, pedometers, trail guides, Nikons and other essential gadgets without which there can be no natural return to nature.

The emphasis on 'genuine', 'authentic' and 'natural' products is an important selling point for this kind of sports wear, appropriate to the kind of lifestyle such an activity is meant to evoke. The goods described above might appeal to someone who actively wants to reject branded sports clothing, preferring instead to exhibit a kind of 'cultural capital' by their consumption of unbranded, handmade, locally crafted goods or perhaps even army surplus. The 'unbrandedness' of these goods actively reinforces their value as 'authentic'. At the same time, the codes at play in them are also found in brands that trade on an image of outdoor pursuits and rugged individualism, such as Timberland, Karrimor and Range Rover. Lifestyle is not merely a product of advertising and branding, nor is advertising a straightforward reflection of readily available lifestyles. Rather, they are dependent upon one another.

RUNNERS. YEAH, WE'RE DIFFERENT.

*Remarkably light and exceptionally flexible, the new Universal is something different too.*

How do brands fit in with the view of goods as signifiers of social meanings? They represent very well the ways in which things become encoded with social values. Advertising may successfully turn a social message into a brand value over time – such as the established association of 'whiteness' with cleanliness in ads for washing power, which has traded on this metaphor for most of this century. In a mobile and fragmented society, the marketing of consistent and reliable values is seen as a benefit by the consumer. Throughout this century, brands have been marketed with the message that they can reassure us in a world that is not always comforting or familiar. Famous historical marketing campaigns such as the slogan for a Strand cigarettes: 'You are never alone with a Strand', and the long-running 'If Only Everything in Life Was as Reliable as a Volkswagen' spoke to consumers of their need for reassurance.

The late twentieth century saw an increased focus on the meaning and image-value of goods, sometimes referred to as the 'aestheticisation of everyday life'.[31] Aesthetic considerations are now applied to a much broader range of goods, services and experiences than before, so that any selection is seen as an expression of taste, a sign of style. The corollary of this, of course, is the expansion of the professional sector devoted to 'style' and image-rich products – advertising, design, fashion, media and other creative industries. Lifestyle industries such as these tend to promote the idea that goods are part of the process of individuation. A 1999 series of ads for Adidas running shoes used the strapline 'Runners. Yeah, we're different.' Another successful campaign for L'Oréal hair products always ends with 'Because you're worth it' or even 'Because I'm worth it'.

The function of advertising is to sell us things, by telling us that one brand of jeans, T-shirt, cigarettes, marmalade or soap powder is more suited to our daily lives than another. Advertising shows us, by implication, that our loft apartment, kitchen, workplace or dining table is the right location for a particular commodity, one that can be slotted in among others to create a coherent sense of self or place. Furthermore, lifestyle ads suggest that, while we may only be able to aspire to the loft apartment, we can at least own the type of goods associated with it. Assigning particular brands to people, places or actions is part of the process of defining lifestyle.[32]

Advertising is successful in linking particular brands and goods with lifestyles and experiences, but it does not construct those lifestyles in the absence of other processes. Advertisements, like the goods themselves, can act as the vehicle for a message. They are a means of embodying social and cultural values, and of temporarily fixing an experience to a brand, such as a sporting activity to a soft drink, or a mode of family life to a ready-prepared meal. Some critics of advertising in the twentieth century characterised it as deceptive, devoted to the encouragement of a wasteful lifestyle.[33] Yet the content of much of it is also moralistic and conservative, providing us with idealistic images of stable family life, the importance of cleanliness and order, the reassurance of safety and authority. Advertising is often a relationship between innovative form and conventional content, sensuous surface and serious undertone.[34]

Advertisements contribute to our desire to project

Opposite: 'Runners. Yeah, We're Different'. Poster campaign for Adidas, 1999. Right: 'Kellogg's Corn Flakes Can Now Help Ease Stress and Aid Relaxation', poster, 1998.

Above: Still from Ronseal
television advertisement,
1998-9.
Below: Billboard with Nike
Swoosh, USA, 2000.

ourselves as purposeful and fulfilled, and 'continue to construct a separate striving self in a world of fascinating but forgettable goods'.[35] Branding and advertising together encourage us that goods are the means by which we differentiate ourselves from others and communicate a sense of personal identity. Advertising might provide a set of normative images of identity in a period when concepts of identity are fluid.[36] Most brand messages are based on essentially conservative values such as reassurance, authority and reliability (no better expressed than in the British advertisement for Ronseal paint and varnish products – 'It does exactly what it says on the tin'). Others, such as fashion and sports goods, as previously discussed, promote self-assurance and the autonomy of the individual. The 'separate striving self' is told to 'Just do it'™, suggesting that human will and strength of character are the means to success. The same 'self' is asked the question by Microsoft 'Where do you want to go today?'™, intimating that a world of possibilities is freely available and within the grasp of the individual. We are sold goods that are promoted as both a means to success and a reward for it. Yet do brands really leave space for the personalisation of goods?

The autonomous and successful individual, presented in various ad-guises, is typically male – fit, energetic, over-achieving, a 'winner' in either sports or business, but with a softer, gentler side usually intimated by the ad-presence of either children or animals. The female individual is far less likely to be presented as autonomous – her identity is forged in her association with others, as mother, girlfriend or wife, friend and successful businesswoman. This difference in the gendering of the autonomous self was epitomised by a Nike campaign of 1991, which featured lines like 'You were born a daughter. You looked up to your father, ' and ended with the line 'You became significant to yourself.' The campaign targeted what Nike saw as a kind of female empowerment, although the message was that Nike was 'giving the female consumer permission to fashion her own identity'.[37]

Brands exemplify the idea that what the modern consumer buys is experiential as opposed to functional. We need a toaster, for example, to make toast and might choose a Dualit because we think it is stylish, smart and of significant social value. It is also very costly. Unable to justify the expense of one, we suggest it for a wedding list, conferring another meaning upon it, as it comes to signify an important event and remind us of the giver. Once acquired, the toaster might continue to be referred to by its brand name alone, as the 'Dualit'. We perhaps do not need to worry that visitors to our home will wonder why we have this kind of toaster – it feels like a relatively secure purchase, having maintained its status for some time now, still a familiar product in style magazines and advertisements for stylish living. In years to come, however, the Dualit toaster might become rather unfashionable (due to its ubiquity and a number of cheaper imitations). Once that happens, we can smile and say, 'The Dualit? Oh, that was a wedding present' – thus deferring a judgement on our taste.

The Dualit toaster is therefore symbolic of a certain lifestyle, but its meaning is liable to change or be 'misread'. There is a certain amount of social risk

attached to such a symbolic purchase. The pleasure gained from it is perhaps only temporary, and the consumer might then move on, seeking to replicate the experience in the desire for, or purchase of, other experiences.[38] But purchasing experiences packaged up in branded goods is not the only means of identifying with a particular lifestyle. The idea that personal identity has become so reliant on commodities and advertising messages that the 'self' is merely an assemblage of bits appropriated from media imagery is rather reductive.[39]

All commodities, including brands, gain their meaning from their place within a greater lexicon of goods, images, services and social activities. The value of one brand name is relative to others, and complex social categorisations of goods result in the need for the consumer to understand and participate in its organisational structure. The grouping of certain brands may be site specific, such as in the department store, shopping mall or style magazine, or it may be socially implied, as with the class and status-based hierarchies of 'exclusive' fashion brands. Both, of course, are related, so that exclusive stores such as Prada and Hermès are found in similar locations together in different cities. Social categories of goods are found in individual consumer behaviours, so that (in Britain) driving a Range Rover and doing the weekly grocery shop at Marks & Spencer's food store are all (rather clichéd)

Above: Brands in Bond Street, London, 1999. Right: Dualit four-slice toaster.

signifiers of a well-heeled, conservative lifestyle. Similarly, we can play associative games with well-known brand names, perhaps placing a BMW with a Rolex watch, a Montblanc pen and a Psion organiser. The hierarchy of brands, therefore, can be treated as a cultural barometer. The brand name is a short cut to a complex cultural idea or social image.

The brand also acts as a bridge between the world of people and things, and can connect the individual to the collective. Brands are used for framing relationships – they are also like a vocabulary, and we construct phrases and meanings by linking certain ones together in particular ways. In specific times, locations and social groups, brands can make sense as an established 'grammar' – we understand that some brands make sense together, but others are mismatched. We often talk of clothing and goods as language. But, as anthropologist Grant MacCracken has argued, the communicative function of goods is too limited, too arbitrary for it to constitute a language. The use of that term is best meant as metaphoric and is frequently used in this way, as with 'Nicole' who felt her clothes did not 'say' anything.

However, goods do communicate, if not in the specific way implied by the language analogy. Their communicative abilities are also context specific. A pair of trainers worn with a business suit in the street, for example, would not be felt to be unusual, as it could be assumed that the wearer was going to change once in the office and was wearing them for practical reasons. Trainers worn with the same suit in a boardroom meeting of a traditional finance company, though, would be less usual. While a woman combining trainers with a fashionable suit in the offices of a media or arts company would, at least in 2000, be identified as having made a conscious style choice, even if only by her peers. The 'putting together' of branded goods, the assembling of the fashion self, is only successful if the message is understood by others.

This underlines the importance of 'localisation' and context for global products. The homogeneity suggested by the de-personalised mass of branded goods available worldwide is countered by the

different uses, meanings and social practices found in different locations.

So far, our focus has been on the identity of the modern consumer as 'western' or at least concerned with western values, and the idea of globalisation as the 'westernisation' of the world.[40] However, as with personal identity, cultural identity is dependent upon a much more complex set of experiences than the presence of global brands in local shopping malls can bring. The opening up of China to a market economy, for example, has meant new consumer audiences for branded goods. However, as Andrew Bolton's example of the Beijing 'Great Mall of the People' shows, attitudes to both western and Chinese brand names are specific to their local context.

To take another example, the impact of brand names on the new consumer capitals of Europe has been both rapid and conspicuous. The political re-shaping of Europe in the late 1980s and throughout the 1990s brought a flow of consumer goods into the former communist states of Eastern Europe.[41] In Prague British stores such as Next and Marks & Spencer have opened outlets, and there are several branches of McDonald's close together in the city centre. The department store Maj, one of the several state-run shops that were the suppliers of household staples to citizens, was taken over in the early 1990s by the US budget-clothing firm K-Mart, who in turn sold it on to British supermarket chain Tesco a few years later. Prague's out-of-town state furniture store is now occupied by IKEA. Within a decade following the democratic revolutions of 1989, changes like this could be seen throughout the former Eastern bloc.

Yet the impact of global brands has not necessarily meant a homogenising of local consumer experience and expectations. The ability to buy western consumer goods such as cars and household appliances was limited, particularly in the early years, as wages and standards of living could not keep up with their availability. Social re-organisation, the emergence of a new professional class employed in the private sector, the re-claiming of property by private owners and the development of a lucrative tourist industry are among the factors that have precipitated a change in many people's economic status. Furthermore, there has been some resistance to the high visibility of multinational corporations in the former Eastern bloc, which have been quick to capitalise on the possibilities of new markets but slower to invest in the rebuilding of local economies.

Although the western media has made much of the enthusiasm for western goods in these 'fledgling' consumer societies, the new consumer economies have brought some degree of disillusionment to people. In Russia, for example, the conspicuous consumption of western luxury goods has become quickly associated with a new social class that evinces particular dislike – the so-called 'new Russians': 'the business-people, stock-brokers, commodity-traders, Mafiosi, personal assistants, computer specialists, bankers, private hotel owners, masseurs or taxi-men of the metropolis'.[42] Some western consumer goods such as cigarettes, toiletries and certain fashion items have been associated with the black market for a long time.[43] Different social groups will therefore have a different relationship to branded goods, based on aspiration to, or suspicion of, the idea of 'western' lifestyle encoded in them.

Global brand messages can not overcome the power of local contexts. Some seek to capitalise on this, as Russell Belk engagingly describes in his snapshot piece 'Wolf Brands in Sheep's Clothing'. American values are not necessarily absorbed wholesale by other cultures but circulate the world in 'piecemeal, pragmatic, haphazard, flexible and opportunistic ways'.[44] The ways in which goods and brands are appropriated locally tends to invest those goods with new and alternative meanings.

Furthermore, resistance to global brands in local or national contexts is also a way of expressing an oppositional identity. A resistance to American popular goods and values has been evident in the attitudes of some European middle-class intelligentsia since the 1930s, albeit expressed by a narrow proportion of people. French resistance to Coca-Cola in the 1950s was an expression of national identity.[45] The ways in which consumer behaviour is politicised is more deeply explored by Gareth Williams in his concluding piece 'The Point of Purchase'.

The tendency to emphasise the relationship between identity and consumer behaviour eclipses another crucial relationship – with those employed to produce the goods we consume. The parts of the world identified by brands as the most lucrative potential markets tend to be in those areas that have become the centres for production, such as the Far East, South East Asia and South America. The manufacture of sports footwear is concentrated in Indonesia and China, where cheap labour is plentiful.[46] Arguably, their personal identity is just as determined by their relationship to the brand, although we are unlikely to see this identity in terms of personal freedom, longing and desire, rather the opposite. How should we evaluate the attitudes to brands of these consumers in the future?

It is without doubt that consumer choice forms an important part of our sense of individuality and social belonging. Inability to take part in consumer culture can result in an exclusion from the practices of everyday life. However we choose to 'choose' brands, we do so on the basis of a set of power relations that are corporate, political and economic. The brand is revealing of some social relationships, but it keeps others very well hidden.

Nike wearers,
Venice Beach,
Los Angeles.

CELIA LURY

# Moving things

We are sitting on the beach, observing two boys playing in the waves. Both are wearing Nike shorts, the letters NI and KE on each leg. The shorts make the boys larger and smaller versions of each other. Their shorts give a flickering message as they run in and out of the water. This is a visual message, but it has an aural accompaniment like a crowd chanting: NI-KE, NI-KE. The brand communicates using the whole of their bodies: the use of profiles, sound, shapes and the body in movement.

In the shopping malls we visit the next day, I notice the careful positioning of Nike logos. They are often situated on the body in a proper three-dimensional space: the marks and logos at right angles to one another.

I observe someone sitting down, the ankle of one leg resting over the knee of the other, with a Nike Swoosh on the sole of the shoe. Others walk by in shorts and socks, the Swoosh riding high on the side of their ankles. Yet although their legs move in sequential time, while they are clearly in three-dimensional space, they are simultaneously repositioned by the logos or marks. It is as if the mark of the brand collapses the foreground into the background and slides now into then. These Sunday shoppers are moving into and out of multiple planes in space and dimensions in time. The mark, as a conceptual outline or trace of movement, seems pressed against the boundaries of space and time, and

concurrently far away *and* near, right here *and* already gone. In short, the mark of the brand re-calibrates time and space.

In these observations, the brand redefines the limits of the human body by placing it in a newly extended field, as space that is both material and imagined, objective and subjective, mechanical and embodied. The space in which Nike moves is one that we are in and at a distance from; in which the gap between the individual and the mass might be closed, the space of 'life on the screen' (Turkle, 1995). In it, the brand presents observers with manifold ensembles of signs; the observer can attend to the whole of the frame and then its parts or

"This is a visual message, but it has an aural accompaniment like a crowd chanting: NI-KE, NI-KE."

vice versa. In the movements I have described, on the beach or in the mall, the signs are in sequences. These sequences operate not only in three-dimensional space and linear time but also in the articulated frames of the extended field of multiply mediated space. Indeed, the presence of brand logos co-ordinates the articulation of these frames. They organise how the observer sees the movement from one frame to another. In other words, the brand is a form of phatic communication.

In linguistics, the term 'phatic' is given to the signals that maintain dialogue or discourse but have little or no intrinsic meaning, for example, the question 'How are you?' In comics and strip cartoons, for example, the phatic refers to the panels or framing devices such as lines and balloons, and motifs such as arrows or speed lines. These direct the observer's attention, showing the relationship between one frame and the next. They maintain movement and direct the action. The Nike Swoosh directs my viewing and positions me in relation to its use. It shows how to move and how to see movement in space. Moreover, through empty demonstration of effect, it creates a community. The brand is thus also a form of phatic communion or identification. As a phatic image it constitutes the subjective capacities of people and the objective properties of things in new ways.

CELIA LURY

# Thinking with things

Buzz Lightyear, Ultimate Talking Action Figure, made in China (Disney, 1997). 1999 Disney Character © Disney Enterprises, Inc.

As companions to the mundane routines of daily life – alarm clocks, drinking mugs, key rings, pencil cases, clothes and bags – branded merchandise reminds us of our childlike ability to lose ourselves in play. Its design, the use of scale, colour, contour, line and other surface qualities , separates it from any immediate association with utility (Miller, 1987). In this playfulness, there is the suggestion that the routines of waking up, of gulping down breakfast and leaving home to go to work or school are not necessarily one dimensional. There is a pleasure to be found there that lies above and outside the necessities and seriousness of everyday life.

Perhaps then, branded merchandise, with its emphasis on image and style, contributes to the elaboration of concrete thinking. Concrete, as opposed to abstract thinking, involves thinking with things, not concepts: it is immediate, synaesthetic and situated. It is also conventionally associated with a stage in childhood development, one identified and described by Piaget in *Dreams and Imitation in Childhood*. It is a stage, so Piaget argues, that is superseded by adults, formal thinking, thinking that can be done without things. But in *Life on the Screen*, her study of the use of computers, Sherry Turkle suggests that with the rise in importance of the interface in contemporary consumer culture, there has been a re-evaluation of this kind of thinking with objects. Concrete thinking, therefore, is no longer confined to childhood.

In considering this suggestion, let us take the example of the computer-animated film *Toy Story*, released by Walt Disney and Pixar and distributed by Buena Vista in 1995, and the associated popular merchandising campaign of children's toys and other branded consumer products. In the film itself,

computer-generated images are rendered tactile. As Thomas Schumacher, President of Walt Disney Feature Animation, points out (Lasseter and Daly, 1996):

> The tactileness of this world, even though it has never existed – the sense that you can reach out and hold what you see on the screen – is very significant to the appeal of the film. If you tried to make it look like real life, you would fail, because it will never look like real life, but it can be touchable life.

The toy-objects, who are the main characters in the film, are given personalities. The film's director, John Lasseter, says of them: 'The task of bringing *Toy Story* to life began with thinking through each toy's physical and conceptual essence. How is it made? What was it built to do? What are its physical flaws and limitations?' Each of the toy's personalities, he goes on to explain, was derived from the traits of the physical construction, and respected the 'physical integrity of the object'. Mr Potato Head, for example, is a 'natural malcontent'. As Lasseter says, 'you'd have a chip on your shoulder too if your face kept falling off all day.'

This description implies an understanding of the image as the surface of the object, recognised by touch, recalled in habit or renewed in gesture. Certainly, this understanding is given a new solidity of sense in the process of 'imagineering', a combination of imagination and engineering, that is deployed by Disney in the creation of the fantasy environments of Disney theme parks, where the cartoon and the real world are one. As branded merchandise, objects are so designed to be (re)-inserted in the ongoing stories that comprise our everyday worlds. They offer, as *Toy Story* character Buzz Lightyear attests, the possibility

"Branded merchandise reminds us of our childlike ability to lose ourselves in play."

of going 'to infinity and beyond'.

It may appear, then, that the pleasures of concrete thinking made possible by branded merchandise should be welcomed. For Sherry Turkle the re-evaluation of concrete thinking challenges what she describes as the highly charged forgetting or cultural amnesia of concrete thinking in adult, western societies. Yet, in the contemporary re-evaluation of this stage as a style, at the same time as there is a challenge to the cultural amnesia in which adults forget the way they reasoned as children, there may also be a forgetting, an erasure of the cultural history of the object and of its formal properties. In other words, while the imaging of objects is increasing with the pervasiveness of branding, this intensification may not contribute to the realisation of the object.

Through the multiple mediation of promotion, packaging and theming, branded merchandising anticipates perception, foreshortens our perspective, intervenes in habit and reconfigures gesture. In doing so the brand erases the gradually built-up memory of an object's generic or common-sense meanings, de-contextualises patterns of use and replaces such memories with information, a catch phrase or a logo. As critic Paul Virilio writes in *The Vision Machine*, the image is 'no longer solitary (subjective, elitist, artisanal)'. Instead, it is 'solidary (objective, democratic, industrial)'. But in the imagineered image of the brand, the object is played out. ©™® are the proprietary superscript of play today. Concrete thinking is reduced to artefactualism; rather than reaching towards infinity, escaping the necessities and seriousness of everyday life, we confront unlimited finitude.

This page: Hello Kitty branded goods: TV and video recorder, calculator, toaster and coffee-maker, 1999.

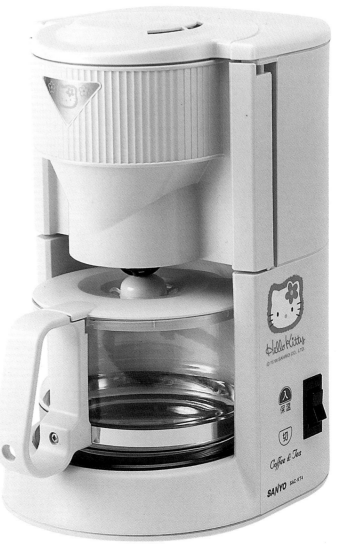

GARETH WILLIAMS

# Hello Kitty

Sanrio

"small gift, big smile!"

From key rings to cars, Kitty adorns over 3000 products, and along with fellow characters produced by Japanese company Sanrio, its products and licences are worth $9 billion annually. Created originally for greeting cards by Sanrio president Shintaro Tsuji in 1974, as a recognisable, patented character Hello Kitty adds commercial value to the most commonplace product,. The company quickly expanded the use of the brand into merchandising: specifically giftware and clothing for children. Sanrio describe their products as 'small gifts that bring big smiles', and as such they play a part in the complex protocol of gift giving in Japanese culture. Like a great deal of merchandising, Hello Kitty products also have a collectors market, which

targets items that are rare or no longer in production.

Kitty's progress has been somewhat different to that of her brand-rivals Mickey, Donald and other cartoon characters. In what we might call 'Disneyfication' in reverse, Kitty began life as a merchandise creation and only recently made it on to the screen in her own animated TV series. She does, however, have her own theme park, Puroland in Japan, which is shared with the stable of other Sanrio brand characters.

Although Hello Kitty is principally marketed at children, in Japan many consumers (particularly women) have grown up with the brand and still identify with it in adulthood. The merchandising available confirms this

view. The product range reflects what Sanrio see to be the main stages of growing up and socialisation for their consumers: there are toy household and beauty products, for example, but these are also available as full size, 'proper' working domestic products, such as toasters, vacuum cleaners and microwaves. In order to produce these, Sanrio entered into a licensing deal with Sanyo, the Japanese consumer-electronics corporation. Hello Kitty is a brand that marks out some of the rituals and behaviours of a contemporary lifestyle: the character appears on credit cards, mobile phones and even wedding dresses. Arguably, in this context, the Hello Kitty brand sells itself as a form of transitional safety for the

"Hello Kitty is a brand that marks out some of the rituals and behaviours of a contemporary lifestyle."

young woman, where the equipment necessary for adult domesticity is reminiscent of the accoutrements of childhood.

Although Hello Kitty is principally marketed for children, she gained a cult following in European club culture. The image of the character and the range of merchandise, including girl's T shirts, hair grips, small purses and handbags, seemed ripe for ironic appropriation. Sanrio have significantly expanded their global reach, targeting fashion stores like Top Shop in Britain, who cater to the teen and pre-teen market. With such market penetration and greater control over the brand image in the UK, less space will be left for the ironic appropriation of 'Hello Kitty'.

**Above: Hello Kitty collectors at home, Japan Right: Hello Kitty promotional event, Top Shop, Oxford Street, London, 1999.**

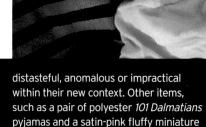

ALISON CLARKE

# Brand not-so-new

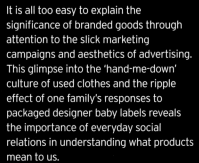

Above: Assorted second-hand children's clothes. Opposite: Child's *101 Dalmatians* pyjamas and *Aristocats* hand bag, Disney characters © Disney Enterprises, Inc.

It is all too easy to explain the significance of branded goods through attention to the slick marketing campaigns and aesthetics of advertising. This glimpse into the 'hand-me-down' culture of used clothes and the ripple effect of one family's responses to packaged designer baby labels reveals the importance of everyday social relations in understanding what products mean to us.

Children's toys, from Barbies to Game-Boys, are frequently in the firing line from the critics of consumerism, given as prime examples of the extent to which we and our children have become embroiled in the world of branded goods. So how do parents make sense of a market full of expensive Disney merchandise and Telly-Tubby jigsaw puzzles? The term 'brand new' connotes a pristine, packaged and mass-produced commodity distinguished only by the mark of its manufacturer. But what happens to branded goods once they have become part of everyday lives and social worlds? This ethnographic snapshot of the second-hand, informal economy in children's wear provides a colourful insight into the post-sale 'lives' of ambiguous branded commodities. In this example popular and familiar branded goods are re-evaluated and interpreted through the particular moral economies of households on an average street in north London.

Jane, a mother of three young children, regularly receives a consignment of second-hand clothes from relatives who live in suburban North America. Along with other 'hand-me-down' clothes given by friends and neighbours Jane sorts through the various articles judging their appropriateness in relation to the values of her own household. Certain items, such as a sequinned party dress and a toddler's white real-fur coat, are rendered distasteful, anomalous or impractical within their new context. Other items, such as a pair of polyester *101 Dalmatians* pyjamas and a satin-pink fluffy miniature Disney handbag, prove more problematic.

In principle, Jane and her partner discourage their children's interest in branded merchandise, which they consider as exploitative and non-educational. Due to its stereotypical connotations the colour pink 'for girls' is also generally avoided. But as a mother Jane is fully aware of the desirability of the pyjamas among girls her daughter's age. For six-year-old Sophie they hold a special premium, operating, as they do, outside the rules that constitute the value system of this household. Certainly Sophie does not need new pyjamas. A hand-made nightdress in 100-per-cent cotton, made by her grandmother as a Christmas gift, lies unused in her wardrobe. For a young girl, despite her affection for her grandmother, the attachment to the magic of a pink sparkly Disney outfit far outweighs the value of a handmade gift. Sophie and her girlfriends frequently covet such items, flicking through the pages of catalogues brought into the school playground. For Sophie's mother the dilemma of the Disney pyjamas is further compounded by its dubious status as a 'synthetic' garment, which she considers to be unhealthy. As a compromise, Jane allows her daughter to keep the pink, fluffy handbag and offers the pyjamas to her daughter, not for her own use, but as a potential gift for her best-friend Rachel (a seven year old living in the same street).

Unfortunately, allowing Sophie to present Rachel with the pyjamas might be construed as insensitive or insulting to Rachel's mother. Why would Jane try to pass off something deemed problematic within her own household to another mother? Both women frequent the local nearly new children's sales and thrift shops together and have often discussed their tastes and preferences as mothers and, in particular, their shared disinclination towards their children wearing branded goods and synthetics. Over a cup of coffee later in the week Jane pre-empts the 'problem' of the contentious pyjamas by assuring Rachel's mother of her own ambiguity towards them and explaining that if unsuitable, they 'can always be sent to the charity shop'. Through their shared views of 'brand' and 'synthetic' products the women generate consensus and sociality around such 'hand-me-down' articles and a particular understanding of 'mothering'.

A week later Jane discovers a pair of Osh-Kosh dungarees in a local charity shop. Overjoyed with her purchase ('fancy finding a designer label in there!') she washes the overalls and proudly dresses her 18-month-old toddler Jeremy in them. The status of the designer label for this particular low-income middle-class group resides in the very contradictions it poses. As a second-hand garment the brand's relation to the manufacturer and advertiser is neutralised to an extent that it can be re-enchanted as a 'bargain find' expressing the knowledge and skill of a wily and ethical mother.

Through swapping values and tastes around children's clothing women create and contest their values as mothers. Bombarded with brand names and designer labels, these mothers circumvent the full-price retail outlets and create an alternative set of values around branded products. Ultimately this trafficking of used children's clothes and the re-interpretation of brand and designer labels generates values (used to enhance the ethical role of mothering) that exist in direct contradiction to the intentions of the marketers and producers.

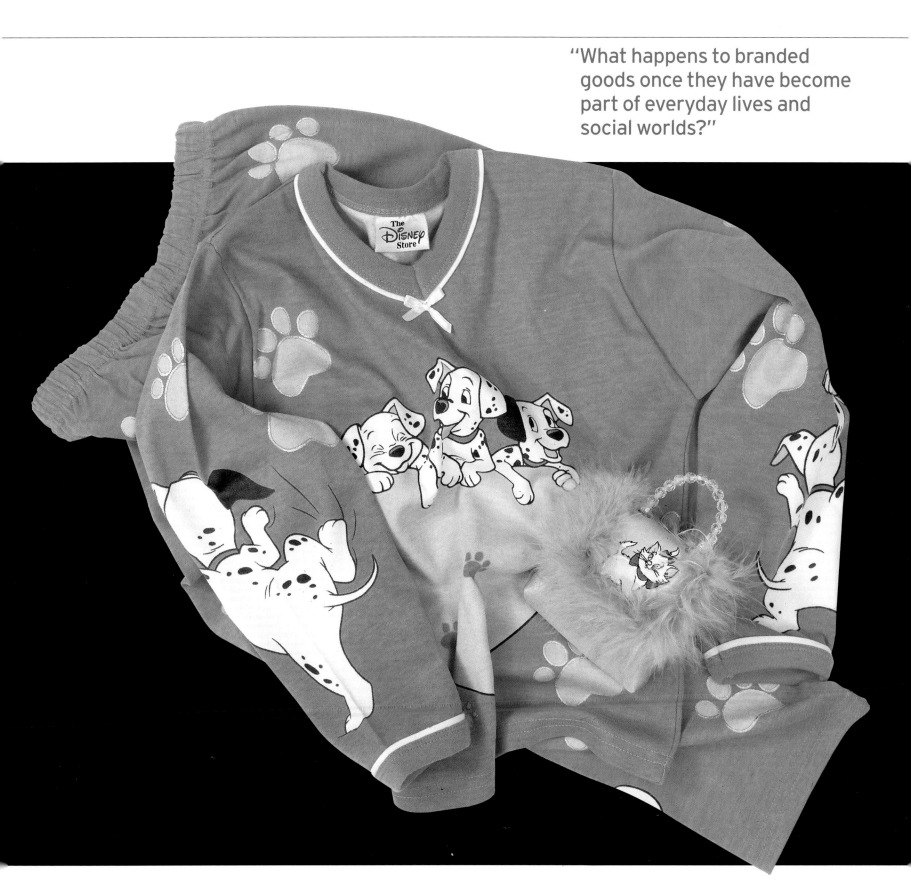

"What happens to branded
goods once they have become
part of everyday lives and
social worlds?"

# OBSESSION

Calvin Kline

## for men

# CHAPTER FIVE

# THE
# POINT
# OF
# PURCHASE

GARETH WILLIAMS

> "Fulfilling the vocation of the consumer means more choosing, whether or not this results in more consumption. To embrace the modality of the consumer means first and foremost falling in love with choice; only in the second, and not at all indispensable place, does it mean consuming more." [1] *Zygmunt Bauman*

Previous page: Adbusters'
'Obsession for Men'
advertisement parody, 1993.

Does branding really define our age? Global brands are claimed to be the top wealth creators in the world. But do they really enrich our societies? In Seattle in 1999, a street protest at the dominance of brands erupted into violence during the World Trade Organisation talks. The power of brands, it seems, is not only to generate wealth and consumer loyalty but also to serve as a focus for our social and political unease.

Buying brands can be a way of defining personal identity, and our individual relationships with them can serve as a metaphor for our broader social and economic relationships. But, although we may enjoy the sense of pleasure or protectiveness that they offer, we are also sceptical about the claims that many brands make. Increasingly, familiar ones have become the target for social and ethical criticism, and even for personal, political action. The pervasiveness of brand names in contemporary society has also made them the target for subversive behaviour and ripe for appropriation and transformation in the social realm.

Why are some of us critical of branded culture? It might be because they often appear to us as the short cut to, or the shorthand for, bigger political ideas. Brands present us with social and personal ideals that we may wish to contest, such as the ideal of physical beauty offered by many fashion and cosmetic brands. Images of status are contained within luxury brands that might challenge us to consider our own social position. The branding of food may be embedded with coded messages about our responsibility toward our own health and that of the planet. Even as consumers question these messages, brand managers try to reassure purchasers of their honest intent, often by shifting their position to counter negative public perceptions. Our readings of branded messages require us to make choices between them, and each choice is an exercise of our critical faculties. To be critical may actually mean not choosing to consume a particular brand at all. For example, we may opt not to buy branded products we believe to be manufactured in countries with oppressive regimes, or by child labourers or exploited women.

Criticism may be merely the querying of brand statements ('How is this washing powder fresher?' or 'Why is this brand of toothpaste cheaper?'). Or it may be a more profound questioning of the values and economic conditions underlying the product (questions such as 'Who makes this and where?' and 'Could these materials harm the environment?'). We are all of us critical to a lesser or greater degree, and at times most of us have followed some of the strategies outlined here. Critical reactions to brands vary from mild scepticism to effrontery and even hostility.

Criticism of particular brands and products enfranchises consumers with a political and social voice that they may feel denied to them within conventional political processes. Conversely, the right to consume has been asserted as evidence of democratic human freedom, as with the American gun lobby's support for carrying handguns. Consumer culture is far from neutral; it is a political arena, a battlefield for activists and ideologies, fraught with moral choices and ethical concerns.

A traditional target for consumer concern has been the advertising industry. Advertising surrounds us; it influences our aspirations and our choices. Its primary function is to create needs, but its important secondary function is to ensure these needs are not fulfilled, in order to guarantee continued, even escalated consumption. As the German philosopher and Marxist critic, Wolfgang Fritz Haug, writes: 'Appearance always promises more, much more, than it can ever deliver. In this way the illusion deceives.'[2] One way of being critical of branded culture is to question the validity of advertising.

The post-war economic boom was fuelled by consumer demand for new commodities. In 1957 Vance Packard, a popular sociologist and critic of American consumer society, wrote of 'the hidden persuaders' in his famous book of the same name.[3] These are the advertisers who make us want what we do not need and buy what we can not afford. Writing in 1950s America, the acme of the consumer society, Packard believed advertisers were manipulating public desire and demand for new goods, using techniques of motivational research learnt from psychoanalysis. According to Packard and other critics of this 'new' consumer society, the function of advertising was the creation of false needs, fed by the constant arrival of new products on the market. The 1950s saw the advent of rapid obsolescence in some manufacturing industries, whereby seasonal style changes encouraged consumers frequently to replace the models of their products, long before they may actually have ceased to function. Rapid obsolescence in the automobile production became a focus of criticism from a variety of parties including consumer journalists, insurers, safety experts and legislators who perceived that changes in style were not the same as exponential enhancements to performance.[4] Ralph Nader, an important and vocal defender of consumer rights in the USA, went so far as to equate rapid obsolescence with 'designed-in dangers'.[5]

Yet even though there was a growing scepticism of advertising's claims, post-war American society was increasingly defined by its consumer goods. The emigré German philosopher of the New Left, Herbert Marcuse, wrote of commodity fetishism: 'People recognise themselves in their commodities; they find their soul in their automobile, hi-fi set, split-level home – social control is anchored in the new needs which [the consumer society] has produced.'[6]

If social control was exerted through the allure of material goods then perhaps happiness was found there too, particularly in contrast to what was felt to be the miserable austerity of Soviet socialism against which the American consumer society defined its values. While Packard believed 'free' Americans were as brainwashed as anyone inside the Iron Curtain was, he suggested advertising was as coercive as Stalinist politics.[7] American politics has always defined itself against external enemies, and from the 1950s to the 1980s this enemy was the spectre of communism and 'the evil empire' of the Soviet bloc. Advertising can be seen as expressing the power of pure American-style market economics, an ideology that underpins the 'land of the free'. Yet its critics viewed it not as a force for individual liberation (through the promotion of personal choice) but as a repressive agent of social control exerted by corporate powers. To misquote Karl Marx, perhaps we should view commodities, not religion, as the opium of the people, as they distract us from questioning the social and economic status quo. Packard viewed the American public as duped by advertisers, but the question remains whether, or to what degree, consumers have been convinced to buy products that could not fulfil the advertisers' promises of happiness?

Packard's criticisms were largely concerned with advertising, but other critics perceived the advertising industry as symptomatic of a greater social and corporate malaise. Wolfgang Fritz Haug

Below: Environmentalists
promote International Buy
Nothing Day in Seoul, South
Korea, 24 November 1999.
Below right: Adbusters'
Christmas Gift Exemption
Voucher, 1997
Opposite: Adbusters poster
for Buy Nothing Day.

argues that advertising is merely part of a larger
exploitative system:[8]

> Since the vast majority of people can find no worthwhile
> goal within the capitalist system, the distraction industry
> appears to be a good investment for the system as a
> whole.... With shades and shadows the illusion industry
> populates the spaces left empty by capitalism, which
> only socialism can fill with reality.

Antipathy towards advertising is therefore,
perhaps, a natural position for the political left that
distrusts the motives of capitalism. Ralph Nader
equates the consumer with the citizen but
acknowledges the disillusionment many have
in political processes.[9]

> Citizen cynicism is a corrosive asset of democracy. Yet
> democracy is the only instrument we know of that can
> comprehensively build a happier, more prosperous
> society. That's why a lot of people like democracy – in
> theory. But when they become cynical they no longer
> practice it. They don't join local groups. They don't
> participate in electoral campaigns.

Nader believes democracy demands engagement
by the individual citizen. John Harms and Douglas
Kellner have developed a critical theory of advertising
and concluded, like Nader, that it is non-democratic
as it promises to provide commodity solutions for all
problems without the need for personal engagement
in the political process.[10]

Critics of advertising, therefore, position their
activity as the defence of the individual and
democracy against the corporate machinations of
big business and the state. 'Subvertisers' are critics of
advertising who take on the advertisers at their own
game, by defacing or spoofing 'real' advertisements.
In so doing they are critical of a mass culture that has
been dominated by big corporations.

The most famous of the 'subvertisers' is Adbusters,
now a global organisation that grew out of anti-
advertising actions in Vancouver, Canada. Adbusters
publish a quarterly magazine with the twin goals
of raising consciousness about commercial excess
and elevating the media awareness and skills of the
environmental movement.[11] Targeted brands include
Camel cigarettes and Calvin Klein underwear. Rather
than defacing existing advertisements, Adbusters
produce elaborate spoofs mocking the values of
existing ad campaigns and the inflated importance of
the corporations that produce them. They challenge
the advertisers on their own territory, using their own
tools. Adbusters also promote the annual
International Buy Nothing Day every November,
exhorting shoppers to 'Participate by not
participating' (that is to buy nothing, in protest

CELEBRATE

BUY NOTHING DAY

NOVEMBER 26, 1999

A 24 hour moratorium on consumer spending

> adbusters.org <

Impotent

WARNING: SMOKING CAUSES IMPOTENCE
California Department Of Health Services. © 1998 California Department of Health Services

OUTDOOR SYSTEMS

Too good to be true?

DEATH™ CIGARETTES
13mg TAR 1.0mg NICOTINE

™ LIGHTS
0.7mg NICOTINE

Health Departments' Chief Medical Officers
**SMOKING KILLS**

Previous pages:
'Impotent Man' billboard,
California, May 1999.
Above: Death cigarettes
and promotional leaflet,
1991.
Below: Billboard showing
a beer advertisement with
graffiti by BUGA-UP,
Sydney, c. 1980.

against the values and methods of the manufacturers of branded goods and the shops that sell them). In 1999 the day was celebrated in twelve world cities as far afield as Boston in the USA and Seoul in South Korea. Another strategy is to issue 'Christmas Gift Exemption Vouchers', which can be downloaded from Adbusters' website, for individuals to exchange in lieu of purchased gifts. In a sense, like Packard in the 1950s, Adbusters and the other 'subvertisers' believe that shoppers are powerless to resist messages in advertising.

Billboard-Utilising Graffitists Against Unhealthy Promotions (BUGA-UP), a movement formed in Australia in 1979 by a surgeon, Dr Arthur Chesterfield-Evans, targeted among others the tobacco industry. Supporters of BUGA-UP's aims defaced billboard advertisements for cigarette brands in protest against what Chesterfield-Evans described as 'a cold-blooded and systematic campaign of deception waged by monied interests against less-informed consumers'.[12] Like Packard and Nader, Dr Chesterfield-Evans clearly associates advertising solely with the interests of capital rather than society. He is now a member of the New South Wales parliament.

In parallel to the kinds of subversion practised by campaigners, some advertisers and brand managers have incorporated irreverence and even 'playful' criticism into their own marketing. Such promotional campaigns diffuse the 'subvertisers'' critique, at the same time exploiting the potential associations. Death cigarettes, for example, could be a creation of Adbusters, but it was in fact a genuine tobacco brand in the early 1990s that 'packaged' the criticism of the tobacco industry and sold it as novelty, appealing (it hoped) to the consumer's sense of irony. This approach invites the consumer to collude with the brand-owner in the subversion of the product.

A noteworthy recent twist in the fortunes of 'subvertising' and its relationship to cigarette advertising is the case of the famous 'Marlboro' Man' billboard in Hollywood. The billboard, a 'more enduring urban monument than almost any other building in Los Angeles'[13] has stood on the Hollywood hills for many years, a symbol of masculinity and part of American folklore. When the USA banned tobacco advertising in 1998, tobacco companies were also forced to hand over their remaining billboards for use by State health and education agencies but had to maintain payments on these sites until January 2000. The sites were to be used for creative work with a health message instead. The Marlboro' Man was transformed – instead of the Marlboro name running beside him, the word 'Impotent' was produced in an appropriate red type, and his cigarette hung limply from his mouth. The emasculated cowboy 'subvertised' the brand message, parodying the values of virility and Americanness that Marlboro' traditionally embodied.

The boundaries between the activities of marketers and the activities of consumer pressure groups are fragile. No longer perceived as the passive victim of advertising claims, the consumer has been 'repackaged' by the media in recent years as demanding, discerning and pro-active. In turn, this shift has provided ample opportunity for brands to target the consumer's conscience. In no other area of marketing and consumption has this been as clear as in the case of Green consumption, where grassroots politics have impacted upon product development and new directions in marketing.[14]

SHAKE HANDS WITH A COLD GOLD KB

MASTURBATION FANTASY #37

Green consumerism has clearly captured the popular imagination to an unprecedented degree. This is because it offers ordinary people access to a new and immediate democratic process: 'voting' about the environment can take place on a daily basis. People are not only not duped, they are able through their shopping to register political support or opposition.

During the last decade, Green issues have moved increasingly towards the centre stage of consumption debates. More and more shoppers are aware of complex ecological and social effects wrought by the manufacture and consumption of the brands they use. Their awareness affects their feelings toward the brands that they buy and ultimately demonstrates the political power of purchase.

*The Annual Survey of British Green Activism*, conducted by MORI in 1994, revealed the following behaviour by shoppers.[15]

In answer to the question, 'Which if any of these things have you done in the last 12 months as a result of concern for the environment?' 45 per cent said they had bought products in recycled packaging, 52 per cent had bought products made from recycled materials, 35 per cent had bought environmentally friendly detergents or cleaners, and 33 per cent products in bio-degradable packaging. Overall, 42 per cent of people participating in the survey said they had selected one product over another because of its environmentally friendly packaging, formulation or advertising.

**Above right: Packaging showing a range of Green symbols, c. 1992.
Right: Signage for organic food, Tesco, West Kensington, London 1999.**

These figures reveal the broad extent of low-level green shopping in the UK by the mid-1990s. Other studies suggest a hard-core of some 10 per cent of British shoppers who integrate ecological issues very consistently into their buying behaviours, while a further 70 per cent occasionally consider the environment.[16] Green consumers' choice of one product over another is dependent on their level of awareness and their inclination towards Green claims by manufacturers. What affects this choice?

Shoppers' most immediate source of environmental information is on the packaging and products they buy. A panoply of symbols and marks are used to validate Green claims. The International Standards Organisation's Strategic Advisory Group on the Environment has identified two types.[17] The first are claims for the product made by a third party, often a governmental agency, but sometimes another body or a private company. Consumers International, a global network of consumers' associations from over 80 nations, sees the endorsement of products by independent specialists as generally a good thing but is doubtful of the efficacy of environmental marks. This is because the messages can be confusing to the shopper. For example, more than 30 schemes are run worldwide incorporating the Mobius loop used to mean 'incorporating recycled materials' or the converse 'recyclable'. National and transnational schemes include Germany's Blue Angel and the EU's flower symbol. However, the proliferation of these symbols, and the variety of criteria for their use, mean environmental marks are difficult to implement with any meaningful clarity.

A newly arrived marker upon products is the Humane Cosmetics Standard logo. Leading animal protection groups such as the British Union for the Abolition of Vivisection (BUAV) have joined forces to endorse the logo that identifies 'cruelty-free' cosmetic products and brands: companies will be independently assessed to judge their compliance. The mark is intended to help consumers to choose cosmetics that have not been tested on animals, and although this issue is aside from green consumerism per se, the logo will act in much the same way as ecological marks, an aide to ethical consumerism.

The second type of marker denotes the claims made by manufacturers themselves. A response to the Green shopper's arrival in the 1980s was a marked increase in the quantity and range of Green products. Advertisements making Green claims in the period 1985 to 1991 increased, while ecological statements have diminished through the rest of the 1990s.[18] Green claims have been most extreme in areas of intense competition, for example in the market for washing powders where environmentalism invigorated the tired advertising of such products. This leads to the sceptical view that the manufacturers were, after all, most concerned for their profit margins and market shares. Green imagery often includes trees, flowers, the Earth held in a pair of caring hands and the sun. They are clearly intended to reassure the consumer and, as it is virtually impossible to differentiate between quasi-official marks and manufacturers' own claims, the marks do not particularly aid the Green shopper. Imagery suggestive of nature's bounty and freshness, such as leaping dolphins, wild flowers and waterfalls are used in the design of much packaging to suggest a 'natural' or 'organic' basis for the product. Often the imagery is unconnected to the product's function, as with the inclusion of dolphins on the label for Reckitt & Colman's Down to Earth washing up liquid. Natural imagery employed in packaging extends to advertising, as with the use of waterfalls in the long-running campaign for Timotei shampoo. The

inference for the consumer in both these examples is that the products are non-polluting and derived from natural ingredients, and to use them re-connects the user with nature.

Many claims on packaging substantiate the manufacturers' efforts to ensure the sustainability of their products, indicating the ingredients or materials included, although most often those that they have excluded. CFC gases (chloroflouro carbons, alleged to contribute to ozone depletion and global warming) are now commonly understood by consumers to be undesirable. Although they have been phased out of aerosol production since 1989 manufacturers still boldly claim the absence of CFCs as a specific selling point. Additionally they may stress that the propellant in their aerosols is harmless compressed air, neglecting to point out this needs thicker, stronger cans using more material and energy to manufacture. Green claims reassure consumers, even if they are at best misleading and at worst economical with the truth.

Much eco-labelling on general household products now implicates the consumer, not the manufacturer, to take responsibility through recycling or safely disposing of waste. Cleverly, this strategy implies responsibility by the manufacturer without delivering it, while the social and economic networks for adequate retrieval of materials and commodities such as aluminium are not in place. Yet the potential of recycling post-consumer waste is enough to persuade most shoppers that they are contributing to improving the environment. A statement such as 'This carrier bag is biodegradable or recyclable' can only be effective if the consumer acts upon it. Little information is published to show that landfills, where most so-called 'biodegradable' waste ends up, are specifically managed to reduce biodegradation and so control the emission of harmful gases. The recycling advice alleviates the responsibility of the supplier, whether or not it is heeded, and using the Green product relieves the consumers' environmental guilt. Both parties in the transaction are vindicated by the green claims.[19]

Vague claims such as 'Environmentally Friendly'

Below: Humane Cosmetics logo, 1999.
Opposite: Packaging showing environmental imagery, 1999.

are even more effective at persuading consumers to buy products, although they may be meaningless in their non-specificity. UK trading and advertising standards inefficiently combat them, although the law in the USA and in other European Union countries such as Sweden has proved better equipped. Ironically it is rival manufacturers, not consumers, who often complain about the accuracy of Green claims for products, implying they perceive environmental responsibility as another marketing tool. In 1994 Lever Bros complained to the Advertising Standards Authority (ASA) about claims made by their rival, Reckitt & Colman, for Down to Earth washing-up liquid. The wording of Reckitt & Colman's advertisement was 'our washing up liquid … looks after rivers. We get independent experts to conduct stringent tests for biodegradability, on the whole product, to ensure we're reducing the harm to the environment.' Lever complained the advertisement implied that competitors' products were less biodegradable and therefore did more harm to the environment. Since Reckitt & Colman was unable to demonstrate its claims relative to

other products, the ASA upheld the complaint.[20]

Consumer confusion about and ignorance of Green issues plays into the hands of manufacturers and marketers. The supermarket shopper may find it near impossible to make informed, critical decisions about green claims, however concerned he or she is to make the right choices for the sake of the environment. Manufacturers employ tried and tested techniques such as the use of 'independent experts' to verify their environmental practices, perhaps as a way of countering cynicism about unendorsed product claims. Mostly, the shopper responds to the manufacturer's claims with complicity and is made to feel better about his or her environmental responsibility by buying what is ostensibly a 'natural' or 'eco-friendly' product. This relationship between the shopper and the brand is a collective mitigation of guilt, in which the palliative of Green consciousness assuages the environmental responsibility of the consumer and the supplier. It is a 'disacknowledgement' of environmental issues, where consumers match manufacturers' Green claims with tokenistic ecological responses. This Sheffield shopper typifies many consumers' approach to Green shopping; 'I don't mooch, ferreting for environmentally friendly ones. If they really stand out then I'll go for it and think, I've done my bit.'[21]

'Light Green' supermarket shoppers seldom deny themselves through their product choices, choosing to consume differently rather than reduce their consumption.[22] However, proactive consumption also takes the form of a refusal to buy certain goods and protest against their presence in the market. Increasingly, we are witnessing the targeting of brands by political activists. Boycotts, for example, are organised for reasons that often transcend the product or manufacturer to make broader social or political points, and they may inconvenience or even threaten those who undertake them. As one critic has put it 'consumer boycotts … have specific goals that do not necessarily operate to the material advantage of the consumer'.[23] Ultimately the environmental movement and economic boycotts combine high-

*week we price check hundreds of everyday*

BAG
FOR
LIFE

RECYCLABLE BAG, REPLACED FREE

Opposite: 'What's Wrong with
McDonald's?' Leaflet
published by London
Greenpeace, UK, 1986-90.

level political concerns with low-level commercial ones. The consumer is political, and the 'vigilante consumer' can effect change.[24]

Not every boycott succeeds, and it is not the only method for consumers to register their criticism. One study of commercial boycotts found that they are most likely to succeed if the target organisation is highly visible and closely involved with the principal cause of the action. The bull's-eye is 'a consumer good or service, low cost, frequently purchased, branded, substitutable, perishable, distributed through retail outlets, and publicly (visibly) purchased and consumed'.[25]

The boycott of Barclays Bank was organised by the Anti-Apartheid Movement in the 1980s. The protest was against the bank's investment in what was perceived as the repressive South African regime. Its specific aim was to persuade Barclays to withdraw from South Africa, and the long-term goal was the overthrow of the apartheid system through the economic isolation of South Africa itself. The campaign encouraged potential customers, particularly students, not to have Barclays accounts. Therefore, boycotters were able to use commercial action to register political dissent, especially as the Anti-Apartheid Movement was also critical of the British government's reluctance to act on the issue. Barclays was not the only British institutional investor in South Africa, but as a prominent High Street brand it became the focus for the action.[26] A direct result of the boycott was a reduction in the bank's share of the student market from 27 per cent in 1983 to 17 per cent in 1985.[27] Barclays also largely withdrew from South Africa, although it claimed this was for a raft of economic reasons, not exclusively due to the sanctions.

A consumer boycott may be deemed a success if it damages a company's representation of itself (its brand image), forcing a fundamental public reappraisal of the corporation's activities. One such example was the action taken by a small pressure group known as London Greenpeace (not related to the environmental pressure group Greenpeace) against McDonald's in the late 1980s. From 1986

activists distributed a leaflet titled 'What's Wrong With McDonald's?' that entreated customers to boycott its fast-food restaurants and questioned the corporation's own environmental and labour relations claims. In this instance, it was not the boycott *per se* that became the focus of media attention or consumer action, but the resulting court case when McDonald's sued two of the activists for libel.[28]

At 313 days, the so-called McLibel trial became the longest court case in English legal history, and the media scrutiny this engendered worked against the successful image of McDonald's. Far from quieting criticism, as had been intended, the case sharply focussed public attention upon the corporation's practices and core values. The defendants, Helen Steel and David Morris, were found guilty of libel against McDonald's as they were not able to substantiate their claims that the corporation caused starvation in the third world, destroyed rain forests, lied about recycling, poisoned customers or maintained poor conditions for their workers. However, Justice Bell ruled that McDonald's had exploited children in its advertising, was cruel to animals, and that its restaurants paid low wages to British workers.[29] Despite the complexity of the case and the inability of the defendants to make it stick, McLibel can be interpreted as a public-relations disaster for McDonald's as it drew public attention to aspects of the corporations activities it did not wish to publicise. The fact that issues surrounding McDonald's activities were discussed openly in the media is evidence of the activists' success, even if they had to go to the High Court to defend their views. This was no 'light Green' consumer activity, therefore, but a committed, politicised action against the values and policies of corporate, branded culture.

For the McLibel activists, their court case symbolised the greater injustices of a world controlled by corporate interests, of which McDonald's was the metaphor. Their protest was essentially about freedom of speech, which they

# What's wrong with McDonald's?

## Everything they don't want you to know.

Above: Sainsbury's loyalty card and Unilever disloyalty card, 1998.
Below: 'No to GM Food, Yes to Organic Food', True Food campaign logo, Greenpeace, UK, 1999.
Opposite: True Food campaign, Greenpeace, UK, 1999.

felt to be suppressed by corporate interests. After the court case they wrote:[30]

> People should have the right to put forward their honestly held beliefs to draw attention to what they see as the problems with the way society is run. It is only through the expression of alternative views and ideas that injustice is remedied and society progresses. It is in the public interest that there be the widest possible dissemination of critical information about those institutions which dominate our lives and environment. There also needs to be vibrant public debate about what is really happening around us, and about the alternatives.

McLibel bears comparison with a previous, successful boycott of a multinational. In 1974 Nestlé, the world's leading manufacturer of powdered baby milk with half the global market, won a libel suit but lost valuable public support. The company was countering claims that their baby-milk products were being marketed in poor countries incorrectly and leading to 'commerciogenic malnutrition'. A full-scale boycott of Nestlé in the USA was organised in 1977 by a coalition of protestors under the banner of the Infant Formula Action Coalition (INFACT). The action of one boycotter illustrates how personal choices have a larger political and social dimension. Her letter to Nestlé read:[31]

> My children love Nestlé Quik. My husband and I are virtually addicted to Nescafé. But we will no longer be buying these or your other products. We have learned about the suffering your advertising of infant formula causes. You are a large company. Individually, we don't have much power over your actions. But our outrage joins with that of many others and together we will boycott Nestlé products until you change.

Like McDonald's, Nestlé responded initially with legal action to refute accusations. Under intense pressure from activists, who along the way recruited establishment support from the World Health Organisation (WHO), Nestlé eventually took on board the criticism aimed at it and amended its practice. The boycott was suspended in 1984 but demonstrated how effective consumers could be

when they call corporations to accountability, and it stands as the model for successful consumer action.

In the 1990s other issues with food have shaken consumers' confidence. So-called 'Mad Cow Disease' (Bovine Spongiform Encaphalopathy, or BSE) was connected to the fatal human degenerative condition Creutzfeldt-Jacob disease (CJD). The ensuing collapse of public faith in British beef, along with European boycotts of its products, led to the virtual collapse of the beef industry itself. By the summer of 1999 the BSE scare appeared to be gradually subduing,[32] only to be replaced in the public arena by a new food fear, that of untested genetically modified (GM) ingredients in processed food.

GM food raises ecological and ethical questions, ranging from potential damage to the ecosystem and human DNA, to concern about animal (and ultimately human) cloning and accusations of 'playing God'.[33] International corporate brands such as Monsanto have been accused of developing new strains of crops to withstand biological and other threats without thoroughly testing the environmental- and human-health implications. Monsanto identified a potential threat to its business activities and public relations from protests in Britain. Interestingly, the American general public have remained unconcerned by the inclusion of genetically modified ingredients in food, and the US agricultural industry has until recently embraced the new technology. By issuing full-page advertisements in the British national press in early 1999, Monsanto countered its critics, an action that has been identified as the strongest possible reaction to a boycott by a target organisation.[34] However, Monsanto is (or was, until the current public debate arose) an 'invisible' corporation, rather than a consumer brand, and consumer action has tended to focus on the better known makers and retailers of food. Unsurprisingly, therefore, the introduction of ingredients such as genetically altered pulses into familiar supermarket branded foods has raised intense criticism from quarters as diverse as dieticians, food writers, ecologists, middle-class housewives and advocate groups like the Consumers'

AVOIDING GM FOODS

GREENPEACE

THE GUILD OF FOOD WRITERS
ACADEMY OF CULINARY ARTS
EUROTOQUES • SLOW FOOD

Association. In June 1999 even the conservatively minded Women's Institute voted to join more radical groups such as Friends of the Earth and Greenpeace in calling for a freeze in growing GM crops.[35]

Activism has taken the now familiar form of product boycotts. An affiliation of Green groups issued a 'Unilever Disloyalty Card' to shoppers outside a north London supermarket in 1998, to protest against that company's unlabelled use of genetically modified soya in brands such as Bachelor's Beanfeast meals. The activists' ironic appropriation of the supermarket loyalty card mocked a popular method of encouraging brand loyalty by incentives. Mimicking advertisers' own use of 'independent experts', the card quoted an influential food retailer (Malcolm Walker, Chair of Iceland Foods) as saying, 'This is Frankenstein Food.' This emotive image of a 'manmade' monster was an appropriate metaphor for the complexity of GM food science and has become an enduring but negative summary image in the debate. The debate crystallised around two issues: the demand to end GM testing and use of GM foodstuffs in Britain, and the more immediate request for efficient labelling of foods to enable shoppers to make informed personal choices. These issues result in lively debate between consumers, suppliers, scientists, government ministers and activists.[36] Supermarket retailers, attempting to pre-empt or deflect possible consumer action, began removing genetically modified products from their shelves before the debate has concluded. Unilever also bowed to pressure. Van den Bergh, the Unilever subsidiary that makes Beanfeast meals, and sister company Birds Eye Walls both announced the withdrawal of GM soya from their products in April 1999. On 28 April, Britain's biggest supermarket retailer Tesco announced it had banned GM ingredients from its own-brand food. Iceland was the first chain to ban GM foods, followed by Sainsbury's, Asda and Safeway. At the same time Tesco conducted a survey of customers and found that one in four wanted GM products removed from the shelves. A Consumers' Association survey found that 94 per cent of shoppers wanted food packaging to contain information on GM ingredients. European Union legislation may enforce the labelling of genetically modified ingredients, though it will not suppress their use. The British government advocates a cautious approach to the licensing of GM foods, but the environmental pressure group Friends of the Earth suspects commercial lobbying and political leverage from the United States are at play. 'If that type of pressure has occurred, as we expect,' said Charles Secrett, the executive director of Friends of the Earth, in the *Times* newspaper, 'then it helps to explain why the Government is doing all that it can to rush through these potentially very dangerous crops and foods before adequate testing has been carried out.'[37]

The furore about GM food embraces the integrity of science, commercial interests, political expediency and citizens' rights. The consumer is torn between these contrary positions. Critics of GM food express various social and ethical points of view, and come from all walks of life, from ordinary shoppers to the Prince of Wales.[38] 'Middle Englanders' have been encouraged by the tabloid press to band together against GM food with events such as 'The *Express* Great Organic Picnic', which took place over the August bank holiday in 1999 as a form of peaceful mass demonstration. Less peaceful was the destruction of a trial crop of genetically modified maize by Greenpeace, an action that resulted in the arrest of prominent activist Lord Melchett.

Consumption, it appears, has become the central metaphor, or leitmotif, of debate in modern society.

Charitable giving, like buying green products or boycotting companies, is a way of empowering people to express opinion over ethical, social concerns. There are approximately 180,000 registered charities in the UK with a total income in 1998 of almost £20 billion. But about five per cent of all the charities receive over 85 per cent of the total annual income, and a tiny percentage (271 charities, or 0.17 per cent of the total register) attract approximately 40 per cent of the total annual income.[39] The big charities, therefore, are big business, and they are increasingly behaving as major brands to attract and maintain their share of public and corporate support. Some have their own credit cards, issued by conventional financial corporations who pay a small commission on each transaction to the charities. These cards may also be vehicles for promoting a particular cause of the charity, for example the PVC-free card issued by Greenpeace. For many of the larger ones, charity shops have gained a major role in promoting their activities and in raising revenue. Dealing with both second-hand goods and new products from alternative sources, charity shops also represent an important alternative to shopping for branded goods usually found in conventional retail outlets.

Oxfam, the acronym of the Oxford Committee for Famine Relief, is one of Britain's best-known humanitarian charities dedicated to relieving hunger and poverty. Its annual income of £91.7 million in 1996/7 included over £17 million raised through its shops.[40] Oxfam shops have become the paradigm of charity shops. The first was opened in Oxford in 1948 and sold everything from feather boas to false teeth, the guiding principle being that the public donated all the stock. Mixing the thrift of the jumble sale with the commercial sparkle of the High Street boutique, Oxfam shops have more recently moved away from their bric-à-brac origins and are now managed as efficiently as other major retailers. With over 850 outlets in the United Kingdom and Ireland, Oxfam has become a branded retailer in its own right.

Oxfam has now created a number of niche outlets, dedicated to particular kinds of goods, such as furniture. Reflecting super-saver own-brands in supermarkets, Oxfam operates 100 Super Savings shops that sell only very low-cost clothes and household goods. Some high value second-hand goods, such as designer clothes, are creamed off for other more 'up-market' outlets. At the other end of the scale, Oxfam also operates Wastesaver in the English town of Huddersfield, a recycling plant that sorts all the unsold clothes from the charity shops. These goods that have failed to re-enter the market are recycled for their materials, earning nearly £2 million for Oxfam in 1997/8.

Traditionally charity shops like Oxfam only sold second hand-items given by the public. More recently the stores have included new goods such as decorative objects, candles, basketry and food, originated in the parts of the world where the charity's humanitarian aid is most active. Not only do the shops raise revenue for the charity but also public awareness of its core activity. The customers participate in the charity's work through purchasing goods. Most of these new products are part of Fair Trade schemes, which are intended to benefit the producer (often in the third world) as much as the consumer. The Green shopper expresses a concern for the natural environment and makes choices of products accordingly. As an extension of this sensibility, ethical shoppers choose products and services because of their impact upon other people. Often, green and ethical issues may co-exist or overlap. For example, at Oxfam coffee drinkers can buy CaféLatino, ground coffee supplied by Peruvian

Right: Greenpeace PVC-free credit card, 1997
Following pages: 'Oppressive Regimes', advertisement for the Co-operative Bank, 1999.

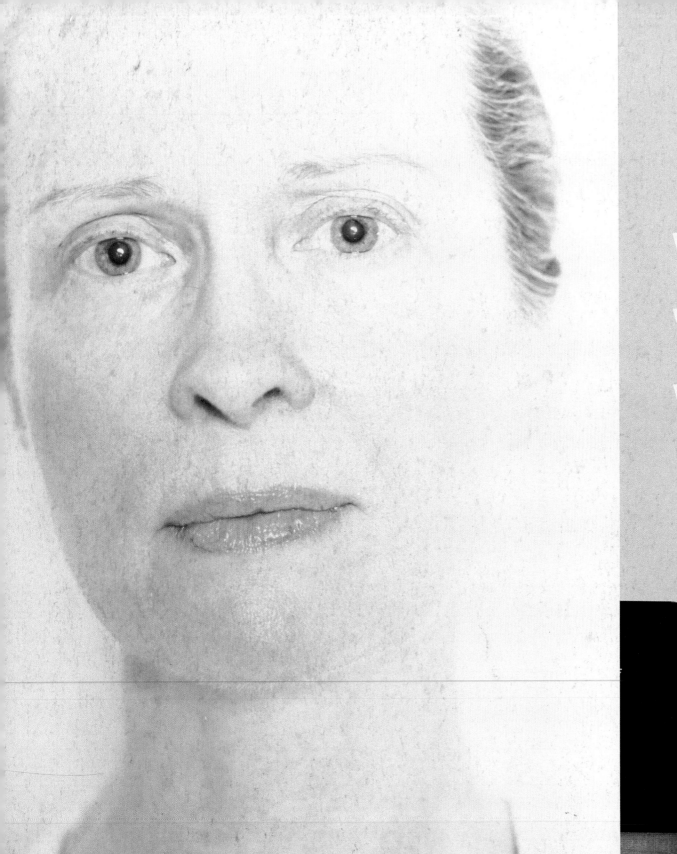

Who fu
Who g
Who th

Not me

The COOPERATIVE BANK
After all, it's your money
nds these people?
ves them money?
e hell funds these people?
The Co-operative Bank will never invest its customers' money in the finance of arms to oppressive regimes. It's part of an ethical policy that states what we will and won't do with your money. After all, it's your money.
0800 90 50 90
www.co-operativebank.co.uk

and Nicaraguan co-operatives made from organically grown beans.

One recent example of a service brand responding to the demands of ethical consumers is the Co-operative Bank in Britain. The bank grew out of the Co-operative movement of the nineteenth century, in which business enterprises were owned and managed by and for the benefit of customers or workers, but by the late twentieth century it was perceived as down-market and old-fashioned. The Co-op appealed to a new generation of customers by drawing upon its own humanitarian origins. The bank differentiated itself from its competition by promising its customers that it would not invest their money in ecologically harmful industries or oppressive regimes, a message forcibly made through advertising. This standpoint is in contrast to the activities that brought Barclays Bank into disrepute in the 1980s. Co-operative Bank customers, therefore, are able to express their political and social values through their choice of bank. Ethical consumption both empowers the consumer and reinforces the brand's image.

This is the context in which Fair Trade products operate. The Fair Trade Foundation is an independent body founded by a coalition of commercial producers and charities to oversee the awarding of the Fair Trade mark. Producers such as Gourmet Percol, who fulfil the criteria for ethical trading, are able to mark their

products. In theory the Fair Trade mark informs consumers who wish to purchase commodities ethically. In reality, as with the confusion about Green marks, officially sanctioned Fair Trade products can easily be confused in consumers' minds with those bearing imagery of one-world unity, or which claim to be 'fairly traded'. Co-operatives or their representatives market "Fair Trade" products and seek to guarantee the subsistence of regional growers and suppliers who are threatened by the economic and political might of global corporations. The best-known examples include Cafédirect in the UK and Max Havelaar in the Netherlands, brands of coffee produced in the developing world but sold in competition with global brands such as Nescafé in the first world.[41] Another example is Divine chocolate, 'Heavenly chocolate with a heart', produced by the Day Chocolate Company in London on behalf of cocoa growers in Ghana. The company claims to offer 'A fair deal for cocoa growers'. The African growers and workers own a part of the company that makes the chocolate. Profits are ploughed back into the community, rather than siphoned off for foreign investors and shareholders. Fair Trade products can be more expensive than more familiar brands (due to their economies of scale), but they offer the shopper the chance to make a purchase in the knowledge that

Packaging for Gourmet
Percol Fairtrade Latin
American organic arabica
coffee, 1999.

the profits will reach the producer directly. Oxfam shops stock over 70 Fair Trade food products, including Swazi Hot Chilli Sauce made by an all women kitchen in Swaziland, organic honey from Zambia and Bolivian Pasta Twirls.

Beyond the range of charity shops and Fair Trade products, some retailers have strong ethical practices for their own-brand goods. The Body Shop, for example, aims to oppose the conventions of the mainstream cosmetics industry with highly visible policies on organic and ethical sourcing of products (including using Fair Trade suppliers), animal welfare and recycling. It purports to respect peoples in the third world, their traditions and products. This ethic is manifested in the 'Eau No!' range of travel products, available for so-called eco-tourists who go to 'places where water, not adventure, is in short supply', and includes dry shampoo and body wipes to reduce the need to use limited local water supplies. The range is backed-up by in-store pamphlets, published by The Body Shop in association with the Centre for Environmentally Responsible Tourism, that advise would-be ethical tourists to 'use locally owned transport, accommodation and services' and 'learn a few words of the local language'.[42] In the larger context of the first world's relationship to the third these products and suggestions may appear at best limited and at worst patronising.

Underlying the concept of ethical consumption, therefore, is a notion that consumers are citizens of the world with responsibilities to one another as well as to the Earth. However, taken to its logical end, ethical consumption is potentially the most critical practice of all. Ultimately it demands that we consume less in order to minimise the detrimental effects of our consumption on the planet and on society.

In some consumer societies, increasing signs of 'consumer fatigue' may mean that the call to consume less finds advocates and supporters. 'Voluntary simplicity' may also result from discriminating choices of purchase and from revised concepts of product and service development that build-in longevity, not obsolescence. Despite a

number of commercial initiatives that reflect a 'one-world' philosophy, the implications of globalisation for developing countries remain largely negative. Global brands are still likely to locate their production sites in areas where labour is cheap and conditions can be poor. Finding their markets in the developed world to be saturated with goods, international companies are seeking ways of penetrating potential new ones, such as China. Global sustainability may be achieved through a reduction in consumption in developed countries, and by investment in the economies of developing countries. However, the global call to consume less is fraught with risks of imperialist moralising. The Malaysian consumer activist Martin Khor says:[43]

> The most important changes required are changes in mentality about happiness and pleasure. But this can only happen if the developed countries offer an example here, because they disseminate their culture to the developing countries. So massive change in consumption patterns, in motivation and in the meaning of life itself are very important. But that can only come about if we can change the distribution of commercial and therefore political power world-wide, between countries and within countries, so that the local communities can have their fair share of resources, so that they can vote in the marketplace or in their communities on how to fulfil their needs.

Many of the ethical consumption practices described so far are aligned to the politics of the left. But politicised consumption can also be an expression of right-wing politics, when the issue at stake is the right of the individual to choose to consume and to resist what is perceived as 'despotic' centralised governmental control. Consumer activism, and a claim to the moral high ground of consumer rights, is not only the preserve of the left. In the United States legislation that is seen as limiting the rights of the individual to consume is frequently criticised as being 'anti-American'. The National Rifle Association (NRA), for example, associates the right to own firearms with the 'American way.' Citing the Second Amendment of the American

Constitution, Charlton Heston, actor and President of the NRA, argued:[44]

> But our essential reason for being is this. As long as there is a Second Amendment, evil can never conquer us. Tyranny, in any form, can never find footing within a society of law-abiding, armed ethical people. The majesty of the Second Amendment, that our Founders so divinely captured and crafted into your birthright, guarantees that no government despot, no renegade faction of armed forces, no roving gangs of criminals, no breakdown of law and order, no massive anarchy, no force of evil or crime or oppression from within or from without, can ever rob you of the liberties that define your Americanism.

Each time we make a purchase, its effects ripple out like rings of water on a pond. Buying and owning goods may be viewed as an inalienable right and a demonstration of our personal autonomy. Beyond this, our personal consuming choices can have implications for others. Whether we are choosing the best value for ourselves or the best deal for the planet, the transactions described so far are predicated on an exchange of money and operate in a commercial environment. The alternative to this is the growth of alternative economies that do not rely on money at all.

In recent years Local Exchange Trading Systems (LETS) have proliferated with over 200 formed in the UK in the early 1990s. LETS originated in British Columbia in 1982, but the idea has spread to the USA, Australasia and Britain. These cashless economies trade services and commodities between members on a barter basis, using a notional currency (for example, the LETS scheme in the London borough of Camden uses 'Locks'). A related cashless economic system is Time Dollars, where different services are offered in exchange for time-equivalent labours. Such schemes provide invaluable services within the communities that support them. The citizenship of the consumer is central, and the trading of services and commodities, from baby-sitting to computer training, food and even architectural design, strengthens community relations. LETSLINK, the British development agency for LETS schemes, promotes them as social mortar:[45]

Capital flight deprives an area of a means of trade with itself. Many low-income areas, however, still possess skills, human energy and potential, and all kinds of material resources. All the components of real wealth are there, locked away, alongside a myriad of unmet needs. All that is missing, essentially, is a medium of exchange. We simply need a communication system, linking supply and demand.

The sociologist Zygmunt Bauman has examined the relationship of consumers to economic power and sees two types of consumers. The 'seduced' are those who have the economic power to make the choice to consume and who respond to the messages of brands and their advertising. The 'repressed' are those consumers who are subjected to the allure of brand messages through mass communications, but who are not able to partake in the consumer society because poverty disenfranchises them. Alternative economies might enfranchise Bauman's repressed consumers by circumventing the need for currency that underlies all other acts of consumption.

The boundaries between consumption and resistance to consumption are porous.[47] Most consumption relies on personal choices, affected by advertising and social convention. Economic power will also effect the ways in which a consumer is able to choose. A growing body of opinion, however, is arguing that our ability to exercise choice as consumers is now more than ever under the control of global corporations. In November 1999, the most serious organised critical action focussed against consumerism and corporate interest took place in Seattle. The World Trade Organisation (WTO), a coalition of 135 nations dedicated to promoting global free trade, met for talks in Seattle. A highly organised protest, combining a mixed coalition of anti-capitalist activists, anarchists, church leaders, human-rights and consumer-rights groups, successfully disrupted the conference and forced the city to declare a state of civil emergency. Whatever the future for global brands in the twenty-first century, it seems clear that they will have to deal with the actions of increasingly politicised consumers.

# NOTES

**CHAPTER 1: IN GOODS WE TRUST**

1   Jane Frost, in interview with author, 1999
2   Bryson, p.288.
3   See later in this chapter, Charlotte Cotton, 'Brand Associations through Advertising', pp. 60–63.
4   Jean-Christophe Agnew questions the extent to which products such as Coke might inspire a loyalty 'beyond the market place' in his essay 'Coming Up for Air: Consumer Culture in Historical Perspective' in Brewer and Porter, pp.33–4.
5   Pendergrast, pp.292–3.
6   Ibid., pp.305–6.
7   Ibid., p.395. However, only a small percentage of the original cast could be traced.
8   Ibid., pp. 56–60. Coca-Cola's name denotes its original ingredients – extract of coca leaf, or cocaine, with extract of cola nut. Although the traces of cocaine were completely removed from the recipe a few years later, the rumours of its cocaine content persisted, which both jeopardised sales and, in some quarters, encouraged them.
9   Ibid., p.13.
10  Ibid., p.64.
11  Lears, p.11.
12  Ibid., pp.162–95.
13  Kathy Peiss, 'Making Up, Making Over: Cosmetics, Consumer Culture and Women's Identity' in de Grazia with Furlong, p.322.
14  Pendergrast, p.170.
15  Batchelor, p.72.
16  Agnew in Brewer and Porter, p.32.
17  Christina Fowler, 'Change in Provincial Retail Practice during the Eighteenth-century, with Particular Reference to Central-Southern England' in Alexander and Akehurst, p. 38. For a discussion of the development of branding in the seventeenth and eighteenth centuries, particularly proprietary medicines, see John Styles, 'Product Innovation in Early Modern London', Past & Present (2000).
18  Goodman, pp.99–102.
19  Cissie Fairchilds, 'The Production and Marketing of Populuxe Goods in Eighteenth-century Paris' in Brewer and Porter, p.239.
20  John Styles, 'Manufacturing, Consumption and Design in Eighteenth-century England' in Brewer and Porter, p.541
21  Carrier, p.101.
22  Strasser, p.52.
23  Gareth Shaw, 'The European Scene: Britain and Germany' in Benson and Shaw, p.31.
24  Carrier, pp.100–1.
25  Hermann Levy, 1942. Quoted in Matthew Hilton, 'Retailing History as Economic and Cultural History' in Alexander and Akehurst, p.119.
26  Martin Kettle, 'The Candy Man', Guardian, 6 July 1999, G2, pp.2–3.
27  Rachel Bowlby, 'Supermarket Futures' in Campbell and Falk, p.94.
28  Miller, 1998.
29  Frank Mort, 'Paths to Mass Consumption: Britain and the USA since 1945' in Nava et al., p.24.
30  Scitovsky, 1976.
31  Pasi Falk, 'The Benetton–Toscani Effect: Testing the Limits of Conventional Advertising' in Nava et al., p.68.
32  Celia Lury and Alan Warde, 'Investments in the Imaginary Consumer: Conjectures Regarding Power, Knowledge and Advertising' in Nava et al., p.93.
33  The ideas put forward by the founder and creative directors of Diesel, in interview for this book, show how brand, product and advertising are seen as intertwined. See pp. 64–7.
34  Slater, p.193.
35  Featherstone, 1991.
36  Ewen, 1988, p.79.
37  Lury, p.232.
38  McCracken, 1990.
39  Colin Campbell, 'When the Meaning is Not a Message' in Nava et al., p. 343.
40  Michael Piore and Charles Sabel, 1984. Quoted in Pine II, p.105.
41  Quoted in Pine II, p.41.
42  Roland Robertson, 'Mapping the Global Condition: Globalization as the Central Concept' in Featherstone, 1990, pp.26–7.
43  Marshall McLuhan and Quentin Fiore, War and Peace in the Global Village, 1968; repr. McLuhan, Fiore & Agel, 1997.
44  Jean-François Lyotard, quoted in Slater, p.196.
45  Miller, Worlds Apart.
46  Appadurai, 1996.
47  Harvey, 1989. See also Giddens, 1984 and 1991. Also Lash and Urry, 1994, pp.223–51.
48  Miller, Acknowledging Consumption, p.9.
49  Gabriel and Lang, pp.173–86.

**CHAPTER 2: TIES THAT BIND**

1   John E. Sherry, 'Marketing and Consumer Behavior: Into the Field' in Sherry, pp.3–44.
2   Peter H. Farquhar, 'Managing Brand Equity', Marketing Research, September 1989, pp.24–33.
3   Jones, 1988.
4   Richard Elliot, 'Exploring the Symbolic Meaning of Brands', British Journal of Management, 5, 1994, pp.13–19.
5   Aaker, 1991, p.7.
6   Kapferer, p.11.
7   Aaker, 1991, p.1.
8   Arvind Rangaswamy, Raymond R. Burke and Terence A. Olivia, 'Brand Equity and the Extendibility of Brand Names', International Journal of Research in Marketing, March 1993, pp.61–75.
9   Room, 1982. See also Tedlow, 1996.
10  Keller, 1998.
11  Ibid. Keller identifies five interrelated roles for brands from a consumer perspective.
12  Robert B. Zajonc, 'Attitudinal Effects of Mere Exposure', Journal of Personality and Social Psychology, 8, 1968, pp.1–29.
13  Harris, 1998.
14  McCracken, 1990.
15  Oliver, 1987.
16  Carol J. Simon and Mary W. Sullivan, 'The Measurement and Determinants of Brand Equity: A Financial Approach', Marketing Science, 12:1, 1993, pp.28–52.
17  Rodgers, 1970; Foy, 1974.
18  Tim Ambler and Patrick Barwise, 'The Trouble with Brand Valuation', Journal of Brand Management, 5:5, May 1998, pp.367–77.
19  Danny Quah, 'The Weightless Economy in Growth', Business Economist, 30:1, March 1999, pp.40–53.
20  McPhee, 1963.
21  Andrew Ehrenberg, Gerald Goodhardt and Patrick Barwise, 'Double Jeopardy Revisited', Journal of Marketing, 54,1990, pp.82–91.
22  Barbara Olsen, 'Brand Loyalty and Consumption Patterns: The Lineage Factor' in Sherry, pp.245–81.
23  Patrick Barwise and Thomas Robertson, 'Brand Portfolios', European Management Journal, 10:3, September 1992, pp.277–85.
24  Sloan, 1965.
25  See, for instance, Aaker, 1991; Kapferer, 1992; Keller, 1998.
26  Andrew Ehrenberg, 'Repetitive Advertising and the Consumer', Journal of Advertising Research, 14:2, 1974, pp.25–34. Demetrios Vakratsas and Tim Ambler, 'How Advertising Works: What Do We Really Know?', Journal of Marketing, 63, 1999, pp.26–43. Patrick Barwise, 'Advertising for Long-Term Shareholder Value' in Barwise, 1999, pp.1–8.
27  Andrew S. C. Ehrenberg and Neil R. Barnard, 'Advertising and Product Demand', Admap, 373, 1997, pp.14–18.
28  Demetrios Vakratsas and Tim Ambler, 'How Advertising Works: What Do We Really Know?', Journal of Marketing, 63, 1999, pp.26-43.
29  Barwise, Higson, Likierman and Marsh, 1989.
30  Patrick Barwise, 'Editorial: Brands in a Digital World', Journal of Brand Management, 4:4, spring 1997, pp.220–3.
31  Cairncross, 1997.
32  Gates, p.158.
33  Peppers and Rogers, 1993.
34  Barwise and Hammond, pp.45–51. Dyson, 1997.
35  Negroponte, 1995.
36  Shapiro and Variam, 1998.
37  Schor, 1991.
38  D. Mario Nuti, 'Making Sense of the Third Way', Business Strategy Review, 10:3, autumn 1999, pp.57–67.
39  Charles Handy, 'The White Stone: Six Choices', Business Strategy Review, 7:1, spring 1996, pp.1–8.
40  Aaker, 1996, pp.108–10.
41  See, for example, Ortega, 1999.
42  Clifton and Maughan, 1999.

## CHAPTER 3: ALL THE WORLD'S A STORE

1   Giddens, 1991, pp.148–9.
2   Margaret Crawford, 'The Fifth Ecology: Fantasy, the Automobile and Los Angeles' in Crawford and Wachs, pp.222–3, 231.
3   The phrase derives from the work of Harvey Green, which is perhaps best represented in his *The Light of the Home*, though he uses the phrase not here, but in lectures.
4   For a wonderfully nostalgic recent evocation of the socialising power and its internal contradictions of the spaces of shopping, see Nicholson's novel, *Everything and More*.
5   The excavations of the agora in Athens have led to various interpretations of the uses of this space.  For the most complete description of the nature of such possible activities, see Wycherley, 1978.
6   Wycherley, pp.91–103.
7   Girouard, p.17
8   Jacobs, 1984.
9   There has not to my knowledge been a thorough study of the history and character of traditional marketplaces with respect to their architecture.  This is perhaps because of their ephemeral nature.
10  Hanawalt and Reyerson, 1994.
11  Weiss and Westerman, 1998.
12  Girouard, pp.18ff.
13  The most complete history and analysis of the arcade is to be found in Geist.  For the social uses of the arcades, see Walter Benjamin, *Paris, Capital of the Nineteenth Century*, as well as the fragments of his *Passagen*, both in Benjamin, 1978.
14  Peter Gay, *Pleasure Wars*, volume 5 of *The Bourgeois Experience*.
15  Quoted in Buck Morss, p.292.
16  Miller, *The Bon Marché*.
17  For a discussion of Zola's attitude to the department store, see Miller, *The Bon Marché*.  See also Zola's novel *Au Bonheur des Dames* (Paris, 1883), published as *The Ladies of Paradise* (trans. B. Nelson), OUP, 1999.
18  Crossick and Jaumain, 1999.
19  Barth, 1980.
20  Longstreth, p.11.
21  *Ibid.*, p.92.
22  There is still no monograph on Victor Gruen.  He did write a short article, 'Shopping Centers: The New Building Type', *Progressive Architecture*, 33:6, 1952, pp.67–94, and *Shopping Town USA*, 1960.  For a somewhat unscholarly survey of the emergence of the shopping mall, see Severini Kowinski.
23  The best review of the type is to be found in Rowe, pp.109–47.
24  For the relationship of malls to global culture, see Castells, pp.376–428.
25  For a review of the type, see Sudjic, pp.215–32.
26  For a review of the 'science' of mall planning, see Beddington, 1981, and Howard Gillette, Jr., 'The Evolution of the Planned Shopping Center in Suburb and City', *Journal of the American Planning Association*, 51:4, 1985, pp.449–60.
27  Ellen Barry, 'The Mall Doctor', *Metropolis*, May 1999, pp.21–5, 53–5.
28  Koetter and Rowe, 1984.
29  Jerde, 1999, and Anderton *et al.*, 1999.
30  Marcus Field, 'Tragedy in the Chalk Pit', *Blueprint*, 61, May 1999, pp.42–5.
31  Conversation with author, 21 April 1988.
32  See also Gottdiener, 1997.
33  I described this place extensively in 'Ontario Mills, California: Castle of Consumption in the Empire of Signs' in Moore, pp.192–203.
34  Allen Hess described with great verve and scholarship this world in *Viva Las Vegas*, but the city has developed at such a rapid pace that the book is already somewhat out of date.
35  Conversation with the author, 12 July 1998.
36  Jackson, pp.171–86.
37  For a recent speculation on how e-commerce will reshape both our virtual and our physical realities, see Mitchell, especially pp.85–97.
38  Conversation with the author, 24 February 1998.
39  The best description of such design parameters is to be found in Wurman's *Information Architects*, but it also already needs updating.
40  For example Kurzweil, 1999, and Stephenson, 1996.
41  The most recent analysis of the place of shopping is by Paco Underhill, though it has a profoundly pro-shopping bias.  The result of Rem Koolhaas' five-year project at the Harvard Graduate School of Design, to be published this year, should offer a critical counterpoint to such analyses.
42  Giddens, 1991.

## CHAPTER 4: BRANDING THE INDIVIDUAL

1   Sir Michael Perry, Director of Unilever, 1994.  Quoted in Gabriel and Lang, p.36.
2   Douglas and Isherwood, p.65.
3   For a discussion of different types of shopping and shopping analysis, see Campbell and Falk, pp.1–14.
4   Zygmunt Bauman, quoted in Campbell and Falk, p.3.
5   Bauman, 1992, p.223.
6   Robinson, p.46.
7   There are a number of historical and social analyses of the female consumer, for example de Grazia with Furlong, 1996. Also Sparke, 1995.
8   Louis Macniece, 1938, quoted in Carey, p.52.
9   Colin Campbell, 'The Sociology of Consumption' in Miller, *Acknowledging Consumption*, p.101.
10  *Ibid.*, pp.21–30, for Daniel Miller's analysis of the myths of consumption in 'Consumption as the Vanguard of History'.
11  See the idea of the 'modern hedonist' in Campbell, 1987.
12  *Ibid.*, p.203.
13  Gabriel and Lang explore the representations of the consumer under the following 'guises': chooser, communicator, explorer, identity-seeker, hedonist, victim, rebel, activist, citizen.
14  De Certeau, 1988.
15  Ewen, 1988, p.79.
16  Message posted on chat site, 14 July 1999: http://wackywet.com/messages/4387.html.
17  The Abercrombie & Fitch brand is, in fact, a re-branding of a sportswear brand that has existed for 60 or 70 years.  Now popular with high-school and college kids in the USA, it signifies a clean-cut, informal brand of clothing rather like its better-known rival, The Gap. Alongside Nike, Tommy Hilfiger and Old Navy, The Gap and Abercrombie & Fitch effectively constitute the standard apparel of many American teenagers.
18  Veblen, p.111.
19  See Brewer and Porter, 1993, and McKendrick, Brewer and Plumb, 1982.
20  Mukerji, 1983.
21  As outlined in the introduction to this book, pp. 18–51.
22  Leora Auslander, 'The Gendering of Consumer Practices in Nineteenth-century France' in de Grazia with Furlong, p.81.
23  Georg Simmel, 'Fashion' (1904) repr. in Levine, p.322; quoted in Gabriel and Lang, p.52.
24  Lury, 1996, p.44.
25  'It is standard ethnographic practice to assume that all material possessions carry social meanings and to concentrate a main part of cultural analysis upon their use as communicators,' Douglas and Isherwood, p.59.
26  For an analysis of five types of shopper and shopping, see Lunt and Livingstone, 1992.
27  Lury, 1996, p.80.
28  Hebdige, 1979.
29  Bourdieu, 1999.
30  *Ibid.* p.220.
31  As outlined in the introduction to this book.
32  See Pasi Falk's discussion of the 'experiential' nature of advertising in Nava *et al.*, 1997, chap. 4.
33  See Gareth Williams, 'Hello Kitty', pp.180–1 of this chapter.
34  As described by Lears, p.11.
35  *Ibid.*
36  See Kathy Peiss, 'Making Up, Making Over: Cosmetics, Consumer Culture and Women's Identity' in de Grazia with Furlong, pp.330–1.
37  Goldman and Papson, p.127.
38  Campbell, pp.85–9.
39  Kathy Peiss, 'Making Up, Making Over: Cosmetics, Consumer Culture and Woman's Identity' in de Grazia with Furlong, p.312.
40  As outlined in the introduction to this book.
41  See Caroline Humphrey, 'Creating a Culture of Disillusionment: Consumption in Moscow, A Chronicle of Changing Times' in Miller (ed.), *Worlds Apart*, pp.44–68.
42  *Ibid.*, p.61.
43  'The black market trade in jeans or nylon stockings are probably the best known examples of this phenomenon. (In the 1930s, Parker pens and imported cigarettes played a similar role in

Soviet culture.)' See Gronow, p.50.

44  Appadurai, 1996, p.174.

45  A historical example frequently cited is that of France in the 1950s, which resisted the expansion of Coca-Cola into the French market on the grounds that it 'diluted' French culture and threatened the wine trade. See Pendergrast, pp.241–4, and Richard Wilk in Miller, *Worlds Apart*, p.114.

46  'Whereas South Korea and Taiwan accounted for a combined 76 per cent of Nike shoewear production in 1987, by 1997 78 per cent of Nike's shoes came from Indonesia and China while the share produced by South Korea and Taiwan had shrunk to 7 per cent.' Goldman and Papson, pp.6–7.

CHAPTER 5: THE POINT OF PURCHASE

1   Bauman, 1998, p.30.

2   Haug, p.50.

3   Packard, 1957.

4   For example, *Consumer Reports* (1952) and the *Journal of Optical Society* (1955) criticised tinted windscreens as hazardous to night driving, even though General Motors continued to promote them as a safety feature until 1965. Woodham, p.228.

5   Nader, 1965. Cited by Woodham.

6   Marcuse, p.24.

7   'Americans have become the most manipulated people outside the iron curtain,' Vance Packard, preface 'To British Readers' of *The Hidden Persuaders*, Penguin Special Edition, London, 1960.

8   Haug, pp.120–1.

9   Ralph Nader, 'Upsizing Downsized Americans', quoted from the following website: www.fatdawg.com/ralph.

10  J. Harms and D. Kellner, 'Towards a Critical Theory of Advertising', www.uta.edu/english/dab/illuminations/kell6.

11  *Adbusters*, Adbusters Media Foundation, Vancouver.

12  Dr Arthur Chesterfield Evans, quoted in Millwood and Gezelius, p.14.

13  Aaron Betsky quoted in Thomas Sutcliffe, 'At Least He Died With his Boots On', *Guardian*, London, 20 August 1999, G2, p.9.

14  Mica Nava, 'Consumerism Reconsidered: Buying and Power', *Cultural Studies*, 5:2, 1991, p.168.

15  Smallbone and Sutcliffe, p.9.

16  Wagner, p.1.

17  Winward, p.13.

18  Smallbone and Sutcliffe, p.14.

19  For more detailed information about consumer responses to green claims described in the paragraphs above, see Smallbone and Sutcliffe, pp.43–54. For more detail about CFC markings see T. J. Olney and Wendy Bryce, 'Consumer Responses to Environmentally Based Product Claims' in R. H. Holman and M. R. Solomon

(eds), *Advances in Consumer Research*, 18, Association for Consumer Research, Provo, UT, 1991, pp.693–6.

20  Smallbone and Sutcliffe, p.69.

21  *Ibid.*, p.45.

22  *Ibid.*, pp.50–2. 'Light green' shoppers are defined as those who are more knowledgeable than most shoppers about green and environmental products available in general retail environments.

23  Nava *et al.*, p.168.

24  Peter Lunt, 'Psychological Approaches to Consumption: Varieties of Research: Past, Present and Future' in Miller, *Acknowledging Consumption*, p.245; Gabriel and Lang, p.145.

25  Smith, p.253.

26  For a full examination of the Barclays' boycott see Smith. For an analysis of corporate strategies to combat boycotts see Dennis E. Garrett, 'The Efficacy of Marketing Policy Boycotts: Environmental Opposition to Marketing', *Journal of Marketing*, 51, April 1987, pp.46–57.

27  Smith, p.241.

28  For a full account of the trial proceedings see Vidal. www.mcspotlight.org contains analysis by supporters of the defendants in the case.

29  Reported in the *Daily Telegraph*, London, 20 June 1997.

30  Dave Morris and Helen Steel: quoted in Vidal, p.342.

31  Cited by Smith, p.249.

32  David Brown, Agriculture Editor, 'Barbecues Mark End of Nightmare for Farmers over EU's Export Ban', *Electronic Telegraph*, www.telegraph.co.uk, 1529, 2 August 1999.

33  Alan Simpson MP, 'A First Victory against Those Who Want to Play God', *Evening Standard*, London, 10 February 1999, p.13.

34  Dennis E. Garrett, 'The Effectiveness of Marketing Policy Boycotts: Environmental Opposition to Marketing', *Journal of Marketing*, 51, April 1987, pp.46–57.

35  John Vidal, 'Power to the People', *Guardian*, London, 7 June 1999, G2, pp.2–3.

36  'Tesco Bans GM Food in Own Brands', *Electronic Telegraph*, www.telegraph.co.uk, 1433, 28 April 1999; 'Tesco and Unilever Join High Street GM Boycott', *Metro*, London, 28 April 1999, p.15; '"Genetically Modified" must be on the Label', *Design Week*, London, 12 March 1999, p.6.

37  Philip Webster and Nigel Hawkes, 'Blair Resists Calls for Ban', *The Times*, London, 13 February 1999, p.10.

38  HRH the Prince of Wales, 'My 10 Fears for GM Food', *Daily Mail*, London, 1 June 1999.

39  Charity Commission, © Crown Copyright.

40  www.oxfam.org.uk.

41  Gabriel and Lang, p.167.

42  'Take Away Tips For Responsible Travelling', in-store leaflet, The Body Shop, 1999.

43  Gabriel and Lang, p.162.

44  Extract from the President's closing remarks at the NRA Meeting of Members, Denver,

Colorado, 1 May 1999, www.nrahq.org.

45  Cited in Gabriel and Lang, p.147.

46  Zygmunt Bauman develops the notion of 'seduced' and 'repressed' consumers in *Legislators and Interpreters*. See also Alan Warde, 'Consumers, Identity and Belonging: Reflections on Some Theses by Zygmunt Bauman' in Keat, Whiteley and Abercrombie, pp.58–74.

47  Lisa Peñaloza and Linda L. Price, 'Consumer Resistance: A Conceptual Overview' in L. McAlister and M. L. Rothschild (eds), *Advances in Consumer Research*, Association for Consumer Research, Provo, UT, 1993, 20, pp.123–8.

# BIBLIOGRAPHY

Aaker, D. A., *Building Strong Brands* (New York, Free Press 1996)

— *Managing Brand Equity* (New York, Free Press 1991)

Alexander, N., and Akehurst, G., eds. *The Emergence of Modern Retailing: 1750–1950* (London, Cass 1999)

Anderton, F., with Bradbury, R., Crawford, M., Klein, N. M., and Hodgetts, C. *You Are Here: The Jerde Partnership International* (London, Phaidon 1999)

Appadurai, A. *Modernity at Large: Cultural Dimensions of Globalisation* (Minneapolis, University of Minnesota Press 1996)

Appadurai, A., ed. *The Social Life of Things* (Cambridge University Press 1986)

Assael, H. Consumer *Behavior and Marketing Action* (Cincinnati, OH, South-Western College Publishing 1995)

Barth, G. *City People: The Rise of Modern City Culture* (New York, Oxford University Press 1980)

Barwise, P., and Hammond, K., eds. *Predictions: Media* (London, Phoenix 1998)

Barwise, P., ed. *Advertising in a Recession: The Benefits of Investing for the Long Term* (Henley-on-Thames, NTC 1999)

Barwise, P., Higson, C., Likierman, A., and Marsh, P. eds. *Accounting for Brands* (London, Institute of Chartered Accountants in England and Wales 1989)

Batchelor, R. *Henry Ford: Mass Production, Modernism and Design* (Manchester University Press 1994)

Baudrillard, J. (trans. Ritzer, G.) *The Consumer Society: Myths and Structures* (London, Sage 1998)

— (trans. Foss, Patton and Beitchman) *Simulations* (New York, Semiotext(e) 1983)

Bauman, Z. *Imitations of Post-Modernism* (London, Routledge 1992)

— *Legislators and Interpreters: On Modernity, Postmodernity and Intellectuals* (Cambridge, Polity 1987)

— *Work, Consumerism and the New Poor* (Buckingham, Open University Press 1998)

Beck, U., Giddens, A., and Lash, S. *Reflexive Modernization* (Cambridge, Polity 1994)

Beddington, N. *Design for Shopping Centers* (London, Butterworth Scientific 1981)

Benjamin, W. (trans. E. Jephcott) *Reflections: Essays, Aphorisms, Autobiographical Writing* (New York, Schocken 1978)

Benson, J., and Shaw, G., eds. *The Evolution of Retail Systems c. 1800–1914* (Leicester University Press 1992)

Benson, S. P. *Counter Cultures: Saleswomen, Managers and Customers in American Department Stores* (Urbana and Chicago, University of Illinois Press 1986)

Bhabha, H. *The Location of Culture* (London, Routledge 1994)

Bloch, P. H., Bush, R. F., and Campbell, L. 'Consumer Accomplices in Product Counterfeiting', *Journal of Consumer Marketing,* 10:4, 1993, pp. 27-36.

Bourdieu, P. (trans. R. Nice) *Distinction: A Social Critique of the Judgement of Taste* (London, Routledge 1999); first published in French as *La Distinction: Critique sociale du jugement* (Paris, Minuit 1979)

Bowlby, R. *Shopping with Freud* (London, Routledge 1993)

Brewer, J., and Porter, R., eds. *Consumption and the World of Goods* (London, Routledge 1993)

Brown, S., and Turley, D., eds. *Consumer Research: Postcards from the Edge* (London, Routledge 1997)

Bryson, B. *Made In America* (London, Minerva 1994)

Buck Morss, S. *The Dialectics of Seeing: Walter Benjamin and the Arcades Project* (Cambridge, MIT Press 1989)

Cairncross, F. *The Death of Distance* (London, Orion 1997)

Campbell, C. *The Romantic Ethic and the Spirit of Modern Consumerism* (Oxford, Blackwell 1987)

Campbell, C., and Falk, P., eds. *The Shopping Experience* (London, Sage 1997)

Carey, J. *The Intellectuals and the Masses: Pride and Prejudice Among the Literary Intelligentsia, 1880–1939* (London, Faber 1992)

Carrier, J. *Gifts and Commodities, Exchange and Western Capitalism since 1700* (London, Routledge 1995)

Castells, M. *The Rise of Network Society* (Oxford, Blackwell 1996)

Certeau, M. de. *The Practice of Everyday Life* (Berkeley, Los Angeles and London, University of California Press 1988)

Clarke, A. *Tupperware: The Promise of Plastic in 1950s America* (Washington and London, Smithsonian Institute Press 1999)

Clifton, R., and Maughan, E., eds. *The Future of Brands: Twenty-five Visions* (London, Interbrand/Macmillan Business 1999)

Corrigan, P. *The Sociology of Consumption* (London, Sage 1997)

Crawford, M., and Wachs, M., eds. *The Car and the City: The Automobile, the Built Environment and Daily Urban Life* (Ann Arbor, University of Michigan Press 1992)

Crossick, G., and Jaumain, S., eds. *Cathedrals of Consumption: The European Department Store, 1850–1939* (London, Ashgate 1999)

Debord, G. *Society of the Spectacle* (Detroit, Black and Red 1977)

Douglas, M., and Isherwood, B., eds. *The World of Goods: Towards An Anthropology of Consumption* (London, Allen Lane 1978)

Dyson, E. *Release 2.1: A Design for Living in the Digital Age* (London, Penguin 1998)

Eicher, J. B., ed. *Dress and Ethnicity* (Oxford, Berg 1995)

Ewen, S. *All Consuming Images: The Politics of Style in Contemporary USA* (New York, Basic 1988)

Ewen, S. *Captains of Consciousness: Advertising and the Social Roots of the Consumer Culture* (New York, McGraw Hill 1976)

Featherstone, M. *Consumer Culture and Post Modernism* (London, Sage 1991)

Featherstone, M., ed. *Global Culture, Nationalism, Globalization and Modernity* (London, Sage 1990)

Fine, B., and Leopold, E. *The World of Consumption* (London, Sage 1993)

Forty, A. *Objects of Desire* (London, Thames and Hudson 1986)

Foy, N. *The IBM World* (London, Eyre Methuen 1974)

Gabriel, Y., and Lang, T., eds. *The Unmanageable Consumer, Contemporary Consumption and its Fragmentations* (London, Sage 1995)

Gates, B. *The Road Ahead* (New York, Viking 1995)

Gay, P. *Pleasure Wars*, vol. 5 of *The Bourgeois Experience: Victoria to Freud* (New York, Norton 1999)

Geist, J. F. (trans. Newman, J. O., and Smitt, J. H.) *Arcades: The History of a Building Type* (Cambridge, MIT Press 1983)

*Gendai Yogo Kisò Chishiki* [Modern Terminology Basic Knowledge] (Tokyo, Jiyokokuminsha, 1997)

Giddens, A. *The Constitution of Society* (Cambridge, Polity 1984)

— *Modernity and Self-Identity: Self and Society in the Late Modern Age* (Stanford University Press 1991).

Gilmore, F. Brand *Warriors: Corporate Leaders Share their Winning Strategies* (London, HarperCollins 1997)

Girouard, M. *Cities and People: A Social and Architectural History* (New Haven, Yale University Press 1985)

Goldman, R., and Papson, S. *Nike Culture: The Sign of the Swoosh* (London, Sage 1998)

Goodman, J. *Tobacco in History: The Culture of Dependence* (London, Routledge 1993)

Gottdiener, M. *The Theming of America: Dreams, Visions and Commercial Spaces* (New York, HarperCollins 1997)

Grazia, V. de, with Furlong, E., eds. *The Sex of Things: Gender and Consumption in Historical Perspective* (Berkeley, Los Angeles and London, University of California Press 1996)

Green, H. *The Light of the Home: An Intimate View of the Lives of Women in Victorian America* (New York, Pantheon 1983)

Gronow, J. *The Sociology of Taste* (London, Routledge 1997)

Gruen, V. *Shopping Town USA: The Planning of Shopping Centers* (New York, Reinhold Winston 1960)

Hanawalt, B. A., and Reyerson, K. L., eds. *City and Spectacle in Medieval Europe* (Minneapolis, University of Minnesota Press 1994)

Harris, J. R. *The Nurture Assumption* (New York, Free Press 1998)

Harvey, D. *The Condition of Post-Modernity* (Oxford, Blackwell 1989)

Haug, W. F. *Critique of Commodity Aesthetics* (Minneapolis, University of Minnesota Press 1986)

Hebdige, D. *Hiding in the Light: On Images and Things* (London, Methuen 1987)

—*Subculture: The Meaning of Style* (London, Methuen 1979)

Hess, A. *Viva Las Vegas: After-hours Architecture* (San Francisco, Chronicle 1993)

Hitchcock, H. R., and Johnson, P. *The International Style* (New York, Museum of Modern Art 1932; repr. 1995)

Homer, T., and Wycherley, R. E., eds. *The Agora of Athens* (New York, American School of Classical Studies 1972)

Jackson, J. B. *A Sense of Time, A Sense of Place* (New Haven, CT, Yale University Press 1994)

Jacobs, J. *Cities and the Wealth of Nations* (New York, Random House 1984)

Jameson, F. *Postmodernism, or, the Cultural Logic of Late Capitalism* (London, Verso 1991)

Jerde, J. *The Jerde Partnership International: Visceral Reality* (Milan, L'Arca 1999)

Jones, J. P. *What's In a Name? Advertising and the Concept of Brands* (Lexington Books 1988)

Kapferer, J-N. *Strategic Brand Management* (London, Kogan Page 1992)

Keat, R., Whiteley, N., Abercrombie, N., eds. *The Authority of the Consumer* (London, Routledge 1994)

Keller, K. L. *Strategic Brand Management* (Saddle River, NJ, Prentice Hall 1998)

Klein, N. *No Logo* (London, Flamingo 2000)

Koetter, F., and Rowe, C. *Collage City* (Cambridge, MIT Press 1984)

Kracauer, S. (trans. Y. Levin). *The Mass Ornament: Weimar Essays* (Cambridge, Harvard University Press 1995)

Kuronuma, K. *Enjo kōsai: jochūkosei no abundai na hōkago* [Assisted dating: the dangerous after-school pursuits of middle- and high-school girls] (Tokyo, Bungei Shunjū 1996)

Kurzweil, A. *The Age of the Spiritual Machines* (New York, Viking 1999)

Lash, S. *The Sociology of Postmodernism* (London, Routledge 1990)

Lash, S., and Urry, J. *The End of Organized Capitalism* (Cambridge, Polity 1987)

—*Economies of Sighs and Spaces* (London, Sage 1994)

Lasn, K. *Culture Jam: The Uncooling of America* (New York, Eagle Brook, Morrow 1999)

Lasseter, J., and Daly, S. *Toy Story: The Art and Making of the Animated Film* (New York, Hyperion 1996)

Lears, J. *Fables of Abundance, A Cultural History of Advertising in America* (New York, Basic 1994)

Leonard, M. *Britain ™ Renewing Our Identity* (London, Demos 1997)

Levine, D. *Georg Simmel: On Individuality and Social Form* (Chicago University Press 1971)

Leyda, J., ed. *Eisenstein on Disney* (London and New York, Methuen 1988)

Lloyd-Jones, P. *Taste Today: The Role of Appreciation in Consumerism and Design* (Oxford, Pergamon 1991)

Longstreth, R. *The Drive-In, the Supermarket, and the Transformation of Commercial Space in Los Angeles,* *1914–1941* (Cambridge, MIT Press 1999)

Lunt, P., and Livingstone, S., eds. *Mass Consumption and Personal Identity: Everyday Economic Experience* (Buckingham and Bristol, Open University Press 1992)

Lury, C. *Consumer Culture* (Cambridge, Polity 1996)

Lury, G. *Brand Watching: Lifting the Lid on the Phenomenon of Branding* (Dublin, Blackhall 1998)

McCracken, G. *Culture and Consumption: New Approaches to the Symbolic Character of Consumer Goods and Activities* (Bloomington, Indiana University Press 1990)

McKendrick, N., Brewer, J., and Plumb, J.H., eds. *The Birth of a Consumer Society: The Commercialization of Eighteenth-century England* (London, Europa 1982)

McLuhan, M., Fiore, Q., and Agel, J. *War and Peace in the Global Village* (San Francisco, Hardwired 1997).

McPhee, W. N. *Formal Theories of Mass Behavior* (New York, Free Press 1963)

McRobbie, A. *Feminism and Popular Culture* (London, Routledge 1994)

McRobbie, A., and Nava, M., eds. *Gender and Generation* (London, Macmillan 1984)

Marcuse, H. *One Dimensional Man: Studies in the Ideology of Advanced Industrial Society* (London, Routledge 1964)

Marling, K. A. *As Seen on TV: The Visual Culture of Everyday Life in the 1950s* (Cambridge, Harvard University Press 1994)

Marling, K. A. ed. *Designing Disney's Theme Parks: The Architecture of Reassurance* (Paris and New York, Flammarion 1997)

Mauss, M. *The Gift: The Form and Reason for Exchange in Archaic Societies* (London, Routledge 1925, repr. 1990)

Miller, D. *A Theory of Shopping* (Cambridge, Polity 1998)

—*Capitalism: An Ethnographic Approach* (Oxford, Berg 1997)

—*Material Culture and Mass Consumption* (Oxford, Blackwell 1987)

Miller, D., ed. *Acknowledging Consumption* (London, Routledge 1995)

—*Worlds Apart: Modernity through the Prism of the Local* (London, Routledge 1995)

Miller, D., Jackson, P., Thrift, N., Holbrook., B., and Rowlands, M. *Shopping, Place and Identity* (London, Routledge 1998)

Miller, M. B. *The Bon Marché: Bourgeois Culture and the Department Store, 1869–1920* (Princeton University Press 1981)

Millwood, D., and Gezelius, H., eds. *Smart Promotions* (Sweden, Konsument 1989)

Mitchell, W. J. *E-topia: 'Real Life, Jim, But Not As We Know It'* (Cambridge, MIT Press 1999)

Miyadai, S. *Seifuku shōjotachi no sentaku* [The Uniform Girls' Choice] (Tokyo, Kōdansha 1994)

Mollerup, P. *Marks of Excellence: The History and Taxonomy of Trademarks* (London, Phaidon 1997)

Moore, R., ed. *Vertigo: The Strange New World of the Contemporary City* (London, Laurence King 1999)

Mort, F., Miller, D., and Lowe, M.Lowe, eds. *Commercial Cultures* (London, Berg 2000)

Mukerji, C. *From Graven Images: Patterns of Modern Materialism* (New York, Columbia University Press 1983)

Nader, R. *Unsafe at Any Speed: The Designed-In Dangers of the American Automobile* (New York, Grossman 1965)

Nava, M., Blake, A., MacRury, I., and Richards, B., eds. *Buy This Book: Studies in Advertising and Consumption* (London, Routledge 1997)

Negroponte, N. *Being Digital* (New York, Knopf 1995)

Nicholson, G. *Everything and More: A Novel of Shopping and Terrorism* (London, Gollancz 1994)

Olins, W. *Corporate Identity* (London, Thames & Hudson 1989)

Oliver, T. *The Real Coke, The Real Story* (New York, Viking Penguin 1987)

Ortega, B. *In Sam We Trust: The Untold Story of Sam Walton and How Walmart is Devouring the World* (London, Kogan Page 1999)

Packard, V. *The Hidden Persuaders* (London, Longmans 1957)

Pendergrast, M. *For God, Country and Coca-Cola: The Unauthorised History of the World's Most Popular Soft Drink* (London, Phoenix 1994)

Peppers, D., and Rogers, M. *The One-to-One Future* (London, Piatkus 1994)

Piaget, J. *Play, Dreams and Imitation in Childhood* (London, Routledge and Kegan Paul 1962)

Pine, B. Joseph II, *Mass Customisation* (Cambridge, Harvard Business School Press 1999)

Piore, M., and Sabel, C., eds. *The Second Industrial Divide: Possibilities for Prosperity* (New York, Basic 1984)

Redhead, D. *Products of Our Time* (Basel, Boston and Berlin, Birkhäuser; London, August 2000)

Robinson, J. *The Manipulators: Unmasking the Hidden Persuaders* (London, Simon and Schuster 1999)

Rodgers, W. *Think: A Biography of the Watsons and IBM* (London, Weidenfeld and Nicolson 1970)

Rogers, M. F. *Barbie Culture* (London, Sage 1999)

Rojek, C. *Capitalism and Leisure Theory* (London, Tavistock 1985)

Room, A. *Dictionary of Trade Name Origins* (London, Routledge and Kegan Paul 1982)

Rowe, P.G. *Making a Middle Landscape* (Cambridge, MIT Press 1991)

Safranek, R. 'The McDonald's Recipe for Japan' *Intersect*, 2, October 1996, p. 7.

Schor, J. B. *The Overworked American: The Unexpected Decline of Leisure* (New York, Basic 1991)

Scitovsky, T. *The Joyless Economy: An Enquiry into Human Satisfaction and Consumer Dissatisfaction* (New York, Oxford University Press 1976)

Severini Kowinski, W. *The Malling of America: An Inside Look at the Great Consumer Paradise* (New York, Morrow 1985)

Shapiro, C., and Variam, H. R. *Information Rules: A Strategic Guide to the Network Economy* (Cambridge, Harvard Business School Press 1998)

Sherry, J. *Contemporary Marketing and Consumer Behaviour* (London, Sage 1995)

Shields, R., ed. *Lifestyle Shopping* (London and New York, Routledge 1992)

Skoggard, I. 'Transnational Commodity Flows and the Global Phenomenon of the Brand', in Brydon, A., and Niessen, S., eds. *Consuming Fashion – Adorning the Transnational Body* (Oxford, Berg 1998)

Slater, D. *Consumer Culture and Modernity* (Cambridge, Polity 1997)

Sloan, A. P. Jr. *My Years with General Motors* (London, Pan 1965)

Smallbone, T., and Sutcliffe, M. *Green Claims: A Consumer Investigation into Marketing Claims about the Environment* (London, National Consumer Council (NCC) 1996)

Smith, C. N. *Morality and the Market: Consumer Pressure for Corporate Accountability* (London, Routledge 1990)

Sparke, P. *As Long as It's Pink: The Sexual Politics of Taste* (London, Pandora 1995)

Stephenson, N. *The Diamond Age* (London, Roc 1996)

Stern, B., ed. *Representing Consumers: Voices, Views and Visions* (London, Routledge 1998)

Strasser, S. *Satisfaction Guaranteed: The Making of the American Mass Market* (New York, Pantheon 1989)

Sudjic, D. *The 100 Mile City* (New York, Harcourt Brace 1992)

Tallents, S. *The Projection of England* (London, Faber 1932)

Tedlow, R. S. *New and Improved: The Story of Mass Marketing In America* (Cambridge, Harvard Business School Press 1996)

Turkle, S. *Life on the Screen: Identity in the Age of the Internet* (New York, Simon and Schuster 1995)

Turkle, S. *The Second Self: Computers and the Human Spirit* (New York, Simon and Schuster 1986)

Uhrich, R. *Super-marchés et usines de distribution: Hier aux Etats-Unis, aujourd'hui en France?* (Paris, Plon 1962)

Underhill, P. *Why We Buy: The Science of Shopping* (New York, Simon and Schuster 1999)

Veblen, T. *The Theory of the Leisure Class: An Economic Study of Institutions* (London, George Allen and Unwin 1925)

Vidal, J. *McLibel: Burger Culture on Trial* (London, Pan 1997)

Vihma, S. *Products as Representations: A Semiotic and Aesthetic Study of Design Products* (Helsinki, University of Art and Design 1995)

Virilio, P. *The Vision Machine* (London, British Film Institute 1994)

Wagner, S. A. *Understanding Green Consumer Behaviour: A Qualitative Cognitive Approach* (London, Routledge 1997)

Warde, A. *Consumption, Food and Taste* (London, Sage 1997)

Watson, J. L., ed. *Golden Arches East: McDonald's in East Asia* (Stanford University Press 1997)

Weiss, W. M., and Westerman, K. M. *The Bazaar: Markets and Merchants of the Islamic World* (London, Thames and Hudson 1998)

Winward, J. *Environmental Labelling in Central and Eastern Europe* (London, Consumers International 1996)

Woodham, J. M. *Twentieth-century Design* (Oxford University Press 1997)

Wurman, R. S. *Information Architects* (New York, Watson-Guptil 1997)

Wycherley, R. E. *The Stones of Athens* (Princeton University Press 1978)

Zukin, S. *Landscapes of Power* (Berkeley and Los Angeles, University of California Press 1991)

Zukin, S. *Loftliving: Culture and Capital in Urban Change* (London, Radius 1988)

# CREDIT LINES

# INDEX

Page numbers in *italic* indicate a
reference in an illustration caption

Abercrombie & Fitch 160
Adbusters *186*, 188–92, *188*
adidas *86*, 151, *156*, 169, *169*
advertising 30, 32–3, 37–8, 51, 140
  brand associations and 60–3, 80–2
  brand strategy and 92–3
  Green claims and imagery 194
  lifestyle and fashion 29–44, 169–74
  subversion of 102–3, *102*, *186*,
    188–92
  tailored to local conditions 51, 68–9
  validity of questioned 187–92
  web pages 141, *141*
  *see also* billboards; hoardings;
    marketing; newspaper; radio;
    television
advertising agencies, multinational
  51
Advertising Standards Authority
  (UK) 199
AEG 52
aerosol cans 194
aestheticisation, of everyday life 44
airports, mass retailing 135
Alessi 46
Alfa-Romeo 82
Amazon.com 94, 96, 141, *141*
American myth 26, 30, 78
Americanisation 32, 48
Anderson, Pamela 39
Anti-Apartheid Movement 200
Appadurai, Arjun, on globalisation
  48
Apple, iMac and iBook *41*
arcades 116–17, *117*, 126, 127, *160*
architecture
  brand signatures 53
  branded buildings *21*, 128, 144, *144*
  roadside petrol stations 144, *144*
  shopping environments 110–43,
    *110*, *126*, *132*
Arden, Elizabeth 32
*Arena 60*
Armani, Eau Pour Homme *39*
Asda 45, *45*, 204
Aaker, David, on trademarks 73
aspirin 23
Audi 92

Batchelor's Beanfeast meals 204
Baleno 151
Barclays Bank 200, 208
Barnes & Noble 96
Bauhaus 126
Bauman, Zygmunt 156, 211
bazaars 114–16, 126
BBC, brand structure 21–3, *23*
BBH advertising agency 60
Beatles 56
beauty products 30–2, 39, *39*, 73

*see also* cosmetics
Beckham, David *86*
beef, and BSE 202
Beer, Henry (architect) 139, 140
Behrens, Peter (designer) 52
Bellagio, The Resort (Las Vegas) 139,
  *139*
Ben & Jerry 56
Benjamin, Walter, on Paris arcades
  116–17
Bercy shopping mall (Paris) 135
Beverly Center (Los Angeles) 128
Bezos, Jim 141
Biba 56
Big Box retail centres 128, 129–32,
  140
Bijvoet and Duiker (architects) 127
Billboard-Utilising Graffitists
  Against Unhealthy Promotions
  (BUGA-UP) 192
billboards 30, 37–8, *159*, *170*, 192, *192*
  *see also* hoardings
Birds Eye Walls 204
Black and Decker 52
Blair, Tony 56–7
Bloomingdales 121
Blue Angel symbol 193
Bluewater (Kent) *110*, 135, *135*
BMC 56
BMP DDB advertising agency 106
BMW 48, 83, *171*
  Rover purchase 92
Body Shop 96
  Eau No! range of products *208*, 210
Boileau, L A (architect) 117
Bon Marché 117, *117*, *120*
Bonzo Dog Doo-Dah Band 56
Boots 93
Bossini *150*, 151
Boucicaut, Aristide 117
Bourdieu, Pierre, on
  'cultural capital' 44, 167
  taste 167
Bovril 33
Boycott, Rosie *204*
boycotts, by consumers 199–204
brand
  associations 60–3, 70–97, 171
  equity 75–8, 82, 83, 92–4, 95–6
  image *21*–3, 39–51, 64, 73–8
  loyalty 88–9
  portfolios 92
  strategy 89–93
  valuation 93–4
  value *21*–3, 33–8, 64, 169
  *see also* trademarks
branding 21, 38–45, 73
  and authenticity 58–9
  consumer perceptions 75–88
  role in consumer choice 80–9,
  94–5, 140, 170
  'brandlands' 149
brands

critical response to 186–211
  discounted designer brands 45, *45*
  individualisation and 159–66,
    169–71
  as phatic communicators 176–7
  social signifiers 169–74
Branson, Richard 39
Breuer, Marcel (architect) 127
Britain, rebranding of 56–7
British Airways 39, 56, *56*
British Broadcasting Corporation
  *see* BBC
British Telecom, rebranding 56
British Union for the Abolition of
  Vivisection (BUAV) 194
BSE 202
BSkyB 92
Budweiser *175*
BUGA-UP 192
Buick 92
Burberry, in China 150
Business Improvement Districts
  (BIDs) 140
Buzz Lightyear 178–9, *178*

Cadbury 33, 36
  *see also* chocolate
Cadbury World 148, 149, *149*
Cadillac 92
Caesar's Casino (Las Vegas) 139
Cafédirect, Fair Trade coffee 208
CaféLatino, Fair Trade coffee 205–8
Cairncross, Frances, on online
  shopping 95
Calvin Klein 151, 188
Camel cigarettes 188
Campari 52
Campbell's soup 26
Canal City Hakata (Fukuoka, Japan)
  139, *139*
Carling, sport sponsorship *73*
Carnaby Street 56, *56*
Carrefour 125, 132
Carrier, James, on 19th-century
  advertising 32–3
cashless economies 211
catalogue shopping 95, 128, 140
  *see also* mail-order companies
CCTV surveillance 106
celebrities, branding of 73, *86*
Center Parcs 148, *149*
Centre for Environmentally
  Responsible Tourism 210
Certeau, Michel de, on consumerism
  159
CFCs 194
chain stores 128
Chanel, counterfeit perfumes *99*
charities 205
charity shops 205
Charles, Prince of Wales 204
Cheng Siu Chung 151
Chesterfield-Evans, Arthur 192

Chevrolet 92
China 150–1, *150*, *151*, 174, 175, *175*
chocolate 36
  Fair Trade schemes 208
  *see also* Cadbury
Christmas Gift Exemption Vouchers
  *188*, 192
Churchill, Sir Winston S *23*
cigarettes 33, 36, 169
  anti-smoking campaigns 188, 192,
  *192*
cinema complexes 140
cities
  de facto malls 140
  markets and 114–16
Citroën 30, 32
Clinton, Bill *21*, 45
Co-operative Bank *205*, 208
co-operatives 208
Coates, Nigel 57
Coca-Cola 23, 26–30, *27*, *30*, 47–8, 50,
  94, 160, 174
  advertising 92
  bottle design *76*
  brand and logo 75–8, *75*
  corporate identity 52
  Diet Coke *21*, 45
  global marketing 69, *69*
  market value 94
  New Coke 82–3
  transnational expansion 32
  Virgin cola and 39
coffee, Fair Trade schemes 205–8
collectables 180, *181*
Communication Arts Inc *135*, 139
communications, and global culture
  48–50
concrete thinking 178–9
consumer choice
  branding and 80–9, 94–5, 140,
  70–1, 175
  ethical considerations 96, 186,
  205–11
  and Green issues 192–9
  in the home 107
  individualism and 158–60, *171*, 175
consumer proactivity 102–3, *102*,
  192, 199
consumer protests 51
consumer research 51
consumer response, to advertising
  38, 102–3, *102*, 186
consumer terrorism 51
consumerism
  Green consumption 192–9
  and human rights 32, 51, 211
  identity and 44–5, 51, 156–75
consumers, behaviour analysis
  106–7, 175
Consumers' Association 202–4
Consumers International 193
consumption, alternative systems
  51, 166

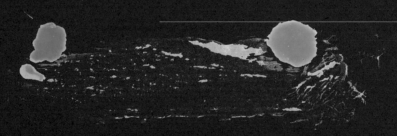